The Story of
The Bahamas

Islands of the Shallow Sea

The Story of The Bahamas

Paul Albury

ST. MARTIN'S PRESS
NEW YORK

Printed in Hong Kong

Library of Congress Catalog Card Number: 75-15490
First published in the United States of America in 1976

Library of Congress Cataloging in Publication Data

Albury, Paul.
    The Story of the Bahamas.

    Bibliography: p.
    Includes index.
    1. Bahamas--History.   I.   Title.
F1656.A42   1976   972.9'6   75-15490

Contents

List of Illustrations and Maps

Colour Plates

Acknowledgements

The publishers wish to acknowledge the following photograph sources:

Joan Albury   p. 205
Bahamas Historical Society   pp. 50, 83, 87, 136, 151
Bahamas Tourist News Bureau   pp. 235, 239, 242, 251, 282
Bahamas News Bureau   pp. 118, 119
Mrs Audrey Boyce   p. 155
S. G. W. Benjamin, from *The Atlantic Islands*, New York 1818   p. 243
Lady Virginia Christie   p. 105
Robert D'Arville   p. 46
Monroe Dreher   p. 95
Etienne Dupuch, Jr. Publications   p. 226
Frank Leslie's *Illustrated Newspaper*, May 25, 1878   pp. 152, 224
The Mansell Collection   pp. 23, 64, 66–67
Frederic Maura   p. 44
B. P. Malone   p. 42
Nassau Guardian (Centenary No. 1944)   pp. 162, 222
William Pemberton   pp. 189, 211
Port Authority, Freeport   pp. 259, 260
Radio Times Hulton Picture Library   pp. 167, 173
J. H. Stark   pp. 123, 124 from *The History of and Guide to the Bahamas*
   (Boston 1891)
John Sandbrook   pp. 138–139
Marie J. (Thompson) Knight   p. 244
Stanley Toogood   pp. 277, 278
H. De W. Wigley from *With the Whiskey Smugglers*

Colour plates

Islands of the Shallow Sea. From the Pictorial Book *The Bahama Islands in Full Colour* by H. W. Hannau.
Woodes Rogers and Family at Fort Nassau—Lady Virginia Christie
Unloading Cotton at Nassau—Paul Albury
Nassau, Freeport, and Independence Day at Clifford Park—by the Bahamas News Tourist Bureau

The publishers have made every effort to trace the copyright holders but if they have inadvertently overlooked any, they will be pleased to make the necessary arrangement at the first opportunity.

Introduction

by the Hon. L. O. Pindling, Prime Minister of
The Commonwealth of The Bahamas.

Dr Paul Albury has more than an interest in Bahamian history, and more than an affection for it; his attachment to the subject is obviously a case of true love. Here in The Bahamas, he is well known as an active member of the Bahamas Historical Society, of which he is now President, as well as a speaker and writer. By the use of these media, he has endeavoured, for many years, to impart to his fellow Bahamians some of his own enthusiasm for this fascinating study.

Readers and listeners who have been delighted with Dr Albury's stories on various aspects of our checkered past, have frequently expressed the hope that one day he would put it all together in book form. And for some years now he has let it be known that he planned to do that. This book, therefore, will be greeted with pleasure and satisfaction rather than surprise.

Whether the timing with respect to publication was deliberate or not I am unable to say. However, it does seem to come at a time when there is an unprecedented surge of interest in Bahamian history, both at home and abroad. For our Bahamian people it will supply a deeply felt need, for never before have they been so anxious to gain some knowledge of their ancient and historic roots.

It takes considerable talent to tell *The Story of The Bahamas* in little more than 300 pages without omitting much that is important, but the author has not resorted to overcrowding his pages, which makes the average history book so tiresome to read. As the title suggests, it is history in story form. From the earliest beginnings to the moment of our Independence, he tells it all in a free-flowing style which is both vigorous and captivating.

In completing this work, Dr Albury has done a great service to the country he loves and I wish him all success with his first sizeable literary venture.

I

Islands of the Shallow Sea

North of the Greater Antilles and east of southern Florida there is a region of great natural beauty, abounding in islands, reefs and shoals, banks and deepwater channels.

The Spanish were the first Europeans to explore that area and, in communicating with their New World territories, they were the first to use it as a maritime highway. But they found little time to marvel at nature's wonders. They looked with awe at a sea-bed which often seemed to rise beneath them. Coral growths of fantastic shapes and abundance reached for the surface and threatened their ships and lives at every turn. Appropriately, they called it *bajamar*, shallow sea. And from this word derives the name Bahama Islands—islands of the shallow sea.

Much of the mystery and danger has gone from the Bahama sea. And even though the reefs and shallows are as numerous as ever, the safe passages through and around them are now well charted. Many lighthouses have been built and seagoing craft are now equipped with an assortment of safety devices. Present day explorers cruise the Bahamas with delight and leave it with genuine regret.

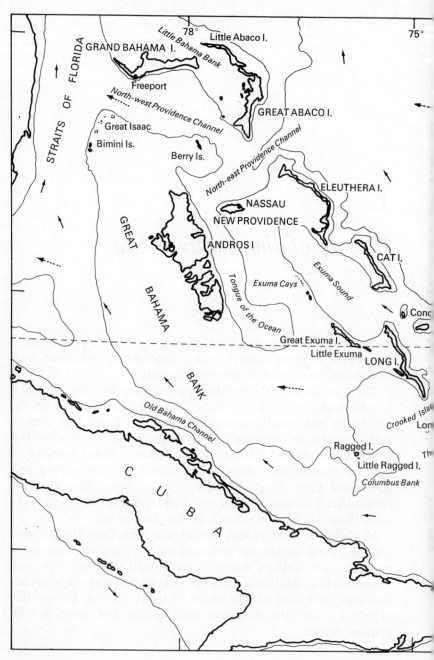

The Bahamas

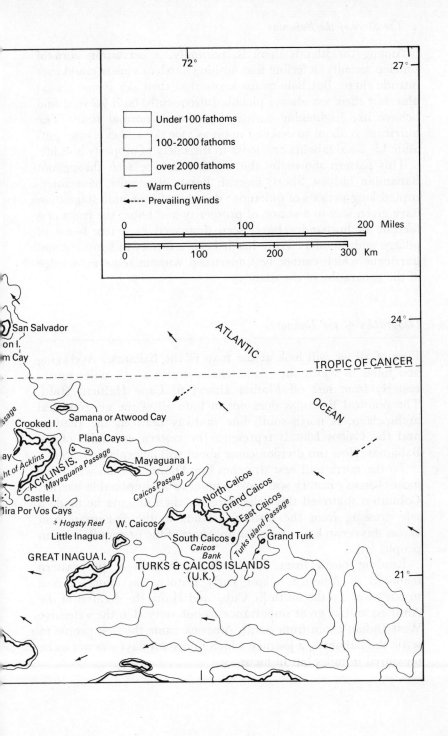

72°   27°

Under 100 fathoms
100-2000 fathoms
over 2000 fathoms
← Warm Currents
◄--- Prevailing Winds

0   100   200   Miles

0   100   200   300   Km

24°

San Salvador
on I.
m Cay   ATLANTIC

TROPIC OF CANCER

OCEAN

Crooked I.   Samana or Atwood Cay
                  Plana Cays
ht of Acklins   ACKLINS IS.   Mayaguana I.
                  Mayaguana Passage
Castle I.   Caicos Passage   North Caicos
lira Por Vos Cays   Grand Caicos
        * Hogsty Reef   W. Caicos   East Caicos
        Little Inagua I.   South Caicos ●
                              Caicos
GREAT INAGUA I.   Bank
                  TURKS & CAICOS ISLANDS
                        (U.K.)   Grand Turk

Turks Island Passage

21°

Among the islands there is, normally, a pervading aura of timeless serenity; a feeling that nothing harsh or violent could ever intrude there. But Bahamians know that their sky is not always blue nor their sea always placid. Infrequently both go wild and behave like frightening caricatures of their normal state. 'The hurricane is about to descend upon us', we say and everyone puts aside his usual labours and looks to the safety of property and life.

This pattern shown by the weather can be seen throughout Bahamian history. Short, feverish bursts of activity have interrupted long periods of quietude; decades of economic stagnation have given way to a season of prosperity and hope; the fruits of a lifetime of husbandry have been destroyed in a few hours of pillage and plunder. Truly has it been a history of sunshine and hurricane which cannot be understood without some knowledge of the geography of the islands.

Geography of the Bahamas

First of all we will look at the map of the Bahamas. Averaging 200 miles in width the island chain stretches 550 miles south-easterly from just off Florida almost to Cape Haitien, Haiti. The political Bahamas does not include all of the geographical archipelago. A north–south line midway between the Inaguas and the Caicos Islands represents the eastern extremity of the Bahamas. How this division came about will be explained later.

To the north and east stretches the Atlantic Ocean which for most of man's history was looked upon as an impassable barrier. Columbus shattered this belief forever when in 1492 he made a safe crossing from the Canary Islands to the Bahamas. And across this ocean have come the ancestors of the present Bahamian people.

Leading north from the Florida peninsula is the eastern seaboard of America, whose early history was closely linked to our own. To the south lie Cuba and Haiti, the greatest of the Antilles, and of great importance to our story. Up the extensive West Indian chain from South America came the first people to settle the Bahamas, a journey which in distant days was not to be measured in miles but in lifetimes.

Between the West Indies and South America, the legendary Spanish Main, lies the Caribbean Sea, sometimes called the 'Mediterranean of the Americas'. To the north-west of this is the Gulf of Mexico. These seas and the lands they wash were the centre of early Spanish exploitation and of the intense European rivalry which later developed. The Bahamas, lying nearby and in such a strategic position, could not escape the violence and bloodshed.

When we speak of the Bahamas we think not only of islands, but of submarine banks and the sea. Therefore it is important to understand the nature of these geographic features.

If you could walk the bed of the Atlantic Ocean toward the Bahamas you would see a majestic mountain rising nearly three and a half miles to the surface of the sea and a little above. This submarine mountain has an interesting and unusual shape. About half way to the top it divides and redivides to form twenty or more flat topped summits of almost equal altitude. The tops of mountain above sea level are the islands; the summits are submarine table-lands or shallow water banks on which the islands rest; and the gorges separating the summits are deep water embayments or passages.

A frequent question is, 'What is the size of this country, and how many islands are there?' The stock reply is, '700 miles and 700 islands.' We have already seen that 700 miles for the length of the chain is a gross overmeasurement. But 700 for the number of islands is a good estimate, once it is understood what is meant by an island. The majority of the units which comprise the Bahama archipelago are considered too small to be called islands. They are grey or brown coloured outcroppings of limestone and are called 'rocks'.

Apart from the thousands of rocks, there remain some hundreds of larger units. To classify these, the word 'cay' was adopted from the Arawakan *cairi*. In the Indian tongue it meant 'island', but in the English form pronounced 'key', it means 'a small island'. Each individual who engaged in naming, decided for himself whether he was dealing with an island or a cay. Inevitably this produced some interesting anomalies. For example, Rum Cay has an area of 30 square miles and Harbour Island only 1½ square miles. And this is why, in the Bahamas, one often hears seemingly confusing, but perfectly logical remarks, such as 'Pigeon Island is a small cay'.

In 1864 the Governor of the day had the islands, cays, and rocks counted for inclusion in his annual report to the authorities in England. The figures he gave were 29 islands, 661 cays and 2387 rocks. The logic of this grouping or the accuracy of this count cannot be judged until something new is officially produced. The islands cover about 5382 square miles in area. Thus collectively they are a little larger than Jamaica and about the same size as the State of Connecticut.

Andros (2300 square miles) occupies forty-three per cent of all Bahamian land. But there are several channels, navigable by small vessels, that pass right through this island, and future enumerators will have to decide whether to consider it a single island or a cluster of islands.

Other islands of more than 100 square miles in area are Great Inagua, Grand Bahama, Great Abaco, Long Island, Eleuthera, Acklins Island, Cat Island and Mayaguana. These eight, together with Andros, account for eighty-six per cent of the land. But New Providence, site of the capital, is only eighty square miles, so size alone cannot be taken as a gauge of political, economic or historical importance.

Land and Vegetation in the Bahamas

The larger islands consist of extensive areas of flat land, a few feet above sea level, sometimes rising to slightly higher ground or sloping into brackish ponds. Andros has no land higher than seventy-five feet, and Grand Bahama none higher than forty feet. But the long, narrow islands which front the Atlantic are marked by a range or series of ranges of hills on the ocean side and parallel to the length of the islands. Eleuthera and Long Island have the most hills above 100 feet, while the 'Everest' of the Bahamas is at Cat Island standing 206 feet above the sea.

The hilly parts and the low parts of the land were formed by quite different processes. The flat land was formerly sea-bed which became elevated not long ago, as geologists count time. The hilly areas were formed of windblown sand, a process which is still going on. Inland the sand particles have become cemented into limestone, while near the coast, the newer hills show the loose consistency of dunes. Thus there are two distinct types of surface rock, the soft sea-bed rock which has weathered into a pitted configuration called 'honey-comb' and the harder hill rock called 'plate rock' or 'flint rock' which the elements have split into boulders.

Many years ago a man with no kind feelings toward the Bahamian people referred to their country as a 'land of cursed rock and stones'. The rock and stones, cursed or uncursed, are indeed abundant, and the soil is pitifully scant. Exceptions are to be found in certain coastal areas where wind-blown sand accumulates to considerable depths. This is called 'white land'. After vegetation takes hold, the cycle of growth and decay darkens and enriches the sand and the resultant mixture is locally known as 'provision land'. But most of the land is very poor which accounts for the low population figures.

Extensive forests of Caribbean Pine are found on Grand Bahama, Abaco, Andros and, to a reduced extent, on New Providence. The trees grow to a diameter of twenty-four inches or more and in certain places are so dense as to present the appearance of a solid wall. On some of the islands hardwood forests, locally called 'coppices', are to be found. Interesting among these trees are the strong and durable *lignum vitae*, mahogany, horseflesh, the logwood used in times past for dyeing and the aromatic cascarilla. The woody vegetation of the smaller islands and cays and parts of the larger islands is comprised mainly of dense shrubs and low trees, commonly called 'scrub lands'.

Passing from the interior, a world of difference is seen between windward and leeward coasts. To windward, there is a blustery and exhilarating freshness occasioned by the prevailing winds and oncoming waves. Creeping vines and low shrubs grow to the water's edge. In times of rage and hurricane they are ripped up and hurled back with savage ferocity. But they never surrender and soon begin to advance again toward the sea.

To leeward, a calmness prevails. The water is still and the breezes gentle and there the dark green mangrove reigns supreme. This remarkable tree rooted in the sea-bed, raises its trunk through several feet of sea-water. Its branches are so dense and intertwined that it is difficult to say to which tree they belong. From a distance, mangrove growth has the appearance of dry land vegetation, and it is hard to determine where the land ends and the sea begins.

Early sailors knew of the mangrove's liking for sheltered water and sought safety there from an approaching storm. Even today when a hurricane threatens, local seamen prefer to place their vessels in mangrove thickets.

Animals and Birds in the Bahamas

In exploring the eastern Bahamas Columbus' men spoke of seeing 'dogs, mastiffs and hounds'. This formidable array of canines seems to have been represented only by a small yellow dog which was unusual because it had no bark. It is now extinct, but the indigenous inhabitants kept it both as a companion and a food supply.

The almost extinct utia, a rodent related to the agouti, was also much relished by the Indians for its meat. Protected by law, it now lives on one or two islands only. In New Providence and Grand Bahama the racoon is frequently seen and rats abound throughout the Bahamas as elsewhere. Wild horses and pigs roam the forests of Abaco and wild donkeys and pigs the savannahs of Inagua.

An interesting reptile, the iguana, lives on some of the islands. Growing about three to four feet in length, it has a frightening, prehistoric appearance, but is, in fact, a harmless vegetarian. It has come under protection because Bahamians look on it as a savoury ingredient of the stew-pot. Several interesting species of bats are found in caves throughout the islands, but frogs, lizards and snakes comprise the bulk of animal life. None of the snakes is poisonous.

A number of interesting birds are to be seen, among them the flamingo, the spoon bill, the Bahamian parrot and the Bahama woodstar humming bird being outstanding. The American flamingo is the national bird of the Bahamas and a surviving colony of 20,000–25,000 at Inagua is jealously guarded by the Bahamas National Trust.

The Bahama Sea

We turn now to the sea to find there a beauty and a profusion of life which far excels anything to be found on land. As seen on the map, the majority of deep water chasms pass right through the island chain to form intersecting channels or passages. Exceptions are the Exuma Sound and Tongue of Ocean which end blindly.

Shallow water predominates in the west and north, and deep water in the south-east. The deep water when lit by sunlight is a dark and luminous blue for some depth, but below that is total blackness. On the banks where the depth is normally a few feet, the sea is remarkably translucent. The colour there, determined by the depth of water and the nature of the background, varies from place to place. It is generally turquoise, but a turquoise which beggars description; a panorama of glowing, living blues and greens made resplendent by millions of shimmering facets of reflected light.

A white mantle of sandy ooze covers the banks almost everywhere. Where there is a strong tidal current the sand tends to shift continuously. Obviously very little sea-bed life can exist under these unsettled conditions. The majority of the bank mantle, however, is fairly static from year to year, being agitated only during infrequent ocean rages and hurricanes, and there life takes hold.

Sea-grasses grow in sheltered locations and here the queen conch with its beautiful pink shell feeds and lives. This white-meated mollusc is an important item in the Bahamian diet and can claim a place in Bahamian history. The less discriminating sponges are widely distributed. These lowly animals which spend their lives anchored to the sea-bottom once comprised the most important sector of our economy.

But by far the most important inhabitant of the banks is the simple coral polyp. He is a choosy little fellow, liking only the warm shallow areas of the tropics. He does not like to work at much below 70°F and he will not take on jobs of reef building at depths much greater than eighty feet. The Bahama banks are much to his liking although he might find it a bit chilly in northern parts during winter time.

The coral does not work alone, but he is the chief architect and chief labourer. Work is slow. To build a reef twenty feet high requires some thousands of years. In the early stages when the foundation is first laid it is a gorgeous sight to view from above, particularly through a glass-bottom bucket or through glass in the bottom of a boat.

Twig-like, pink gorgonians; wispy, straw coloured sea-feathers, and lacy, yellow and purple sea-fans, sway to and fro, among myriads of other many coloured tenants of the reef. Dark purple sponges, black spiny sea urchins, yellow and brown sea-stars contribute to the galaxy of shapes and tones.

Coral dominates, and each coral colony has a distinctive hue, scarlet, yellow, purple, rose and a particular design indicated by the common name, finger coral, brain coral, star coral, staghorn coral. Fish, forever on the move and of every imaginable colour, add a vivid brilliancy to the scene.

The coral has built marvellous structures on the Bahama sea-bed. On the interior of the banks these are called 'shoals' or 'coral heads' and in many areas they are so dense as to make it impossible to chart them. There, experience, expert seamanship and broad daylight are the only safeguards against shipwreck.

To windward, on the edge of the banks, between the islands and the ocean, the coral achieves his most ambitious architecture, forests of living stone, known as 'fringe reefs'. There is a fragile appearance about the upper part of these reefs but they can crush the hardest steel plate of a ship's bottom, and the hurricane waves batter them in vain. But strength and endurance are relative qualities and however long these magnificent growths may last, finally they crumble and die.

Without the coral polyp the shallow sea would be a virtual desert; there would be no beautiful sea gardens and the majority of our fish would have no place to live and feed. The islands and banks would lose their protection from eroding waves and there would be no splendid, pink-white beaches. Life swarms about the reef and every plant and animal has a part to play in the overall pattern.

Under rocky shelves and in crevices lives the spiny lobster. During daylight hours, when he rests and hides from predators, only his antennae can be seen, ever ready to signal danger. But both his warning system and his defences are useless against his chief enemy, man, who finds his meat a lucrative commodity.

Fishes, from little pigmies less than an inch in length, to the gigantic jew fish, weighing up to 500 pounds, live among the coral. There are grunts, yellow tails, porgies, snappers, angelfish, parrot fish, turbots, margate fish, groupers, rock fish and many others whose habits are well known to Bahamian line-fishermen. Game fish, too, are abundant in deeper waters, mackerel, kingfish, alison tuna, dolphin, amber-jack, sailfish, barracuda, shark, and the much prized blue-fin tuna and blue marlin weighing up to 800 pounds and more.

Seasonally, shoals of fish leave their deep water habitat to feed on the banks and their arrival is eagerly awaited by net-fishermen. Important among these are jacks, runners and goggle-eyes. The 'passing jack' which is a great delicacy to Bahamians, and whose movements are guided by phases of the moon, appears only briefly, and in selected areas, during July and August.

Climate in the Bahamas

Long ago in tribute to its equable climate someone called the Bahamas the 'Isles of June'. On 21 June, the sun reaches the farthest point in its northward swing and its rays fall directly on Latitude 23° 30′ North, an imaginary line called the Tropic of Cancer. This line passes right through the Bahama Islands. But apart from location these are other factors which greatly influence the climate.

First, the islands are low-lying. This protects against the sudden changes in temperature which are characteristic of mountainous regions. Secondly, sea water which is everywhere and which changes but a few degrees throughout the year tempers both atmospheric heat and cold.

The four seasons are never spoken of. In the Bahamas it is simply winter and summer and the temperature difference between the two averages is only 11°F. The summer temperature seldom rises above 90°F and although the humidity is high, its effects are moderated by cooler sea breezes. In winter the temperature rarely falls below 60°F and usually rises to 75°F during the warmest part of the day. Rainfall averages about fifty inches a year and most of it falls during the summer months in the form of gusty squalls.

Mid-July to mid-November is the hurricane season with the peak of expectancy in September. When a maximum hurricane does strike straight on the destruction can be enormous. Damage results not only from winds of between 75 and 150 miles per hour, with gusts occasionally up to 200 miles per hour, but also from torrential rains and savage ocean waves. Considering that the Bahamas lie right in the middle of their tracks, the wonder is that the islands are not ravaged more frequently.

Geology of the Bahamas

The Bahama Islands were born of the sea. The rock is formed primarily of the cemented skeletal remains of billions of marine organisms. Therefore it is, by definition, limestone. But present also are large numbers of tiny spheres called 'oolites' which were originally precipitated out of the sea-water and which classifies it as 'oolitic limestone'. Geophysicists tell us that, in relation to the sea, the islands once stood ten to fifteen feet lower than now and once 300–400 feet higher than now.

To understand this we must consider a phenomenon which seems far removed from the balmy Bahamas, the accumulation and melting of glacial ice. The time cycles involved are enormous, stretching out into hundreds of thousands, and perhaps millions of years.

Many changes in the configuration of the Bahamas date from the most recent Ice Age, about 50,000 years ago, when water in the form of glacial ice was three times the present quantity and the ocean's surface was about 300 feet lower. The shallow Bahamian sea was gone, all the Bahama banks were exposed and the land area many times greater than today. When the thaw began, the oceans started to rise, slowly engulfing the islands. The process is still continuing at the rate of an inch or more every century. If this goes on until all the glacial ice is melted the oceans will be 100 feet higher than at present and there will be precious little left of Bahama land.

2

Island People

The story of the original American people can never be fully known. It is widely believed that their ancestors entered Alaska from Siberia. After many waves of migration and many thousands of years, they had spread all over the two continents and nearby islands.

Our present knowledge indicates that far-roving Norsemen were the first Europeans to meet with them. This contact took place in Newfoundland and, perhaps, also on the mainland coast farther west. Attempts at settlement failed and by the second half of the fifteenth century, southern European knowledge of these distant Scandinavian discoveries, if it existed at all, existed only in the form of legend. Such was the situation when in 1492 there occurred one of the most momentous voyages of discovery in history. Christopher Columbus sailed from Spain to the Canary Islands and then westward over the unknown ocean to his landfall in the Bahamas.

Those who welcomed him were unlike any people he had ever seen before. And believing himself to be in the East Indies he named them Indians. But they called themselves Lucayans, meaning 'Island People', and that is what we shall call them. They were but a small fraction of the total American people. Nevertheless, they are of interest to the world because they were the first that Columbus met and because of their brutal extermination a short time later.

The Lucayans never developed the art of writing. The history of their ancestors was memorized from generation to generation. And when the entire people died, their history died with them. Thus our knowledge of them is very limited.

A long time ago Indians of South America began to explore and settle the West Indian islands. These early movements are shrouded in mystery and archaeologists are digging away in an attempt to shed some light on them. At the time of discovery the Lesser Antilles, from Trinidad to the Virgin Islands, were occupied by the warlike, cannibalistic Caribs. Peaceful Arawaks inhabited the Greater Antilles (Cuba, Hispaniola, Jamaica and Puerto Rico) and the remnants of a more primitive tribe, the Ciboneys, were found in Cuba.

Living in the Bahamas were the Lucayans who looked on Hispaniola, which they called Haiti, as their ancestral home. The Arawaks who lived there, and who were known as Tainos, were regarded as their kinsmen. They spoke the same language, used the same tools and weapons, built their houses and canoes in much the same way and, in general, followed the same customs and held the same beliefs.

This suggests that the Lucayans were simply Tainos who had settled the Bahamas, but possibly this was not so. Some of those who saw them during the short interval between discovery and death considered them different in both physical appearance and personality. One observer said they were more like Ciboneys than Tainos. Thus we cannot be certain that they did not have in their veins some other blood mixed with Tainan.

Lucayan Life-style and Appearance

The accounts of contemporary Europeans describe them as a gentle, peaceful, happy people. There was, indeed, much that was exceptional about them. They were a handsome people; so

Lucayans—Island People

handsome, in fact, that men from other lands frequently came to the Bahamas to find a Lucayan wife. Their bodies were well proportioned, with a supple strength and healthful glow characteristic of those who spend their lives outdoors and who practise good dietary habits. It was said that what a Spaniard ate in a day would suffice a Lucayan for a week.

Striking to European eyes was the head, which seemed unusually large. This was due to artificial flattening during infancy. The slight pressure of a board on the forehead, applied frequently by the mother, was sufficient to mould the soft bone into the desired shape. The result was that the forehead was widened laterally and sloped sharply back from the brows.

The skin, naturally brown, was usually painted in a variety of colours and patterns. Some were content with a little facial make-up; others painted a part or all of the body. This was done chiefly for cosmetic effect but there were other important reasons. For the warding off of evil or harmful events, designs were painted to represent protective spirits. Certain types of paint shielded the skin from the sun's rays; and sometimes there was incorporated into the pigment, plant extracts that were repellent to insects.

The Lucayans had smooth faces. Their hair was straight and black and as coarse as a 'horse's tail'. It was kept short, falling just below the ears, except for a few strands at the back which were never cut. In front, it covered the forehead to the eyebrows.

Such was the appearance of the naked Lucayan, and nakedness was a state from which he little departed. Girls on reaching puberty wore a small mantle made of cotton netting and leaves, and on becoming married the size of this scanty garment was slightly increased. Headbands and waist bands, elaborately woven of cotton and other fibre, and sometimes adorned with bird feathers, were worn by some. For jewellery, pieces of gold, sea-shell or rock were frequently suspended from the ears and nose which were pierced at an early age.

Houses and Occupations

In exploring the Bahamas we look for Lucayan buildings in vain. Their dwelling houses of wood and leaves have long since yielded to insects and decay. Their villages were small and centred around the dwelling of the head man or *cacique*. Fifteen houses would have been considered a large settlement; the majority were much smaller, and sometimes a single house stood alone.

We can but bow to the skill and talents of a people who were able to build such beautiful and sturdy structures with simple and primitive tools. And we must take note not only of their houses but of other articles of wood such as canoes, spears, bowls and chairs. These objects were handsomely made and often decorated with the most delicate carvings.

Wood Duho *(ceremonial stool)*
used by the Lucayans (found in
a cave at Long Island)

These houses had rounded or polygonal walls with a conical roof, a form aesthetically pleasing and best suited to withstand destructive winds. A single doorless entrance-way broke the continuity of the walls and a small opening at the apex provided ventilation. They were constructed by interweaving strong pieces of timber with slender withes. Sinewy plant fibres were used to bind together the many pieces and the roof was thatched with palm leaves. The wall uprights were firmly planted in the ground and in the middle, a single massive tree trunk rose to the roof-top and lent central support to the entire structure.

Fire, which they coaxed from two dry sticks, was the principal tool in their hands. Live hardwood coals, judiciously placed, did in time fell the largest tree or shape the most intricate of designs. Hard stone axes and adzes, imported from Haiti, were used to remove the charred surface, and final scraping and finishing was accomplished with the aid of sharp-edged pieces of conch shells.

In the mind's eye we can still see the housewife, with her brood of children about her, nimbly weaving and plaiting her cotton and palmleaves into hammocks, baskets and other articles of household and personal use. We see families working their farms together, clearing the land, tilling the soil, and planting and reaping crops of cassava, cotton, corn, gourds and tobacco.

We admire the expertness with which the men speared the fish and dived for the conchs which abounded in the shallow sea. We can imagine with what merriment they hunted the agouti and the iguana, with the help of their little barkless dog. And we are saddened to know that the poor dog frequently ended up in the same cooking pot as the prey. At sea the Lucayans were as much at home as on land. We can but marvel at the sure way in which they navigated their canoes to distant points.

Patience was not so much a virtue with them as it was a way of life. The idea of making every minute count, or of toiling ceaselessly from dawn to dusk, was to be pressed on them later with devastating effect. Crime was unknown among them. They were social creatures who gave freely of whatever they possessed. They were happiest at communal gatherings for sports and festivities. *Batos,* the national game, played with a rubbery ball, was enjoyed by both sexes. The birth of a child, a wedding, or any other joyous event, was celebrated with singing, dancing, feasting and storytelling.

In their daily lives and against the abuses of man and nature they looked for protection from *zemis,* or good spirits which surrounded them everywhere. And up in the skies, in heaven, there was a supreme being from whom all good things came.

The Caribs

But out of the south, there sometimes came evil men against whom both God and spirits seemed to be impotent. These were the Caribs who stole in on the Lucayans as stealthily as the night. So much did they value surprise that if their whereabouts were prematurely discovered they regarded it as a bad omen and abandoned the foray.

An eye witness to one of these raids would have marked how quietly the canoe which brought the cannibals was concealed. He would have noted how each man armed himself with his bow and arrows, his bludgeon and his piece of rope; and how noiselessly they then marched to a selected house. During that darkest hour before the dawn, the doomed house was surrounded and from that moment the fate of the occupants was sealed.

Here it should be understood that the raiding Caribs were ugly to the point of being nauseating to the senses. The Lucayans were terrified beyond measure by their presence. In the first paroxysm of fear the thought of escape dominated every other consideration. Husbands would leave behind their wives, and mothers their children, to escape the dreaded cannibals.

After the first screams of despair, terror took such sole possession of the Lucayan's mind and body that it robbed him of the ability to defend himself. He became a jellied mass of sweating, trembling, helpless flesh. Men, women and children were bound with ropes, stacked in the canoe and taken to Carib land. There the males were mutilated, tortured and finally eaten. The females were kept for breeding purposes. And, it is said, their male offspring, sired by Caribs, were also eaten.

The Lucayans had their medicine men whose job was not only to provide herbal remedies for the sick but to foretell the future. We can assume that with increasing Carib raids they became very important and very busy people. The occupants of a house or village who were warned beforehand could hide themselves in forests and caves until the danger had passed.

But if there had been a medicine man with real prescience on Guanahani on 11 October 1492, he would have told his people that the morrow would bring to their island men such as they had never seen, or dreamt of, before. He would have told them, further, that before 300 moons had passed they would all be dead.

3

Discovery

Far eastward of the Bahamas is another archipelago called the Canary Islands. It lies almost as close to Africa as the Bahamas does to Florida. Between the two groups is the deep and wide Atlantic Ocean. The Canary Islanders had looked out over that ocean for centuries. They had heard of vessels which had been blown far westward during storms. Some never returned. Some of the men on those that did, told wonderful tales of the marvels they claimed to have seen. In 1492 there were many who would testify that on certain days and at certain times they had seen land far to the west.

Occasionally a ship had gone out to look for those lands. They never went very far because of a mortal fear of being forever lost on the watery waste. Nothing was ever discovered, but interest was kept alive because the explorers frequently spoke of seeing land just before nightfall, or just before a squall, and then not being able to find it again.

Thus they were accustomed to think of lands to the west, to the coming and going of ships, and to voyages of exploration. But on 9 August 1492, there arrived from Spain, a fleet of three ships which set them all agog. The crews let it be known that this was no ordinary fleet and they were on no ordinary voyage of discovery. The ships had been sent out by the mighty Sovereigns of Aragon and Castile whose proud standards flew from the masts. On board were supplies to last a year and they planned to sail right across the great ocean sea to whatever there was on the other side.

Columbus

The leader of the enterprise, Christopher Columbus, was a Genoese-born seaman and chart-maker. During his four weeks stay he was entertained by the finest families as befitted an emissary of the King and Queen. We can imagine the rapture with which they listened to him as he told the story of his life. For it was a thrilling story and he was a good talker.

From his earliest boyhood days in Genoa he had been fascinated by ships and the sea. By the time he became a man he was an experienced sailor. He was acquainted with the noise and danger of sea-battle and the terror of shipwreck.

He loved to read books of adventure and especially was he interested in the travels of Marco Polo to the fabled lands of the Far East. Excitedly he read of the gold and silver, pearls, silks and spices which abounded there. And he noted that because of the great distance of the overland route only a trickle of these treasures ever got through to Europe. He pondered on the enormous wealth that would come to the men who could get there and back by some sea-route, and to their nation.

The Portuguese, in fact, were trying to do this. For years they had been sending ships down the west coast of Africa. Every year they went south a little farther. And every year they hoped to come to the end of that great mass of land and sail around it into the Indian Ocean. In Portugal where he spent many years, Columbus studied these voyages, frequently talking with the men who sailed on them. He carefully examined all the new maps that were made and he learned to make them himself. He was particularly interested in globes which showed the earth to be round as all learned men knew it to be.

Suddenly a bold and wonderful thought entered his mind. Would it not be shorter and easier to get to the East by sailing west across the Atlantic Ocean? Once that idea entered his head it ruled his life. Columbus believed in a personal relationship with God. He became convinced that it was His will that he should be the one to open the western route to Asia. But he was

Christopher Columbus

poor and nations were jealous of high-sea ventures by men of other countries. He needed money and he needed the protection of some mighty prince.

The Kings of Portugal and England were approached but they were not persuaded. After many years of consideration Ferdinand and Isabella, King and Queen of Aragon and Castille, decided to lend their support and protection to the enterprise. An agreement was made whereby Columbus would receive certain honours and a share of the proceeds. Three ships were procured, crews enlisted, supplies taken on, and on 3 August the fleet sailed from Spain for the Canary Islands. Columbus in the 100 ton *Santa Maria* was in command and the two smaller vessels of about 60 tons, the *Nina* and *Pinta*, were captained by the brothers Vicente Yanez Pinzon and Martin Alonzo Pinzon.

Voyage into the Unknown

We can be sure that not a minute was wasted in the Canaries. Columbus was anxious to be on his way. All necessary repairs and alterations were completed and supplies stowed on board by 5 September. Early the next morning, a Thursday, the anchors were weighed and the bows of the ships pointed toward the west. But little progress was made until Sunday for there was a calm.

At three o'clock on Sunday morning a stiff breeze blew in from the north-east. The fleet picked up good speed and by nightfall the Canary Islands had disappeared from sight and ships and men were alone on the sea. The weather could hardly have been better for the crossing. On 16 September, Columbus noted that 'the weather was like April in Andalusia', and there was nothing lacking but to hear the nightingales sing. Again on 8 October, 'the breezes were softer than in April at Seville, so that it is a pleasure to be in them: they are so laden with scent'.

The seamen experienced some understandable fears. The trade winds which blew constantly favoured the outward voyage, but knowing the ships could not beat well to windward, they wondered how they would ever get back to Spain. The Sargasso Sea with its broad areas of floating sea-weed caused some concern; they reasoned that this weed might get so thick as to make motion impossible. They were also troubled that the compass needle did not always point directly to the North Star.

The greatest difficulty, however, came toward the end of the voyage. Arriving at a point where they thought Japan should be, there was great disappointment among the men at seeing nothing but a seemingly endless sea. Columbus reasoned that if they had missed Japan they were sure to hit China and he was anxious to go on. But the seamen had never thought much of the enterprise from the beginning. To them it was a waste of money, effort and time. But they were seamen and their wages were guaranteed by the Queen. They had agreed to go west a certain number of leagues where Columbus assured them there would be land. But they had reached that point and gone beyond it and still there was no land.

What did Columbus now have in mind? Did he plan to sail on until the ships rotted or until the men all starved to death? They had fulfilled their share of the bargain and now they had their lives to think about. On Wednesday, 10 October, Columbus wrote in his log-book 'the men could now bear no more; they complained of the long voyage'. It is certain they threatened to take matters into their own hands and turn the ships about. Columbus 'heartened them as best he could, holding out to them bright hopes of the gains which they could make'. But it was probably Martin Alonzo Pinzon who turned the tide with even more persuasive language. He threatened to hang half a dozen of them or throw them overboard, so it is reported. Sullenly they agreed to sail further west for a few more days. The next day, 11 October brought cheer to all. Several green tree branches and canes were picked up, and what was more encouraging, a stick that had been carved by man. 'At these signs,' wrote Columbus, 'all breathed again, and rejoiced.'

The wind blew hard that day and the sea was rougher than at any time during the voyage. Helmsmen were hard put to keep the course and seamen were hard put to hold their footing. But there were no requests that sail be reduced and no complaints, for throughout the fleet there was the electric feeling that success was at hand.

The sun went down and darkness fell. But there was to be little sleep that night. Columbus impressed on all the necessity of a good lookout. The smell of oriental spices was in his nostrils. If land was close by, as it surely was to his mind, there might be offshore reefs.

The night grew very dark indeed as the vessels with the *Pinta* leading, strained forward to their rendezvous with destiny. At ten o'clock, Columbus thought he saw a light and later some few others thought they saw it too. This did not cause much of a stir at the time, but there have been volumes written about it since. The moon rose about 11.00 p.m. and soon illuminated the white-capped sea. The seamen's eyes were heavy with sleep and burning with crusty salt. But they would not yield to drowsiness; they had a feeling that this was to be their night of all nights.

The *Pinta* had increased her lead throughout the dark hours. At two o'clock Rodrigo de Triana, one of her seamen, thought he saw an object on the horizon. There was a moment's hesitation for he was fearful of being mistaken as others had been so often. But there it was—no doubt! '*Tierra! Tierra!*' he shouted 'Land! Land!'

Arrival in the New World

Meanwhile, the Lucayans of Guanahani had climbed into their hammocks at nightfall to sleep away the dark hours as they were used to do. A refreshing breeze blew in from the ocean caressing their bodies into restfulness. In the distance, Atlantic waves pounded the reef and they closed their eyes to the comforting sound of surf. That night, although they knew it not, they slept away the last hours of an era.

At daybreak next morning, they awakened to go about their daily chores and pleasures. But all thought of work or play was soon put aside as they gazed on a sight such as they had never seen before. Floating on the water a few miles eastward of their island were three large objects which moved about like living creatures. They watched with awe and fear as these objects came closer and then stopped with a great furling of wings.

With increasing anxiety they saw strange boats put into the water by strange looking beings who proceeded to paddle them shoreward. Terror gripped the hearts of the Lucayans. Would these unknown people who had come from the east be as bad or even worse than the cannibals from the south? They fled in panic from the seashore and hid themselves in the bushes.

But on that memorable Friday morning Columbus and his men had no evil designs on those naked, terrified people. What they really wanted was to meet them, and make friends with them so that they might ask them some very important questions. And there was so much Columbus wanted to know. The island on which he looked was puzzling. It showed no signs of the oriental splendour he had expected. But China or not, it was land, and that was more important than anything else at the moment, especially to Columbus.

The rowers pulled sturdily on the oars, cutting down the last few yards of the long, long journey that would make the name of Columbus immortal. In the long-boat that was taking him to glory, he must have reflected that he was still Christopher Columbus, Mariner; but soon now he would be Don Christopher Columbus, Admiral of the Ocean Sea, Viceroy and Governor of the Indies. The boat grounded, he stepped on to the beach, fell on his knees and, weeping, gave thanks to God. Next, he formally took possession of the island on behalf of Their Majesties and named it San Salvador.

From their hiding places, the Lucayans looked with astonishment on the finely dressed, white-skinned, hairy-faced people and their mysterious ceremonies. They were relieved to see no signs of hostility. How different these new-comers were to the cannibals! The Spaniards made every gesture of goodwill and friendship they could think of. They held out tempting gifts, brightly coloured beads, tinkling bells and beautiful cloth.

The Lucayans moved toward them, timidly at first, but with increasing assurance. They looked into each others' eyes, touched each other and exchanged gifts. This meeting of Old and New World peoples on a Bahamian coral beach was surely one of the most dramatic events in the history of man.

4
An Infernal Fire

A fire was destined to sweep the Bahamas. The igniting embers were brought across the ocean in the minds of Columbus and his crew. It was not to be the kind of fire which consumes stubble and tinder but an 'infernal fire' which feeds on human flesh.

Before commencing this heart-rending story, however, we will note some pleasant aspects of the Admiral's Bahamian stay.

Columbus in the Bahamas

In many respects these must have been the most exhilarating days of his life. He had crossed the formidable Atlantic Ocean and now a rich new world lay before him. Honours and fame would be his, and wealth untold.

In a buoyant and optimistic mood he sailed the Bahama sea, searching the islands he found for gold. And even though gold was always uppermost in his mind he was excited by the natural beauty he saw everywhere and by the friendly people who greeted him. Those who promote tourism, which is the keystone of the present-day Bahamian economy, frequently say that Columbus was our first tourist.

Like millions of others since, he was fascinated by the crystal clear water of the shallow sea and the colourful fish which live therein.

> There are here fish [he wrote] so unlike ours that it is a marvel; . . . of the finest colours in the world, blue, yellow, red and of all colours, and others painted in a thousand ways, and the colours are so fine that no man would not wonder at them or be anything but delighted to see them.

One night at anchor 'there came from the land the scent of flowers or trees, so delicious and sweet, that it was the most delightful thing in the world'. At another place he remarked that 'the singing of little birds is such that it seems that a man could never wish to leave this place; the flocks of parrots darken the sun, and there are large and small birds of so many different kinds . . . that it is a marvel.'

These flattering observations are interesting enough, but we must now turn to people, for this is essentially a story of people.

The Spaniards and Lucayans Meet

That the Lucayans were at a disadvantage in dealing with the Europeans stands out clearly. This is shown at the very beginning, on Guanahani, when they were unable even to accept the Spaniards as inhabitants of this world.

The Spanish seamen were experienced enough to know that there was considerable variation in the appearance of different peoples. They, therefore, looked on the physical characteristics of the Lucayans as being interesting but not astonishing. In fact, Columbus said that their colour was much as he expected it to be considering the latitude.

The world which the Lucayans knew, on the other hand, was inhabited only by people like themselves. They knew nothing of the yellow Chinese, the blond whites of Scandinavia, or the ebony blacks of Africa. Thus they were mentally incapable of assessing

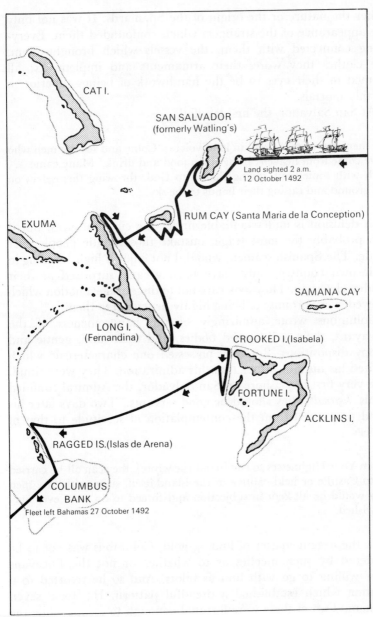

CAT I.

SAN SALVADOR
(formerly Watling's)

Land sighted 2 a.m.
12 October 1492

RUM CAY (Santa Maria de la Conception)

EXUMA

SAMANA CAY

LONG I.
(Fernandina)

CROOKED I.(Isabela)

FORTUNE I.

ACKLINS I.

RAGGED IS.(Islas de Arena)

COLUMBUS
BANK
Fleet left Bahamas 27 October 1492

Landfall and exploration of some of the Bahama Islands

either the nature or the origin of the Spaniards. It was not only the appearance of the strangers which confounded them. Everything connected with them, the vessels which brought them, the clothes they wore, their armaments and implements; all seemed to their eyes to be the handiwork of beings superior to earthly mortals.

At San Salvador, the first landfall,

the men and women cried in loud voices: 'Come and see the men who have come from heaven; bring them food and drink.' Many came . . . each with something, giving thanks to God, throwing themselves on the ground and raising their hands to the sky. . . .

This delusion is understandable under the circumstances, but it was probably the most tragic mistake those gentle people ever made. The Spanish seamen, who did not enjoy a high standing in their own country, must have been greatly surprised at their sudden elevation. They took care not to discourage a notion which showed every promise of being highly beneficial to them.

Columbus wrote admiringly of the handsomeness of the Lucayans, their well-formed bodies, and their kind, gentle and happy dispositions. But they possessed one characteristic which excited his disdain rather than his admiration. They were timid. The very first day ashore on San Salvador, the Admiral confided to his *Journal* 'They should be good servants.' Two days later his mind progressed from the contemplation of servitude to that of slavery.

When Your Highnesses so command [he wrote], they can all be carried off to Castille or held captive in the island itself, since with fifty men they would be all kept in subjection and forced to do what ever may be wished.

In the urgent matter of finding gold, Columbus was not to be hindered by such niceties as to whether or not the Lucayans were willing to go with him as pilots. And so he resorted to a solution which established a dreadful pattern. He 'took' seven of them. Two of these were fortunate enough to escape while the fleet was still in the Bahamas. The remainder, heartbroken in captivity, were taken all the way to Spain and it is doubtful if any of them ever saw Guanahani again.

The Search for Gold

After leaving San Salvador the Spaniards discovered and explored Rum Cay, Long Island and the Crooked Island group but found no gold. On 27 October fifteen days after discovery, the fleet sailed out of Bahamian waters and before nightfall Cuba was sighted. The extent and natural grandeur of that large island caused Columbus to think that he had probably reached Japan or even China. But alas, with the most diligent probing he could find no magnificent cities, no wealthy potentates and no gold.

He therefore abandoned the Cuban search and crossed the Windward Passage to Haiti, arriving there on 5 December. That island appealed to him from the very beginning and he renamed it Hispaniola. The people, who called themselves Tainos, were as kind and generous and timid as the Lucayans.

There he did find gold. He found gold in possession of the common people and more gold in possession of the *caciques,* and a brisk bargaining for these precious ornaments began. But of greater importance, there was persuasive evidence that somewhere in the interior of that island was the source of all the trinkets he had seen thus far, the long sought gold mine.

During the early hours of Christmas day the *Santa Maria* drifted on a reef and was wrecked. This made it necessary for Columbus to leave some of his men behind in Haiti. In order to provide them with a base, a fort was built and stocked with adequate supplies and provisions. The Tainos wept at the disaster and helped the Spaniards in every possible way. Columbus was very touched by their feeling and their generosity. 'A people so full of love and without greed [he wrote] . . . that I believe there is no better race . . . in the world.' Here we will pause to reflect that had the Spaniards returned even one-tenth of the love and kindness which they had received, how different would have been the fate of the unfortunate Tainos, and of the Lucayans too.

Return to the Indies

The Spanish fleet returned home in March 1493 and a much larger fleet set out for the Indies in September of the same year. Columbus was undoubtedly anxious to find out how diligently the thirty-eight men he had left behind had performed during his absence. Had they been able to gather a large quantity of gold or, better still, had they found the gold mine?

But tragedy had befallen the garrison. On arriving at La Navidad, the place of the fort, the mutilated and decomposed bodies of some of the men were found, all of them having been killed some weeks or months before. Spanish blood had flowed and would flow again and again. And Tainan blood was to flow in ever greater volume until there were no Tainos left to bleed.

The Spanish official intention was clear. Hispaniola was to be developed for the Glory of God and the Glory of Spain. The persons sent out to execute this plan added another objective, the enrichment of themselves. These three pursuits were usually seen as one and the same by Spanish eyes, but the last rapidly gained priority.

In the beginning, Indian goods and services were obtained by barter, or by purchase. But the progression from this to enforced demands and finally to slavery, took no great length of time.

The Destruction of a Race

As more and more Spanish colonists arrived and as the military grip became tighter, the entire island took on the aspect of a brutal labour camp. Escape for the Tainos was useless for there was no refuge to be found. Compliance was only better than resistance in that it deferred death a little longer.

It has been estimated that when the Spaniards first came to Haiti there were 300,000 Tainos living in that island. Sixteen years later, only 60,000 remained alive. By 1550 there were probably less than 500. Today there are none. Faced with this rapidly diminishing labour supply the Spaniards turned to the Bahamas to augment it.

It makes a sad but interesting story to say that many Lucayans were lured aboard the slave ships by the promise of being taken to heaven where they would be reunited with their loved ones who had died. This may have happened in some instances. But we have already seen by the seven whom Columbus 'took', that these people dreaded leaving their homeland to go anywhere else—including heaven. Furthermore, the Lucayans were undoubtedly well aware of the sort of 'heaven' then existing in Hispaniola.

The truth is that to Spanish colonists of that day the lives of their own countrymen meant very little, and those of the Indians nothing, except, hopefully, a few months or years of labour. With some notable exceptions, feelings of humanity never troubled their consciences. The rapidity of depopulation is itself indicative of ruthless haste. Irresistible force and terror were undoubtedly the principal weapons of persuasion. The Spaniards would descend on the hapless Island People with cutlasses and savage dogs and drive them on the slave ships, like cattle.

They were then crammed into dark and suffocating holds below decks, frequently with too little food and water. Thousands died even before the ships set sail from the islands and the sea-routes to Hispaniola were strewn with floating corpses. Perhaps those who died so soon were the fortunate ones. For surely death is preferable to a life without a moment of happiness or a glimmer of hope; the kind of life which awaited them as slaves in Hispaniola.

In that wretched island they were set to work to produce quotas. Quotas of farm food were demanded beyond the ability of both soil and man. To make matters worse, so pitifully little of the harvest was allowed the slaves that they lived in a state of perpetual hunger and increasing weakness. There were not enough hours in the day or days in the week to meet the quotas of gold. However feverishly the river beds were scraped or the earth dug up, it just could not be done.

For not meeting the impossible quotas brutal penalties were inflicted on their emaciated bodies. But perhaps it was their tortured minds which hastened death more than their suffering bodies.

Many of them [Peter Martyr wrote] in the anguish of their despair refused all forms of sustenance, fled to untracked woods and desert caves and there in silence, breathed their last. Others made their way to the sea-coast on the north side of Hispaniola and standing upon the shore cast longing eyes over that part of the ocean in which they believed the islands, which were their homes, were situated. When the breeze blew they eagerly drank it in knowing that but a short moment before it had been blowing down their own happy valleys and that it carried the very breath of the wives and children they had left behind. So they lingered for many hours until overcome by exhaustion, they stretched out their arms toward their homes in a last endeavour to embrace their dear ones and sank down upon the sand to die without a groan.

What the good Bishop Las Casas referred to as 'that infernal fire and devastating plague', raged on until the slavers could find no Lucayans to enslave. And this happened within twenty-five years of discovery. At that time Las Casas believed there might yet be some of the islanders left, hidden in forests and caves. He conceived the humanitarian idea of collecting them and settling them in an area of Hispaniola where they would live their last days in company with each other and in freedom. A vessel was hired and commissioned to search the entire Bahamas. After three years, eleven persons only were found. And when these were carried away there was no one left to mourn.

An entire race, which probably numbered twenty to thirty thousand when Columbus came, had been wiped from the face of the earth.

5
A New Beginning

After the Lucayans were taken away to slavery and death, a human silence settled over the Bahamas. The forests once again claimed the land which they had cleared to build their houses, to grow their crops, and to play their *batos*. It was almost as if the Island People had never existed.

European Rivalry in the New World

For the next 130 years the islands were to remain in a kind of historic limbo while great events surged about them. We are obliged to look at these events to gain perspective. But we must do so briefly and try to understand patterns rather than particulars.

The gold found in Haiti served only to whet the appetite of the Spanish nation. In the furious search for this metal, vast areas were explored and conquered. The rest of the Greater Antilles, the Spanish Main, from the Orinoco River to Panama, Central America, the lands of the Aztecs and those of the Incas, all fell to Spanish arms. Ships laden with treasure soon began making their way to Spain. To get into the favouring winds, the 'westerlies', they first had to go north, thereby passing through or near the Bahamas.

Other Europeans looked on Spain's good fortune with jealous eyes. They started a clandestine trade with her colonies and sent out privateers to prey on her treasure galleons. They began to settle the islands of the Lesser Antilles and to plant colonies on the Atlantic coast of North America.

These activities aroused the utmost resentment, for Spain regarded all these lands as her private domain. She claimed them by right of discovery, or by Papal degree, or both. But claiming is one thing and holding is another and this she was unable to do. It soon became evident to all nations that the best title was that of effective occupation.

By 1640, however, the Bahama Islands still remained un-occupied and, it would seem, unwanted. It is true that there was little of intrinsic value to attract settlers. Nevertheless the islands were at the centre of European activity in the Americas and this, alone, might have prompted some nation, and especially Spain, to settle them. But the only interest Spain showed was in sending Ponce de Leon, in 1513, to find and settle the island of Bimini, where there was reputed to be a fountain of miraculous water. Those who bathed in it, no matter how ravaged by age, were instantly restored to the beauty and vigour of youth. Neither Ponce de Leon, nor his successor who carried on the search, ever found the fountain and therefore no settlement was made.

Occupation of the Bahamas

The grant of the islands to Sir Robert Heath in 1629 indicates that by that time the English considered them to be a possession of their Crown. This, however, did not prevent Cardinal Richelieu from granting five of the islands to prominent Frenchmen four years later. These grants are only of the slightest interest to us. Nothing came of them; Bermuda was to be the spring-board for permanent settlement and we must now consider those beautiful islands which are of great importance to our story. The island group stands alone, in the open Atlantic, about 800 miles north-east of the Bahamas, the farthest north of all the coral islands of the world.

Apparently the American Indians never found their way there, for when they were discovered by Spaniards early in the sixteenth century, they were uninhabited. The first permanent settlement was made by an English company in 1612 but it was not prosperous. Farming proved both tiresome and unprofitable. The settlers suffered many hardships and anxiously looked about for ways to make ends meet.

The more adventurous turned to the sea which surrounded them everywhere. On their own banks and among their 300 islands they dived for pearls, fished, searched for ambergris and salvaged the cargo and fittings of an occasional wreck. This kind of life was much to their liking for they were by nature a daring and breezy lot, traits still to be found in their descendants today.

The growth of English colonies on the North American mainland encouraged them to make offshore voyages. Trade with these provided both excitement and profit. It is not known when the bold Bermudians, in their little vessels, first explored the Bahamas. But certainly by 1640 they knew of the large group of uninhabited islands, just four or five days sailing to the south-west.

Religious Quarrels

In that same year the storm clouds of religious controversy were gathering over Bermuda. They had blown across the Atlantic from England where they were soon to burst with tornadic fury.

At that time, a new English Parliament was in session, and its members were inflexibly resolved to bring to a head, once and for all, the long and bitter dispute with the Crown. A train of events was set in motion which was destined to affect the lives of almost every inhabitant of the British Isles. Before the ensuing calm, many prominent men were executed, the country was bloodied by Civil War, and both King and Parliament were destroyed.

We cannot go into the causes of these momentous happenings except, briefly, that of religion which seemed to be the root of all. The great majority of English people believed there should be a

State Church whose uniform ceremonies and tenets would be compulsory throughout the land. The burning issue was the form this Church should take.

While this wrangling was going on, a growing body of men and women challenged the very principle of a State Church. They contended that the Bible, which they assiduously read, was the only guide they needed, or would tolerate, in matters of faith and that the best thing King and Parliament could do for religion was to set it free. Holding themselves responsible only to God, they spurned the ecclesiastical authority of any earthly power.

Many of them abandoned the churches of their fathers and joined with others in setting up 'independent' congregations. The ridicule and persecution meted out to them was so severe as to drive thousands into exile. The most famous group to leave England were those who finally settled in Massachusetts in 1620 and came to be known as the Pilgrim Fathers.

In Bermuda, by 1644, three clergymen, including the Reverend Nathaniel White, had withdrawn from the Church of England to establish an Independent congregation. This group faced the same hostility as did their brethren in the Mother Country. And they conceived the idea of leaving Bermuda and going to settle in the Bahamas where they could 'enjoy Christe in the puritye of his ordinance, without this Bermudian imbitterment'.

With the object of finding a suitable island, a vessel was despatched to the Bahamas in 1644 but it never returned. Another, sent out the next year, returned to report that no suitable island could be found. The idea might have foundered at this point, except for the interest taken in it by a remarkably able and energetic man, Captain William Sayle. Sayle, an ex-governor of Bermuda, was a man of many parts. He was, at once, an able administrator, a successful businessman and an expert navigator. He combined daring and leadership with the ability to plan and undertake unusual and difficult enterprises.

In 1646, he was anxious to pursue the search for a suitable island which had been unsuccessful the year before. For this purpose, he and three others purchased the *William*, a ship of about 100 tons burthen. In addition, they had a small vessel specially built for exploring in shallow water.

But it would seem that events were overtaking the careful plans which Sayle had in mind. As the Bermuda Independents grew in number and determination, the persecution of them became more intense, resulting in near-riotous conditions. Whether Sayle was a member of the Independent congregation we do not know; but we do know that he strongly championed their right to religious freedom. To further this end, he accompanied the Reverend William Golding to England, arriving there late in 1646.

Things going on in England, at that time, were astonishing. The King was a captive and soon to lose his head, but still had considerable influence and hoped for conformity to the old established Church. Parliament was pressing for conformity to Presbyterianism. Oliver Cromwell, backed by the most powerful force ever established on English soil, the New Model Army, was becoming pre-eminent. The soldiers of that Army, predominantly Independents, were insisting that belief and worship should be matters for the individual to decide.

Sayle could see the direction in which the wind was blowing and he could sense that those in Bermuda would soon gain that freedom for which he had come to plead. Of greater importance, his perceptive mind could also sense that the time was most opportune to advance his plan for colonizing the Bahamas. Prominent men, close to Cromwell, lent a sympathetic ear, and some of them were prepared to take an active interest in the Bahamian venture.

The Eleutherian Adventurers

Consequently, Sayle and twenty-five others, who called themselves 'The Company of Adventurers for the Plantation of the Islands of Eleutheria', got together and drew up *Articles and Orders*, a document which was to be, in fact, the first constitution of the Bahamas. The name 'Bahamas' was replaced by 'Eleutheria', a word taken from the Greek and meaning 'freedom'. Ridicule or persecution of any person for his religious beliefs was prohibited. Freedom of religion for all, and an equal distribution of justice to all, were guaranteed. Eleutheria would be a republic, the first in the New World, with a Governor, a Council of twelve and a Senate of 100.

Sayle arrived back in Bermuda in October 1647, bringing with him a few English people destined for the new colony. It was, perhaps, in the early part of 1648 that a ship, probably the *William* and the specially built 'shallop', set sail for the Bahamas. There were about seventy settlers, most of whom were Bermudian.

Sayle undoubtedly gained the interior of the central Bahamas by way of the North-east Providence Channel. He may have landed first at New Providence, Abaco, or one of the cays near Eleutheria (now called Eleuthera). Dissension among the colonists started immediately; in fact, it was boiling up while they were still at sea. There was a Captain Butler who had come out from

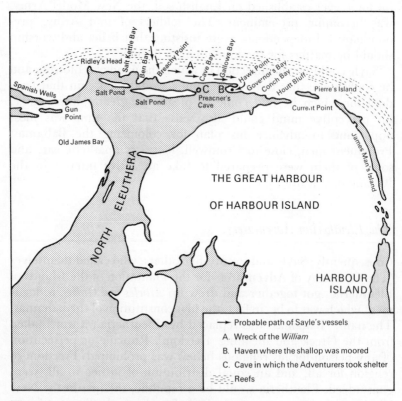

The arrival of the Eleutherian Adventurers

England and who had a strange conception of religious freedom. He seemed to have taken it to mean that he should be free from all religion. Consequently, he violently objected to the preachings, prayers and hymns that went on around him.

Having quickly decided that the colony would be ill-starred with Butler and his adherents in its midst, Captain Sayle thereupon set sail once again, taking with him most of the colonists, and steered for Eleuthera. Butler's group, left to themselves, are lost to history and we can say no more about them.

Shipwreck and Arrival

The northern end of Eleuthera and the adjacent small islands are protected from the ocean waves by fringe reefs of great density. Getting through them is an anxious business even today. Somewhere close to shore the *William* struck and became a total wreck. One man was drowned and all the goods and provisions were lost. Governor Sayle found shelter for his shallop in a little harbour which, appropriately, was named Governor's Bay. The settlers found shelter in a nearby cave.

This cave, traditionally known as Preacher's Cave, because the pioneers used it later for religious services, can still be seen. At the far end is a large boulder which still shows the shaping that was done to make it serviceable as a pulpit. Through circular openings in the roof pour shafts of sunlight which illuminate the interior with a diffuse glow reminiscent of a church-like atmosphere.

The settlers, having lost their provisions, were forced to exist for some months on 'such fruits and wild creatures as the island afforded', which was pitifully little. When it became obvious that they would die of starvation, Sayle decided to go off in his little vessel of only six tons to find food for them. With a crew of eight and after nine days, he arrived at Virginia.* There, the people of similar religious persuasion, loaded a ship with supplies and despatched it to Eleuthera. This act of generosity probably saved the lives of the colonists.

---

* First permanent European settlement established at Jamestown in 1607 by the London Company who had been granted a charter in 1606.

The wreck of Sayle's ship

But two years later they had not been able to raise themselves above the barest level of existence. The Puritans of New England,* on hearing of their plight, collected the magnificent sum of £800, with which they purchased 'provisions and other necessities'. The ship carrying this vital cargo arrived at Eleuthera in June 1650. In return, and '. . . to avoid that foul sin of ingratitude so abhorred of God, so hateful to all men', the Eleutherians went into the forest and cut ten tons of hardwoods and dye-woods and sent it to Boston by the return ship. They directed that the proceeds from the sale thereof should go to Harvard College.

Life on Eleuthera was so very hard that after a few years it was plain that only the most resolute would voluntarily remain there. From 1650 onward, many of the settlers, including the leading men, returned to Bermuda where they were tolerated if not welcomed. Captain Sayle, himself, left the colony in 1657. On the other hand individuals and small groups in search of a greater freedom, drifted in from time to time to join the gallant band.

But not all were volunteers. In 1656 'some troublesome slaves and native Bermudians and all the free Negroes' were sent into exile at Eleuthera. And we believe that both New England and Virginia used the colony for the same purpose. In time those who remained learned to live from the resources their new land and sea afforded. Fishing and farming provided the necessities of life, and occasional good fortune came by way of a conch pearl, a piece of ambergris, or a shipwreck. In 1684, the Eleutherians were descended on by Spaniards from Havana. Their settlement in the vicinity of Preacher's Cave and Governor's Bay was plundered and burnt, never to rise again from the ashes.

But for many years before this the pioneers had been busy establishing other settlements, at Harbour Island and Spanish Wells, and southward along the Eleutheran shore. And as we shall see in the next chapter, fourteen years before this the Bahama Islands came under the control of other people. New Providence became the capital island and the centre of activity and interest.

Strictly speaking, the name 'Eleutherian Adventurers' belongs to the twenty-six proprietors who promoted the venture. But it is doubtful if any of these, with the exception of Sayle, ever saw the

* The first European settlers were the Pilgrims who founded a settlement at Plymouth Massachusetts in 1620.

Interior of Preacher's Cave

Bahamas. To the Bahamian people the Eleutherian Adventurers were, and will always be, that remarkable group of men and women who left their homes and their homelands and came to the Bahamas in search of freedom.

Bahamians have an especial pride in those indomitable few who stayed on to lay the foundation of their country. During the early years, hunger and fatigue were with them always. They suffered every imaginable deprivation and enjoyed no comforts. But nothing could induce them to leave. Sustained only by an unshakeable faith in God, they struggled on to earn a distinction which belongs to few in history.

'After all,' wrote Sir Winston Churchill, 'it is not given to many to start a nation.'

6

The Proprietors

New Providence bursts on Bahamian history with surprising suddenness. In considering Eleuthera, we noted that the settlers had to overcome almost insuperable difficulties in becoming established. After ten years it is doubtful if the total inhabitants numbered more than the original seventy. And by 1670 there were less than 200 people in Eleuthera and the adjacent cays.

Then, with little previous indication that very much was going on there, New Providence moved to the centre of Bahamian affairs and was to remain there. In 1670, a population of 300 or more suffered 'noe want of provisions', and they loved the island because it was 'soe healthful'. This rosy picture, even allowing for exaggeration, is a far cry from that of the starving Adventurers. The question naturally presents itself, 'Why did these pioneer settlers find life so much easier than those of Eleuthera?'

A part of the answer is to be found in certain geographical advantages of New Providence; its central and sheltered location, its accessibility to shipping by way of the Providence Channel, and its fine harbour, which can be entered in almost any weather. But of far greater importance was the type of settler. Those of

Eleuthera were farmers and those of New Providence were mainly seamen. The latter knew how to live from the sea which provided an abundance of food in contrast to the impoverished land.

First Settlement of New Providence

We believe the island was first settled by Bermudian seamen who started to drift in some time before 1666. There was nothing high-minded about the purpose of these men and nothing dramatic about their arrival, as was the case with the Adventurers. They were merely searching for more productive fields in which to ply their trade. Ambergris, Spanish wrecks and salt first attracted them to the Bahamas, and they soon saw that New Providence, then called Sayle's Island, was an ideal headquarters for their ranging activities.

They were experts at gathering the conchs, and catching the fish and turtles which abounded in Bahamian waters. Their flimsy shacks ashore provided rest from the sea and their little farms produced sufficient fruit and vegetables to supplement their diets. Thus, being mainly creatures of the sea, they were immeasurably better off than the early Eleutherians who were tied to the land.

Some time after 1666, however, several groups of farming families came in from Bermuda which was then considered to be over-populated with insufficient farm land for its people. Because these families were very poor, financial assistance was necessary to transport and resettle them. On arriving and finding all the land they wanted and feeling certain that the soil would produce 'good cotton' and 'gallant tobacco', they were filled with gratitude and hope, and they renamed the island 'Providence'. The prefix 'New' was added later to avoid confusion with other Providences.

But throughout this period, it was the seamen who dominated the scene and it was they who either influenced or made the history.

Although enabling legislation for settlement of the islands had been properly passed by the English Parliament it would seem that Sayle and his fellow Adventurers were never given Letters

Patent. Consequently they had no legal claim and we suspect this is why they lost interest in Eleuthera. To complicate the problem the New Providence colony had sprung up with nearly twice as many people and also without a government.

Lords Proprietors

Sayle certainly felt some responsibility for the Eleutherians, and John Darrell and Hugh Wentworth who had stood the cost and arranged the transportation of the poor Bermudian farmers felt responsible for New Providence. As a result, Sayle, Darrell, Wentworth and others wrote to Lord Ashley and suggested that he and the other Proprietors of Carolina should obtain a patent for the Bahamas. They did, and on 1 November 1670, all the Bahama Islands were granted to Christopher Duke of Albemarle, William Earl of Craven, John Lord Berkley, Anthony Lord Ashley,* Sir George Carteret and Sir Peter Colleton.

The object of Ashley and his group, in taking over the Bahamas, was to make money. They envisaged a growing and thriving plantation, the Proprietors' share of which would result in a handsome income. Some money needed to be invested, but here they adopted a cautious attitude. Throughout the period, successive Governors could get little or no assistance for the most essential undertakings. The pattern the Proprietors followed was one of slight spurts of interest followed by months or years of indifference.

Locally, the seamen looked with great distaste on controls of any kind. Especially did they dislike paying shares of their proceeds to absentee landlords who never did anything for them except irritate them. They had been accustomed to gathering ambergris, hardwood, salt and wreck-goods and disposing of them to their best advantage. Their independent and intractable nature was seen at the very beginning when they elected their own Governor, John Wentworth, although they knew very well that the Proprietors had decided to appoint his brother Hugh

* Lord Ashley, later to be the first Earl of Shaftesbury, was one of the most important political figures in the reign of Charles II. He was active in the promotion of plantations and trade and had a personal interest in a number of colonies.

Duke of Albemarle

Earl of Craven

Lord Ashley

Three of the six Lords Proprietors of the Bahamas

to the post. However, Hugh died on his way to the Bahamas in November 1671 and the Proprietors then appointed John as Governor.

John had been a sea-captain himself and, among his adventures, was a spell at privateering. The waterfront crowd undoubtedly looked on him as a kindred spirit. Nevertheless, he was a servant of the Proprietors and felt obliged to try to carry out their instructions. The difficulty was, he had no means of enforcing the laws and regulations he was told to put into effect. And the seamen were not to be moved by sweet reason when it came to telling them where their goods should be sold, to whom, at what price, and what should be the Proprietors' and the Crown's share. They rebelled against the authority which was imposed upon them. The blame fell on the Governor and he was dismissed for not maintaining law and order and for not looking after the Proprietors' interests.

Chillingworth, who succeeded Wentworth, found the people living 'a lewd, licentious sort of life', and he tried to 'bring them to reason'. Poor man! They put him on a vessel and shipped him off to Jamaica, never to be heard from again in Bahamian affairs.

Wrecking Disputes with Spain

On the lonely expanses of the Bahama sea, law was but a word which had no practical meaning. When Bahamian wreckers came upon a wreck, they would not allow man or devil to stand between them and the fortune within reach. Crewmen who survived the wreck, so it was said, could not be sure of surviving the wreckers. If this was true, the evidence was effectively swallowed up by the sea. But indisputable evidence of some other outrages got back to Havana.

It was a custom of the Spaniards, if they knew the position of one of their wrecks, to send their own people to salvage the valuables. Bahamian wreckers regarded them as interlopers and drove them off. Sometimes they did worse than this by taking from them what they had already salvaged. Spanish officials looked on these incidents as blatant outrages, or even acts of piracy. It is not surprising, therefore, that they decided to retaliate.

According to the infuriated Governor Clark, who came after Chillingworth, Spanish ships made a number of incursions in Bahamian waters. They seized vessels, committed robberies, and took away Bahamian farmers as prisoners in Havana. Clark in reprisal commissioned privateers and sent them out to plunder and destroy Spanish ships. They must have enjoyed considerable success for soon Havana was howling with fury. And English officials were incensed that a petty Governor was endangering the peace by starting his own private hostilities. After all, by the Treaty of Madrid, signed in 1670, both Spain and England had agreed to abandon privateering in times of peace.

The Proprietors were called upon by the English authorities to explain the actions of their Bahamian Governor. Apparently they could give no satisfactory explanation. Clark was dismissed and Richard Lilburne sent out in his place. The unlucky Lilburne had hardly arrived when he was awakened by the noise of cannon fire. The Spaniards had struck. Before he could sound the alarm, Government House had been taken, and he was fleeing for his life. The Spaniards were delighted to find their mortal enemy, Clark, still in town, and they roasted him on a spit, so the story goes.

After the Havana fleet left, that same afternoon, the Governor and others who had escaped, crawled back out of the woods to survey the ruin. They set to work to build again what had been destroyed but the enemy returned again, later in the year, to repeat the performance, this time more thoroughly. As noted before, the original Eleutheran settlement was also destroyed that year and the inhabitants dispersed. But the majority of the Eleutherians who were then living elsewhere on the island and nearby cays were unaffected.

Historically, the harbour of New Providence has held an almost magnetic attraction for seamen. A feature of great importance, especially in the days we are discussing, is that there are two main entrances, each of which is provided with an alternative route which can be used by shallow-draught vessels. This natural endowment has saved many a ship, and many a life, both of good men and of rascals. During the Spanish raids, there was little damage to ships in the harbour. Losses to the seamen were mainly shore possessions, without which they could get on very well.

The permanently settled people such as the farmers and the merchants were in a different situation. Those who had not been killed or captured were left destitute and decided to move to other colonies in North America and the West Indies. And the Governor, having neither people nor houses left in his capital, went back home. But scarcely two years passed before a second settlement was made.

Second Settlement of New Providence

This time the immigrants came from Jamaica, and their leader was a preacher by the name of Bridges. Their motives, however, were not thought to be spiritual. Apparently they made the move without the knowledge, and certainly without the permission, of any authority. The Governor of Jamaica was incensed. He was convinced that a privateering or piratical nest would be set up in New Providence. But his orders that they should return to Jamaica were ignored. The Proprietors were not sure what was taking place but, hoping for the best, they confirmed Bridges as Governor.

Again the wheels of commerce began to turn, and salt,* which played such an important part in the Bahamian economy, began coming in from Exuma, woods from other islands, ambergris from the beaches and wreck-goods from the sea. Ships from Carolina brought in provisions, and ships from many places came to take on supplies and to trade as they had done before.

The Proprietors, seeing new hope, decided to show some initiative and appointed Cadwallader Jones to the governorship. This was a terrible mistake, for he exerted a totally disruptive influence. He was a scoundrel of the worst sort who never did anything good for the Proprietors or the Bahamas.

Of different calibre was Nicholas Trott who succeeded him in 1694. He was probably the best of the proprietary Governors and he built a new fort and a new town, both of which were named Nassau in honour of the Prince of Orange-Nassau who then sat on the English throne as William III. The town of 160 houses

* See Chapter 20, p. 61.

must have given much encouragement to the population. A church was also erected, perhaps to counteract the influence of the two public houses. This period of unusual prosperity needs some brief explanation.

Pirates and Privateers

After the 'Glorious Revolution', England had joined with other nations in opposing France whose military might was then the terror of Europe. This allowed Bahamian-based privateers to operate against French ships. But apart from this remunerative business, because of the war inflated prices were obtained for salt and wreck-goods.

The Treaty of Ryswick, 1697, put an end to the war and to Bahamian prosperity. Governor Webb, who came after Trott, found the people economically depressed and miserable. Privateering was at an end, salt brought only one-seventh the price it did during the war, and even wrecks were scarce.

During the conflict, men of foresight had prophesied that the war would breed a swarm of pirates to infest the Caribbean and Atlantic. The reason they gave was that there was no better training for pirates than the privateering school. The physical act of taking and plundering a ship, whether undertaken by privateers or pirates,* was the same. But legally and morally there was a world of difference. That difference was obviously not seen by men to whom law and morals meant little or nothing. Thus, some privateers became pirates with the greatest of ease.

From 1697, these pirates began increasingly to use the port of Nassau. They represented the only prosperity to be seen in those days and, as long as they behaved themselves tolerably well in port, the people of New Providence were not averse to their presence. It was reported, that even the Governors found pirate money irresistible, but these officials usually made an outward show of trying to suppress the rogues.

This causes much confusion in trying to evaluate the Governors of the period. For example, Deputy Governor Elding, a mulatto,

---

* See Chapter 7, p. 193.

who succeeded Webb, had four pirates publicly hanged, but was himself subsequently imprisoned for piracy and for dealing with pirates. To add to the confusion, Elding got himself freed and had his successor and captor, Governor Haskett, clapped in irons and shipped out of the colony. To this act, the people gave their roaring approval. It is hard to say who, if anyone, was free of piratical taint.

In 1701, Europe was again embroiled in a war, this time to decide who would inherit the Spanish crown. Spain, much reduced in power, was little more than a pawn. As before, England and other European nations were allied against the might of France whose Prince was the strongest contender for the vacant throne.

The French and Spanish of the New World had suffered much from Bahamian-based privateers and pirates. In combination, forces of the two nations made a surprise assault in October 1703. Nassau was quickly taken, plundered and burnt. Those who had managed to escape found the same scene of charred and blackened ruins which had faced their predecessors nineteen years before.

As with the first, the second settlement of New Providence had been totally annihilated. Nassau must have reminded the survivors of ancient Sodom, destroyed because of its wickedness. The will of the Proprietors to establish effective government was destroyed too, and for all practical purposes proprietary government ended in 1703.

7
Privateers and Pirates

Privateering, in its pure sense, was considered to be quite an honourable calling, not unbecoming a christian and a gentleman. In fact, some of the more successful of the privateers were looked upon by their countrymen as national heroes. The object of the Government was to encourage private vessels to wage war against the enemy without cost to the public treasury. Privateers were allowed to keep most, and sometimes all, of the captured ships and the valuables they contained, and the proceeds were divided between owners and crews according to agreement.

It must have been a very attractive business for during the War of the Spanish Succession the number of privateers in the Atlantic and Caribbean were estimated by some to exceed the number of merchant ships sailing the same regions.

Every genuine privateering ship was legally commissioned to undertake hostilities against the enemy. The captains held letters-of-marque, issued to them by some competent authority. That piece of paper was obviously of great value, for it meant that the possessor was a privateer and not a pirate. In a manner of speaking, it was insurance against the gallows. Privateers were apt to get into trouble when the pickings were lean. When no enemy ship had been seen for weeks on end, they sometimes plundered a friendly vessel to make something of the voyage. Such an act was, of course, illegal; it was raw piracy.

Thus, among the freebooters, were some who practised piracy when they were badly starved of lawful plunder. Undoubtedly there was, also, a good sprinkling who practised piracy on the slightest pretext, and some others who needed no pretext at all. But, during a war, seamen in general were inclined to prefer the advantages of legal privateering to those of illegal piracy, which carried the threat of the hangman's noose.

Some three months after Nassau was burnt to the ground, Birch was sent by the Proprietors to take up the governorship. Apparently he was quite unaware of the catastrophe which had befallen New Providence. An old writer records that 'finding it deserted, he did not give himself the trouble to open his commission'. After a few months, during which time he was forced to sleep in the woods, he returned to Carolina from whence he had come. Birch was the last Governor to be sent out by the Proprietors. From a practical standpoint, they ceased to exercise even their ineffectual authority after the destruction of Nassau.

Privateers' Republic

The lack of government and the consequent absence of law were not considered a hardship by the bold and ruthless seamen. Ashore and afloat they preferred to be restrained only by their own code of behaviour. Thus, the authority vacated by the Proprietors was promptly filled by the privateers who established a sort of 'Privateers' Republic'. This lasted for eleven years from the destruction of Nassau in 1703 to the end of the War of the Spanish Succession in 1714.

Records of the period are scant, but it seems that a pattern of reciprocal violence was established. New Providence based privateers would plunder and destroy French and Spanish ships throughout the year and, in reprisal, the enemy would pillage and burn Nassau at fairly regular intervals.

The sad fact of privateering was that wars do not last forever.

The Peace of Utrecht, signed in 1713, was followed by other agreements which, together, brought peace in Europe. News travelled slowly across the Atlantic Ocean in the eighteenth century and news of this nature, unwelcome to the privateers, undoubtedly took some time to penetrate their ears.

On 24 July 1715, a Spanish treasure fleet consisting of twelve ships had set sail from Havana for the long voyage home to Spain. Six days later, while in the Florida Straits, it met with a fierce hurricane which wrecked all the ships save one. Over 1000 persons were drowned and about 1500 washed ashore, many of them to starve, on the Florida coast and cays.

When this news got back to Havana, the Spaniards immediately set about salvaging what they could of the sunken treasure. Apparently they were quite successful for by December they had recovered, with the aid of 'diving engines', over 5,000,000 pieces of eight. The following spring they were back on the job, and after some weeks they had fished up an additional 350,000 pieces of eight. This silver was stored ashore under the guard of sixty soldiers.

Captain Henry Jennings

Then from over the horizon came privateer, Captain Henry Jennings, with a fleet of two ships and three sloops manned by 300 bold mariners. Jennings had no difficulty in overcoming the guards and making off with the entire treasure. On the way to Jamaica he met with more good fortune by way of a Spanish ship, laden with a rich cargo including 60,000 pieces of eight. With this additional loot added to his booty, Jennings sailed into Kingston Harbour.

But, whether he knew it or not, the war was over. Far from offering protection, the authorities in Jamaica were intent on punishing the privateers who, by their depredations in time of peace, were guilty of piracy. Jennings then decided to live up to the name with which he was branded. He and his men put to sea as raw pirates, rifling any ship they could take, whatever the nationality. Like other nautical outcasts of the time, they needed 'some place of retreat, where they might lodge their wealth, clean and repair their ships, and make themselves a kind of abode'. They decided upon New Providence partly because of its central location and good harbour, but chiefly because there was no government to interfere with their activities.

Pirates' Republic

Not only New Providence, but the entire Bahamian archipelago was admirably suited to their needs. The Florida Straits, the Bahama Channel and the Windward Passage had developed into regular sea-lanes. North Atlantic shipping routes and those of the Caribbean Sea were but a few days sailing distance, no great challenge to the swift vessels and hardy crews of the pirate fleet. Furthermore, throughout the islands were hundreds of harbours and creeks, secure havens where they could repair their ships, wait out stormy weather, or elude their would-be captors. The pirates had good reason to be satisfied with their domain, and the 'Privateers' Republic' degenerated into a 'Pirates' Republic'.

The swashbuckling nature of these daredevils calls forth an admiration tinged with envy. We admire their sheer courage, the valour with which they faced great odds, the defiance with which they fronted all the forces of law and order, and even death itself. At sea they were capable of frightful deeds, but our major concern is their life style in the Bahamas. On coming home, after a voyage, their first business was to sell, or convert to their own use, the ships and goods they had taken and to restore their own vessels to seaworthiness.

Nassau was, of course, the port for selling and buying. With hundreds of men of the 'Black Flag' headquartered there, it is easy to imagine the raucous bustle which went on in the harbour and along the waterfront. After business had been attended to, they turned to pleasures, chiefly those to be found in liquor and women. The money for which they had risked their lives was squandered in Nassau's public houses and bawdy houses. And many of them set out on a new voyage as poor as they had begun the voyage before.

Nassau provided for an almost explosive release of tension after the discipline and hazards of the high sea. But, being aware that the French or Spaniards might descend on that town at any time, the pirates were never free from anxiety there. Consequently, each commander had his own little retreat, on some lonely island where the ship-work might be done with a greater feeling of security.

But even there, they never quite forgot that they were hunted men. A vessel, careened for the lengthy process of drying, cleaning, caulking and repairing, was in an extremely vulnerable state. To provide for security during the overhaul, it was customary to set up some of the ship's guns on shore as a temporary battery.

Pirate Entertainment

Between spells of work copious supplies of rum set them dancing, singing and exchanging ribald humour. A book appeared in 1724, just a few years after the events we are discussing, entitled *A General History of The Robberies and Murders of the Most Notorious Pyrates*. The author Captain Charles Johnson, records some of their humorous activities ashore, including the performance of a little skit in which a member of the crew was mockingly tried for piracy.

The Court and Criminals being both appointed, as also Council to plead, the Judge got up in a Tree, and had a dirty Tarpaulin hung over his Shoulders; this was done by Way of Robe, with a Thrum Cap on his Head, and a large Pair of Spectacles upon his Nose:
Thus equipp'd, he settled himself in his Place, and abundance of Officers attending him below, with Crows, Handspikes, etc. instead of Wands, Tipstaves, & such like —— The Criminals were brought out, making a thousand sour Faces; and one who acted as Attorney-General open'd the Charge against them; their Speeches were very laconick, and their whole Proceedings concise. We shall give it by Way of Dialogue.

ATTORNEY GENERAL An't please your Lordship, and you Gentlemen of the Jury, here is a Fellow before you that is a sad Dog, a sad sad Dog; and I humbly hope your Lordship will order him to be hanged out of the Way immediately. —— He has committed Pyracy upon the High Seas, and we shall prove, an't please your Lordship, that this Fellow, this sad Dog before you, has escaped a thousand Storms, nay, has got safe ashore when the Ship has been cast away, which was a certain Sign he was not born to be drown'd; yet not having the Fear of hanging before his Eyes, he went on robbing & ravishing, Man, Woman and Child, plundering Ships Cargoes fore & aft, burning and sinking Ship, Bark and Boat, as if the Devil had been in him. But this is not all, my Lord, he has committed worse Villanies than all these, for we shall prove, that he has been guilty of drinking Small-Beer; and your Lordship knows, there never was a sober Fellow but what was a Rogue. —— My Lord, I should have spoke much finer than I do now, but that, as your Lordship knows our Rum is all out, and how should a Man speak good Law that has not drank a Dram. —— However, I hope, your Lordship will order the Fellow to be hang'd.

JUDGE —— Heark'ee me, sirrah, —— you lousy, pittiful, ill-look'd Dog; what have you to say why you should not be tuck'd up immediately, & set a Sun-drying like a Scare-crow? —— Are you guilty, or not guilty?

PRISONER Not guilty, an't please your Worship.

JUDGE Not guilty! say so again, Sirrah, and I'll have you hang'd without any Tryal.

PRISONER An't please your Worship's Honour, my Lord, I am as honest a poor fellow as ever went between Stem and Stern of a Ship, and can hand, reef, steer, and clap two Ends of a Rope together, as well as e'er a He that ever cross'd salt water; but I was taken by one George Bradley (the Name of him that sat as a Judge,) a notorious Pyrate, a sad Rogue as ever was unhang'd, and he forc'd me, an't please your Honour.

JUDGE Answer me, Sirrah, —— how will you be try'd?

PRISONER By G— and my Country.

JUDGE The Devil you will. —— Why then Gentlemen of the Jury, I think we have nothing to do but to proceed to Judgment.

ATTORNEY GENERAL Right, my Lord; for if the Fellow should be suffer'd to speak, he may clear himself and that's an Affront to the Court.

PRISONER Pray, my Lord, I hope your Lordship will consider ——

JUDGE Consider! —— How dare you talk of considering? —— Sirrah, Sirrah, I never consider'd in all my Life. —— I'll make it Treason to consider.

PRISONER But, I hope, your Lordship will hear some Reason.

JUDGE D'y hear how the Scoundrel prates? —— What have we to

do with Reason? —— I'd have you to know, Raskal, we don't sit here to Reason; —— we go according to Law. —— Is our Dinner ready?

ATTORNEY GENERAL Yes, my Lord.

JUDGE Then, heark'ee, you Raskal at the Bar; hear me, Sirrah, hear me. —— You must suffer, for three Reasons; first, because it is not fit I should sit here as Judge, and no Body be hang'd. —— Secondly, you must be hang'd, because you have a damn'd hanging Look: —— And thirdly, you must be hang'd because I am hungry; for know, Sirrah, that 'tis a Custom, that whenever the Judge's Dinner is ready before the Tryal is over, the Prisoner is to be hang'd of Course. —— There's Law for you, ye Dog. —— So take him away Gaoler.

The pirates held undisputed sway in the Bahamas for about three years. But whether there or elsewhere their careers were usually short lived. To quote Johnson, 'I must inform my readers that the far greater part of these rovers are cut short in the pursuit, by a sudden precipitation into the other world.'

Blackbeard

Edward Teach, more commonly known as Blackbeard, the most colourful and well known of all the pirates, is a never-dying legend in Bahamian lore. He was a massive man noted for his boldness, his fiendish appearance and roguish ways. With cutlasses and three brace of pistols slung about him, he resembled a walking arsenal. His long black beard was twisted with brightly coloured ribbons and turned about his ears. Slow burning cords tucked under his hat wreathed his head with demonic smoke. All this, together with his fierce and wild eyes, 'made him . . . such a figure that imagination cannot form an idea of a fury from hell to look more frightful'.

One day at sea he said to a few of his men, 'Come, let us make a hell of our own, and try how long we can bear it.' He took them below, closed up the hatches, and set on fire several pots filled with brimstone and other acrid matter. One by one, close to suffocation, the men were forced to seek the upper deck. Blackbeard held out the longest and was quite pleased that he was better fitted to live in hell than the others.

Edward Teach alias Blackbeard

At the edge of the township, on what is now the Eastern Parade, Blackbeard held his court.

Under a wild figtree [wrote McKinnen, eighty-five years later] the trunk of which still remains and was shown to me . . . he used to sit in council among his banditti, concerting or promulgating his plans, and exercising the authority of a magistrate.

The story goes that under that tree he kept a barrel of rum from which all who passed by were invited to drink. Those who hesitated were given a choice of drinking or being shot.

Other Pirates

Next to Blackbeard, Bahamians show greatest interest in two female pirates, Mary Read and Anne Bonney. These were not fictitious characters but real women who dressed like men and fought like devils. It is claimed that among all the cut-throats they were unsurpassed in bravery. On trial, shortly before her death, Mary Read was questioned as to why she chose a career that carried the certainty of an ignominious death. 'She answered, that as to hanging, she thought it no great hardship, for were it not for that, every cowardly fellow would turn pirate, and so infest the seas, that men of courage, must starve.'

On the day that Anne Bonney's lover, Captain Rackham, was executed, he was permitted to see her before meeting with the noose. The comfort she gave him was that 'she was sorry to see him there, but if he had fought like a man, he need not have been hanged like a dog.'

The pirate commanders who made Nassau their headquarters are listed by Johnson as follows

Jennings, Benjamin Hornigold, Edward Teach, John Martell, James Fife, Christopher Winter, Nicholas Brown, Paul Williams, Charles Bellamy, Oliver La Bouche, Major Penner, Ed. England, T. Burgess, Thos. Cocklyn, R. Sample, Charles Vane, and two or three others.

There were at least twenty commanders based at Nassau and

Anne Bonney and Mary Read

although we know that some of these commanded more than one vessel, we will allow one to each. The average pirate crew seems to have been about seventy men. Thus during this period there

B. Cole sculp.

were about 1400 pirates who operated out of Nassau. Not surprisingly the British Government was deluged with complaints about the menace they presented. Finally something was done.

A proper force was ordered 'to be employ'd for the suppressing the said Pyrates'. Fourteen warships mounting more than 330 guns were placed on station from Barbados to New England. Further, 'the more effectually to put an end to the same', a year later, a general pardon was proclaimed to all pirates who surrendered before 5 September 1718. Pirates of New Providence were thus faced with the choice of being captured or surrendering. Many went to Bermuda and other places with a government to claim the pardon. Others stayed on at their beloved Nassau hoping that somehow or other they might be able to carry on their wicked business.

What of the people in Nassau who were not pirates? In July 1718 it was reported that 'ye greater part of the inhabitants of Providence are already gone into other adjacent islands.' The few who remained could only groan under a brutal tyranny.

8

Woodes Rogers Takes Over

On the hot summer's night of 26 July 1718 the pirates of Nassau were in a dilemma. During the late afternoon of that same day, a number of ships arrived at the bar of Nassau harbour. The fleet included an armed merchantman, the *Delicia*; three naval vessels, *Milford*, *Rose* and *Shark*, and a few Bahamian sloops. Bristling with cannon and crowded with people, the vessels were obviously on some extraordinary mission. After they had come to anchor, small boats from the harbour soon swarmed about them to discover the purpose of the visit. On board the *Delicia*, was a Captain Woodes Rogers, who soon made it plain who he was and what he had come to do.

He had been sent out as the first Royal Governor of the Bahamas, and chief among his priorities was the suppression of piracy, by peaceful means or otherwise. He had with him some able men who would help to establish a government, some industrious settlers who preferred honest work to plunder, and a hundred soldiers who would maintain order. His escort of warships were to remain until the pirate vessels in the harbour had either surrendered or been sent to the bottom.

Woodes Rogers and the War of the Spanish Succession

When this news got back to the pirates they were filled with dismay. They knew that Woodes Rogers was not a man with whom they could trifle. His fame as a courageous commander had been gained during the War of the Spanish Succession, when privateers had taken over the Bahamas. French and Spanish privateers had inflicted such grievous losses on English ships at sea that British mercantile trade was severely crippled. None suffered more than Bristol merchants who were eager to find some way of recouping their losses. Woodes Rogers, a sea-captain of the city, suggested that he should be sent to attack and plunder the enemy in the Pacific Ocean, where English ships were least expected to appear. The prominent men of Bristol were favourably impressed with the bold and energetic Rogers and his scheme. They financed the fitting out and supplying of two ships, the *Duke* and *Duchess,* which were commissioned as 'private men-of-war' that is to say, privateers.

After entering the Pacific the first activity of interest was the rescue of Alexander Selkirk which later became inspiration for Defoe's immortal *Robinson Crusoe.* Thereafter several small enemy ships were taken and the city of Guayaquil plundered and held to ransom. The great objective, however, was to capture the 'Manila Ship', the Spanish treasure galleon which sailed once a year from the Philippines to Mexico. Toward the end of December 1709, when all despaired of ever meeting with it, a sail was sighted, a 'great and joyful surprise'. The encounter lasted about three hours before the galleon surrendered.

The prisoners taken gave news of an even larger galleon, which had left Manila at the same time. This ship was met with and engaged the day after Christmas. During seven hours of hot fighting, the English poured 500 cannon balls into her hull. But she was a new and massive ship and could not be sufficiently damaged to cause her to surrender.

Rogers, who had lost part of his jaw in the previous encounter, was again among the casualties. A part of his ankle was blown away by the explosion of an enemy 'fireball'. And once again, as before, he refused to be carried from the quarter-deck, where he remained throughout the action, giving orders and encouragement to his men. In October 1711 the ships arrived back home with plunder estimated to be worth as much as £800,000. It was, indeed, one of the most successful voyages of English privateering history.

Rogers had shown himself to be a great organizer and a courageous leader of men, not easily intimidated by threats, or frightened by overwhelming odds. After a little more sea-going activity and some years of inactivity spent in Bristol he began to consider several projects to which he might devote his enormous energies. Among these was a plan for the Bahamas.

By 1715, pirates had started to gather there in great numbers. So serious did the situation become that the House of Lords, in an address to the King, stressed the advisability of the Crown taking over the responsibility of Bahamian government. Thus, Rogers' proposal to the Lords Commissioners of Trade, that he should be commissioned to clean up the pirates, was put forward at a propitious time and it received favourable consideration.

One would think that the Lords Proprietors would have been happy to surrender their political rights to the Bahamas, which had never brought them anything but trouble. But much persuasion was needed before their resistance was overcome. The Lords Proprietors surrendered the civil and military government of the islands to the King on 28 October 1717, but retained ownership of the land and this, including quit rents and royalties, was leased by them to Rogers and six co-partners for twenty-one years. The Proprietors agreed to accept from the lessees a total of only £2,450 which indicates that they did not expect very much to come of the venture.

Rogers' motives in this enterprise were similar to those which had moved him to undertake his privateering voyage. He expected to render a service to his country and, at the same time, gain glory and wealth for himself, a way of life accepted by all prominent men during those times.

Rogers' Arrival in the Bahamas

After being duly appointed by the King, Rogers set sail on Friday, 22 April 1718. His arrival was not entirely unexpected by the pirates. Some months before they had found on a captured ship a document called 'A Proclamation, for suppressing of Pyrates', and dated 5 September 1717. Issued in the name of the King it left no doubt that the English Government was determined to eradicate piracy in the New World. After stating that 'we have appointed such a force as we judge sufficient for suppressing the said Pyrates', it went on to offer amnesty to any who would surrender within a year.

Thereupon, the Bahamian pirates who were out cruising were called in and a general council was held. Some were for fortifying New Providence and holding it as a Pirate Commonwealth. Some put forward other ideas. But it was a chaotic meeting and no agreement could be reached. Jennings decided to surrender under the terms of the Proclamation. Apparently, he had much influence among the ranks, and about 150 aligned themselves with his decision. There being no Governor in the Bahamas, they were obliged to go elsewhere to swear the necessary oaths. Thus, the remainder, whose ships Rogers saw in Nassau harbour, were chiefly those who had been unable to decide what to do. But the time had come when a decision had to be made.

What transpired during that night of 26 July is not at all clear. With darkness coming on it seems that Rogers had decided not to enter the harbour until daybreak. But the captains of the *Rose* and *Shark*, feeling confident with good Bahamian pilots, went in that night. Whether they misunderstood Rogers' orders, or whether they were goaded into indiscretion by the insolence of Charles Vane is not known. This pirate captain would only surrender on his own terms and if these were not accepted, he made it plain that he would stand and fight.

After an exchange of gun fire the crafty Vane fired a French prize and set it drifting toward the naval ships. The horrifying blaze threatened to engulf the *Rose,* and Captain Whitney was forced to cut his cables and make for safety. As the fire heated the loaded guns, the ear-splitting noise of discharging cannon made the spectacle all the more terrifying. To Rogers who watched from outside the bar it must have seemed that the entire harbour had exploded in fire and thunder. At daybreak Vane slipped out of the harbour through the Eastern Narrows, to carry on his bloody business, and to be hanged before many years had passed.

After the narrow escape of the *Rose,* Rogers wanted to be certain that there were no more hot-heads like Vane left in the harbour. But all the news he received was reassuring; the remainder of the pirates were prepared to surrender.

In the early morning of 27 July, the long boat of the *Delicia* was rowed into a little cove, in the vicinity of the present Sheraton-British Colonial Hotel, and Woodes Rogers stepped ashore. The pirates had all gathered for the occasion, anxious to see the renowned privateer with the scarred face and limp walk, who had come to put them out of business. Whatever secret thoughts or intentions they may have had, outwardly it was all enthusiasm for their new Commander-in-Chief.

Suppression of Piracy

From the top of Fort Nassau the Governor's commission was read and, 'Our Trusty and Well-beloved Woodes Rogers, Esquire' was duly sworn in as 'Our Captain General and Governor-in-Chief in and over our Bahama Islands in America'. Rogers himself then read the Royal Proclamation of pardon, and nearly 300 pirates took the oath. It is interesting to reflect on how Blackbeard might have behaved had he been in Nassau then. But the fierce rascal was out on a voyage, and was never to see New Providence again. About four months after his friends surrendered in Nassau, he was killed in Carolina.

A Council of twelve was formed, consisting of six men who had come out with Rogers and six selected from among the inhabitants. Rogers was pleased that he had been able to find, locally, six good men 'who had not been pirates'. Before a week had passed, all the important posts had been established and filled and the machinery of government was in good working order.

The problems facing Rogers were tremendous. Filth and garbage were piled high around the dilapidated hovels, and all along the waterfront. It was said that the effluvia which rose from Nassau was a better guide to the harbour than the compass. The pirates had apparently developed immunity to their pestilent surroundings, but newcomers quickly succumbed. Before the end of the year, Rogers had buried a hundred soldiers, sailors and workmen. Therefore, cleaning up the town and building new houses was not so much a matter of improving its appearances, as it was a desperate necessity for survival.

The provision of adequate defence was of extreme urgency. During the previous fifteen years, the enemy had descended on Nassau thirty-four times and at any moment he could be expected again. Yet the fort which guarded the western entrance to the harbour was a complete shambles, and to the east there was no provision for defence at all.

While every available man was kept busy in cleaning up and rebuilding the town, in repairing forts, and in doing guard duty the thought which bore very heavily on Rogers' mind was that of pirates. He realized that those still at sea, far exceeded the number which had surrendered to him. Moreover, of the three hundred who had taken the oath, at least a hundred had gone back to their old profession, and it was questionable how long the others would remain loyal. He knew very well that the war against the pirates was yet to be won.

The pirate threat was very real and the fortifications he was building were protection against them as well as the French and Spanish although he dared not tell his ex-pirate workmen that. For example, Vane, who had escaped when Rogers arrived, was itching for revenge. He had established headquarters at Harbour Island, just sixty miles away, and had sent warnings to Rogers that, in combination with other pirates, he would attack him soon.

In a sense, Rogers was working against time. Measures which might provoke the pirates unduly had to be avoided, however justifiable. Discretion was essential to success and in this respect the Governor proved to be a master.

To begin with, he commissioned sloops manned by ex-pirates to go out and search for pirates; and those brought in were quietly lodged in jail. In November he moved another step forward by sending three to England for trial. By December he felt the hour had come. In the guardroom of Fort Nassau, ten pirates, captured at Exuma, were put on trial and sentenced to be hanged. Rogers decided to test his strength and authority by staging a public execution.

After ascending the gallows platform at ten o'clock in the

morning of 12 December 1718, the men, some of them gaily bedecked with ribbons, were given forty-five minutes to prepare for the next world. There was some singing of psalms, some clowning, some salty humour; one of them kicked off his shoes saying he had once sworn not to die with them on.

We can be sure that everyone who could walk was out that day to witness the grim spectacle. Assuredly it was unsettling to the ex-pirates to see their old friends about to be 'tucked up, and set a sun-drying like a Scare-crow'. It must have crossed many of their minds that the honourable thing to do was to rush the gallows and rescue them from such a horrid death.

The tension was so great that, to Rogers, every minute of that forty-five must have seemed like an hour. The situation was made all the more tense when the condemned men began calling on their former mates to intervene and save their lives, saying it was cowardly not to do so. But no man made an untoward move. A youth of eighteen was reprieved after the noose had been placed about his neck. A minute later the other nine were dropped into eternity.

Rogers knew that, at last, he was really master of New Providence. He had successfully taken over and transformed the greatest pirate den in the world. Perhaps it was then that he thought of a meaningful motto for the colony: *Expulsis Piratis— Restituta Commercia,* Pirates Expelled—Commerce Restored.

Spanish Invasion

Having got his internal affairs under reasonable control, Rogers was faced with an immediate threat of invasion. The beginning of 1719 found England, France, Austria and the Netherlands at war with Spain. The ex-pirates who could hardly be persuaded to work for either love or money were moved to feverish activity by their hatred of the Spaniards. Throughout 1719 there were rumours of an impending invasion, and with every new rumour Rogers was able to get a few weeks of work out of his charges. As a result, by 1720 Fort Nassau was in good condition with fifty cannon mounted.

The Spaniards were slow in getting around to New Providence, only because they had been busy trying to retake other former Spanish possessions. On 24 February 1720, however, the invasion fleet was seen on the horizon. After leaving Havana, the armada of twelve ships had made its way through the Florida Straits, entered the North-west Providence Channel and bore down on New Providence from the north.

The *Delicia,* which had brought Rogers out, was still in the harbour with her thirty-four guns and so, fortunately, was another armed vessel of twenty-four guns. These ships together with the fort could be counted on to give a hot reception to the enemy if he should try to cross the bar. Otherwise, the situation was not too good. On board the Spanish ships were 1300 soldiers and Rogers could muster only 500 men. The majority of these were ex-pirates, however, and on this occasion the Governor was undoubtedly pleased that they were better at fighting than working.

The Spanish fleet, looking formidable indeed, came to anchor off the harbour entrance and out of range of cannon shot. This made it plain to those who anxiously watched from Nassau that no attempt would be made to challenge the bar defences.

That afternoon some of the vessels weighed anchor and worked their way eastward. Rogers, realising what this meant, posted sentries and armed groups all along the eastern foreshore. Late at night soldiers from these ships attempted a landing. 'But two valiant Negro sentries blazed hotly and happily away at the oncoming boats.' The Spaniards having no stomach for the iron balls that were ripping among them quickly returned to their ships.

A party which tried to get ashore to the west of Nassau was equally unlucky. They ran into a detachment of ex-pirates who were overjoyed to meet their hated foes again. The Spanish expedition returned to Havana, having accomplished nothing. It was a miserable performance on the part of a nation which had bred the *conquistadores.* The message they took back to the authorities there was that there was a brave and capable Governor in the Bahamas now, and that Nassau could no longer be plundered and burnt with impunity.

9
The Aftermath

After the pirates were subdued or driven out, peace settled over New Providence. The 'Black Flag' had lost its glory, and the cannon salutes, which heralded its arrival in port, were heard no more. Gone was the excitement of prizes being brought in and of holds filled with plunder.

The word which Rogers had for his ex-pirates was that each should now do an honest day's work for which he would pay a dollar. Nothing speaks more for his persuasive ability than that so many of them tried. And it must have been something of a sight to behold them performing the unaccustomed labours of sweeping streets, felling trees and cutting stones. But old habits proved hard to shake off. Most often they turned up for work late, or drunk, or both. Frequently they did not turn up at all. One by one they drifted off, hoping to find somewhere in the wide world the way of life they loved so well.

To get a plantation going Rogers had hoped to bring with him 500 Palatine refugees whose homeland had been laid waste by the French. He could not get this number, but it seems that he did bring a few hundred including some Swiss and Huguenots.

These settlers were sturdy and hardworking but they had little resistance to Nassau's 'summer sickness', and before many months a number of them had died. The survivors were confronted with land more stubborn than any they had ever tried to work before. In fact nothing looked very promising.

It had been an extremely costly business to rebuild the fort and town, maintain a company of soldiers, and keep the *Delicia* on station. When the co-partners had put out £90,000 and would spend no more, the Governor was forced to use his own savings. And when these were gone, he had to rely on what credit he could get. After two years and nine months of unremitting toil, anxiety and sickness, Rogers went home to England hoping, perhaps, to recoup his health and vigour and to raise more capital. Instead, he was dismissed from office and lodged in a debtor's prison.

Governor Phenney

When his successor, George Phenney, arrived he found New Providence, and indeed all the Bahamas, quiet with nothing very exciting going on anywhere. The population had increased by only a few hundred since the proprietary grant. There were still only three islands with much of a population: New Providence with 750 people, Eleuthera with 240, and Harbour Island with about 175. New Providence had had a great turnover of settlers during the past fifty years, with some always leaving and some always coming in. The people of Eleuthera and Harbour Island, on the other hand, being somewhat removed from the centre of turmoil, were still mainly descendants of the pioneer stock.

After Governor Phenney settled in, he reported that

The Trade consists in cutting the Dye woods, which with the salt, Turtle and Turtle Shell and Fruits in their seasons are exported to the neighbouring colonies of America, for which sometimes, vessels belonging to North America, bring in barter several commodities.

We can with confidence add 'wreck-goods' to Phenney's list, for these were a perennial harvest in peace or war.

Bahamian woods had been cut and exported ever since the Adventurers first settled Eleuthera. As the years went by more and more trees were discovered that had commercial value. Peter Henry Bruce, who came to the Bahamas not long after Phenney, listed those of importance. We will use the names that Bruce used and leave the botanically-minded to consult their *Florae* where better identification is required.

Mastic, madeira, mahogany and cedar were used in building houses and ships, and also in furniture-making. Valued for their strength and durability, these woods were shipped to both England and North America. It is believed that some of the English ships which fought at Trafalgar were partly constructed of Bahamian timber. Also prized were a number of lesser known hardwoods: prince wood, yellow wood, box wood, naked wood, *lignum vitae*, black and red iron-wood, ebony, machinella, black feney and dog wood. These were in demand for the manufacture of small cabinets and curios.

For use in the dyeing of cloth, log-wood, braziletto, and green and yellow fustic were exported. These gave fixed dyes in an age before chemicals. Many tons of wild cinnamon bark were shipped annually to Curacao where it was used in the distilling of cinnamon waters, and the bark of the *cortex winterina* was sent to the Levant to be burnt for incense and perfume. Cutters would scour the islands in search of these woods and sell them to merchants in Nassau who would ship them abroad.

Salt-making* too had been an industry since the Adventurers. Bermudians had tried unsuccessfully to make it at home. In the Bahamas, where there are thousands of shallow, salt water ponds conditions were more favourable and perhaps the first local salt works was at Salt Kettle Bay, Eleuthera, near Preacher's Cave. When an area along the margin of one of these ponds is diked off it is called a 'salt pan'. The water in this pan is continuously evaporated by wind and sun. If the rate of evaporation exceeds that of rainfall, salt crystals result.

Before refrigeration, salt had a much wider use than today. It was essential and much in demand for the preservation of meat and fish. During the period we are discussing there were salt

---

* See Chapter 20, p. 193.

works at Eleuthera and on New Providence and nearby islands. But Great Exuma came to prominence at this time as the chief centre of production. Men from New Providence would go there and work the ponds on a seasonal basis. From the Bahamas many shiploads were exported annually to the North American colonies.

Bahamians had always grown fruit and vegetables for home use. During Phenney's time these products were exported for the first time. The farmers Woodes Rogers had brought in were making a valiant effort to do something with the rocky Bahamian soil.

They have tamarinds [wrote Bruce] equal to any in the world; the Lucca olive, as well as the wild kind; oranges (sweet, sour and bitter), lemons, limes, citrons, pomegrantes, plums, sugar apples, pine apples, figs, papues, sapodylles, bananas, sowersops, water and musk melons, yams, potatoes, gourds, cucumbers, cod and bird pepper, guavas, casava, plantains, prickly pears, oil of castor, sugar, ginger, coffee, indigo, cotton preferable to that in the Levant, and tobacco; Indian wheat, Guinea-corn and peas: besides these all the roots of Europe grow wonderfully quick, and to a surprising size. The flowering shrubs and other plants are so aromatic, that they perfume the air to a great distance.

This long list might lead us to believe that agriculture had blossomed into a substantial industry. It had not done that, but Phenney had advanced the good work which Rogers had set in motion. 'Many families came and settled,' during his time we are told, 'who, by their industry and improvement upon their plantations, furnished the markets with all sorts of provisions.'

In a personal way the Phenneys also contributed to the economy. They invited some Bermudians to come down and teach Bahamian women to plait and sew the leaves of the palm trees into baskets, mats, and other useful articles. 'Straw-work', has remained an important cottage industry to the present day. Phenney never ceased to plead for permission to call an Assembly. Undoubtedly he thought such a body would be of great assistance in providing much-needed money for essential works. Authority was finally granted, but too late for him to do anything about it.

Once more Spanish ships were a threat. The defences caused Phenney great anxiety especially the state of Fort Nassau which was too weak to support the weight of the guns which the Governor had brought with him. His pleas for help from the Home Government seldom brought assistance and he was forced to rely to a large extent on local resources. This, understandably, aggravated the inhabitants who thought defence should be the responsibility of England. Through it all, however, Phenney did his best, with whatever he could muster, to get the colony moving and to make it stable and secure.

More troublesome to him than the lack of an Assembly, the crumbling Fort, or the struggling plantations, was his wife. She was a millstone around his neck which was finally to bring him down. A hard-mouthed, ambitious woman, she dominated and abused everyone she encountered. She monopolized both the import and export trade, charging the inhabitants exorbitant prices for what she sold and often neglecting to pay for what she bought.

The naturalist, Mark Catesby, visited Government House in those days and he must have been surprised at the strange activities of the occupants, what with Mrs Phenney selling rum and biscuits at the back door and her husband examining his feet for chiggers in the parlour. Nevertheless, he liked Phenney; and we are inclined to like him too, or at least to sympathize with him.

Woodes Rogers Again

To the great delight of Bahamians, Phenney's successor was their well-beloved Woodes Rogers. During the past eight years in England, he had endured debtors' prison, bankruptcy and unemployment. Prominent men who knew him tended to esteem him all the more because of the fortitude which he had shown in adversity. His honesty and rectitude were never questioned by his co-partners or even by his creditors. Bahamians had let it be known that they regretted his departure; and they made it equally clear that they welcomed his return.

The Governor arrived in Nassau in August 1729, and one of

his first official acts was to issue a proclamation calling for an Assembly of twenty-four members. The sixteen members for New Providence, four for Eleuthera, and four for Harbour Island were duly elected and met for the first time on 29 September 1729. One of the men elected was John Colebrooke who had arrived on the same ship as Rogers and had become his great enemy. He was chosen to be the Speaker and from the beginning he opposed Rogers at every turn. Colebrooke soon dominated the Assembly and influenced its members against the Governor.

Woodes Rogers was now a salaried Governor at £400 a year and conditions in the Bahamas were more settled. But in many respects his second term was an anti-climax. He was a man of bold and incisive action; his place was on the quarter-deck enveloped by the thunder and smoke and fumes of gunfire. It is almost distressing to think of him caught up in the tedious business of government and political intrigue.

His three years were spent in concern about the ailing plantations, the poor state of defence, an obstructive Assembly, and in litigation with Colebrooke. Through it all he never surrendered his high-minded goals to gain the support of petty and selfish men. His motto *Dum spiro, spero* (While I breathe, I hope) is suggestive of his resolute and optimstic spirit. But time was running out for the gallant privateer.

We are not told, but we suspect that the onset of the hot months of 1732 brought a last recurrence of the 'sickness' which he had shaken off so many times before. On 20 July 1732, the President of the Bahamas Council wrote to the Secretary of State: 'Whereas it pleased Almighty God to take unto himself the soul of Woodes Rogers, Esq., our late Governor, on the 15th day of the inst. We acquaint Your Lordship therewith.'

Governor Fitzwilliam

The Bahamian people could not have expected a successor of the stature of Woodes Rogers. But Richard Fitzwilliam who arrived in 1734 possessed a character more typical of a proprietary Governor. He was a rogue with piratical instincts. He looked on his appointment only as an opportunity to make what he could for himself. Like Mrs Phenney, he monopolized the trade to the detriment of the people. He exempted himself from many taxes while increasing the burden on the population. Judges and juries were subjected to intimidation and he reversed any verdict which was not to his liking.

Soon after his arrival, he informed the Assembly of a threatened slave-uprising which he claimed to have discovered in time to frustrate. It is surprising indeed that such a widespread and well organized plan as he made it out to be, and which had as its objective the destruction of all the whites, had come only to the Governor's ears.

He was fond of saying that he would like to hang a few people in New Providence. A wonderful opportunity to do this came his way when soldiers of the Independent Company mutinied, in March 1736. The reason given for their desperate action was that in the Bahamas they were not given additional pay as were their counterparts in Jamaica and elsewhere. But we suspect there was more to it than this. They planned to seize the Governor and hold him as a hostage to ensure their escape to some other place.

Governor Fitzwilliam's house

The Governor made an unsuccessful effort to retake Fort Nassau which they had captured. When the mutineers left the harbour he devised a plan to surprise them at sea which was successful. The next day 'every man of them was convicted and sentenced to death'. It is a sad reflection that Fitzwilliam found it necessary to hang more people during a tranquil period than Woodes Rogers did while performing the monumental tasks of suppressing piracy and repelling invasion.

Woodes Rogers had planned to replace the bloody doubloons of piracy with the honest rewards of agricultural industry. Much money and human effort had been expended in a persistent effort to bring about this transformation. Because of Fitzwilliams' 'violences, oppression and extortions', the best of these farmers, including 'all the Palatines', gave up everything they had gained through years of toil and quit the Bahamas. Once again the colony was set back on its haunches and no one knew where to look for fresh hope.

10
Boom and Bankruptcy

Since Lucayan times, the resources of the land and sea had been sufficient to feed the population but it had been difficult to stretch them beyond that. Companies and settlers had hoped for reasonable returns for their efforts but both had failed. There seemed to be no way to achieve success from the products of Bahamian sea and soil. When prosperity did come, it was generated by events far removed from Bahamian shores.

From 1721 to 1742, Sir Robert Walpole ruled Parliament and England. He was the first man to be styled Prime Minister, and he had a great passion for peace. Even when Spain began to limit English trade with her American possessions, Walpole was convinced that diplomacy would produce better results than war.

A climax was reached in 1738 when Captain Jenkins appeared before the House of Commons and exhibited an ear which he said the Spaniards had cut from his head. Immediately Parliament and the country were roused to fury. Walpole was forced to give way and war with Spain commenced the next year. The underlying reason for this war was, of course, not Jenkins' ear but the control of trade with the Spanish colonies.

Governor Tinker

No Governor before had taken up his duties under more favourable auspices than did John Tinker, when he arrived in 1741. There was internal peace throughout the islands; England was at war, which allowed for privateering and prosperity once more, and a renowned military engineer was on hand to put the defences of New Providence in order. Within two years, Peter Henry Bruce had completely rebuilt Fort Nassau and had constructed the new Fort Montagu and a complementary sea battery, called Bladen's Battery, at the eastern entrance.

Once again, plunder, prisoners and prizes flowed into the harbour. It must have caused some excitement when Captain Vandeno, the corsair of Havana who had cut off Jenkins' ear, was brought into port. As before, New Providence attracted privateers from many quarters. But it is somewhat surprising to hear that seventeen of the privateering ships were owned and manned by Bahamians.

In 1748, Tinker observed that New Providence had 'increased most surprisingly in strength and wealth, and the town of Nassau grown populous'. Prosperity was so great that some of the new homes and houses of business were grand enough to be 'called sumptuous in the Indies'. The War of Jenkins' Ear merged into the War of the Austrian Succession which dragged on until 1748. After an uneasy truce fighting broke out again in 1756 with the Seven Years' War.

Tinker was Governor of the Bahamas for twenty years, more than any man before or since. He did not find the path entirely smooth nor was his own character always above question. He was thought dictatorial by many, and he had his difficulties with the Assembly which refused to pay him a salary. Certainly he made personal financial gain from dealings in prizes and plunder.

Toward the end he tired of his job. He complained of the narrow sphere in which he had spent so many years of his life, and of the type of people by whom he was surrounded. 'The spirit of privateering has taken possession of these people, and extinguished every other industrious or commercial application. . . .' So wrote the man who had felt something of that spirit himself. In July 1758 he died at his post.

Governor William Shirley

By 1760, the Bahamas was approaching a peak of prosperity and progress. It was the colony's additional good fortune to welcome William Shirley, an ex-Governor of Massachusetts. He was a man of exceptional experience, insight and ability. His patience

Governor William Shirley

and understanding brought about a rapport with the Assembly such as no Governor had enjoyed before. Even the privateers who were despairing of ever being treated fairly in Nassau, found a champion of their legitimate rights in William Shirley. Perhaps his most outstanding quality was that he was never motivated by self-interest. He raised the entire administration to new heights of duty and responsibility.

During his term, Nassau was greatly improved and enlarged. Mosquito-breeding swamp areas along the waterfront were filled in, the town re-surveyed, and many new streets added. One of these streets still honours the name of this Governor who did so much for the colony. Getting old and plagued with 'inveterate scurvy', Shirley felt obliged to relinquish his post in 1768. England was at peace by then and the wealth gained through privateering was fast evaporating. Before leaving, he felt the first strong winds of economic depression which were to blow fiercer than any which had been felt in fifty years.

Privateering during the series of wars in which England had been engaged had brought greater prosperity and growth to New Providence than the island had ever enjoyed before. But the people built their new houses and spent their easily earned money with never a thought of thrift. Governor Tinker, with clear insight, had observed that the war had introduced 'two formidable enemies . . . luxury and sloth . . . the excessive dearness of every necessary of life would make a stranger at first sight imagine we had golden mines no farther off than the Blue Hills'.

Governor Thomas Shirley

William Shirley was succeeded by his brother Thomas who found things so bad as to damp the 'spirit of this Government'. He could hardly do a thing worthwhile in the face of extreme poverty and the listlessness which it bred. There were thirteen men only to garrison Forts Montagu and Nassau, and the Public Treasury could scarcely afford the £20 a month it took to keep them employed.

The Assembly refused to authorize a militia, or even a night watch, and Shirley dissolved it. He could do no better without it;

nor did things improve with the new one which he called. By 1772, the machinery of government had almost collapsed. Even the courts of law had had to close down. In a speech to the Legislature, the Governor referred to the lack of trade and the great poverty of the people. At the earliest opportunity, he said, he would write to the Secretary of State and inform him that the Treasury was empty and that the salaries of officials were in arrears and could not be paid.

The Assembly, in January 1773, agreed that nothing further could be done at the local level and that the duties on the productions of the islands and the taxes on the people were as great as could be borne. Consequently, in a last desperate bid to find relief, a joint committee of the House and Council petitioned the King. In requesting the Governor to forward this petition, the committee informed him of their own failure to find a solution, saying quite plainly that any new imposts would bring ruin upon the colony.

The reply from the King, through the Secretary of State, was that the only fund available for the kind of help sought, was 'so low as to barely answer the present charges upon it'. The Bahamas was bankrupt, and there was no hope of improvement. In fact there were strong indications that things would get worse. There was a drastic fall in trade because American ships were no longer coming to Nassau. The reason for this was that the North American colonies were caught up in a damaging quarrel with the Mother Country.

Relations between the Bahamas and North America

The underlying causes of this dispute were complicated, but it was taxes which set it ablaze. The colonists objected very strongly to being taxed by the English Parliament, saying this was a right which should be exercised only by their own Assemblies in which they were represented. As the quarrel dragged on, there was a steady increase in the number of things to quarrel about. But all these were finally seen to be part and parcel of one all-embracing issue. To state it simply, the British King and Parliament thought they should exercise stronger control over the colonies, and the colonies were determined to have a greater say in their own affairs.

The Bahamian people believed, as did most of those in England and America, that an amicable settlement would be reached. Certainly they hoped so, for a war between England and the mainland colonies would place the Bahamas in a difficult position, politically, economically and militarily. The association between the Bahamas and the continental colonies had been a very close one. Bahamian pioneer colonists had come to Eleuthera for the same reasons that many had gone to North America—religious freedom. We saw how in the days of the Eleutherian Adventurers, the people of both Virginia and Massachusetts had sent help to the struggling colonists, and that the Eleutherians had contributed to the enlargement of Harvard College.

All the Lords Proprietors of the Bahamas were also Proprietors of Carolina, and that colony became something of a second motherland to our own. We looked there for advice, assistance and trade. In fact, trade with the mainland colonies was the lifeblood of the Bahamas. Our enemies were traditionally the same as their enemies, and an attack on one colony was considered a threat to the others. The privateers of all the colonies heard the same call to action, and Nassau became as familiar to many American captains as their own home ports.

Bahamians travelled to Carolina, Virginia and Massachusetts as freely as if those colonies were an extension of their own territory and many of them settled there when conditions were bad at home. There were few Bahamians who had not some relative on the mainland.

Yet, by 1774, it looked as though this association was coming to an end. In both England and America the voices which called for moderation and conciliation were being drowned by more militant voices. The British were building up their military strength in the face of a possible revolt. And some of the colonials were hoarding guns and gunpowder against the day they might be needed.

In April 1775 General Gage, the commander of the British forces, sent a detachment of a thousand men to destroy a collection of war material at Concord. A band of rebel militiamen met them on the way and, in an exchange of gunfire, eight of the rebels were killed. At Concord there was more trouble, and casualties on both sides. The war was on!

Governor Montford Browne

Governor Montford Browne had been in the Bahamas for only four months when hostilities began in North America. What a dismal situation he faced as Captain-General and Commander-in-Chief! The economy was about as low as it could go. To the south, old enemies, the Spaniards in Cuba and the French in Haiti, were likely to attack at any time. And now to the north, America was one big question mark. In August, a few ships arrived from Boston. They had been sent down by General Gage to remove the gunpowder stored in Fort Nassau. Gage feared the powder might be seized by the rebels who were desperately short of this essential commodity of warfare.

The Governor was away but the Council vigorously objected to New Providence being left totally defenceless. And so the powder remained. But from that day forward the people of Nassau were aware that the Americans might strike at any time. A few months later Gage ordered away the small company of soldiers whose duty it was to man the forts. The Bahamian people were thereupon left to ponder which was worse, guns without powder to charge them or guns without a garrison to operate them.

I I

The Americans Strike!

Sunday, 3 March 1776, dawned cool and blustery on New Providence with a stiff north-easter blowing. But long before sunrise Pilot Farr had put his little vessel over the bar to beat up into the North-east Providence Channel. As he tended the tiller and sheets he kept a sharp lookout to windward hoping to sight an incoming sail, for money was scarce and he needed a pilot's fee.

Warnings of Invasion

As night gave way to day, he saw, in the distance, not one sail, but three . . . five . . . seven . . . with billowing canvas and foaming bows, bearing down straight for New Providence. Farr's mind immediately turned to the gunpowder stored in Fort Nassau and the well-known fear that the Americans might attempt to take it. He turned his vessel about, sailed back into the harbour and went straight to Government House.

The Governor, Montford Browne, awakened from sleep, was told that the Americans were not far off. He asked Farr what he thought should be done. Farr replied that he did not know unless the Governor sent away the powder. Browne had had several recent warnings about the certainty of invasion. A week before, a Captain Law had come from America to inform him that a fleet being assembled at Cape Delaware would attempt to capture New Providence. And two days before, a Captain Dorsett had come from Abaco with the news that the American fleet was in Bahamian waters. It was a late hour indeed for the Governor to begin to consider what should be done.

Browne thanked the pilot for his good advice and requested him to tell Major Sterling not to let Chambers sail until he had seen him. Chambers was the captain of a fast sloop, the *Mississippi Packet,* which was about to depart for Jamaica, and the Governor had in mind to send the powder away on this ship.

Browne met most of his Council shortly after 6.00 a.m. in Fort Nassau. A few cannon were fired as an alarm and the militia drum sounded. Samuel Gambier, who arrived late because he was crippled with gout, strongly advised against sending away the powder and insisted that New Providence should be defended.

The Council proposed that first, a fast sailing vessel should be sent to reconnoitre the enemy; secondly, vessels should be prepared for sinking in the channel to block the western entrance; and thirdly, a strong force should be sent to Fort Montagu to protect the eastern entrance. By this time, however, it must have become apparent that the Americans would not attempt the western entrance and therefore the sinking of ships there would be useless.

Evidently some indecision had taken hold of the American fleet. When Farr had sighted the ships, they could have been no more than ten to fifteen miles off. With a strong and fair wind, they should have been over the bar by seven o'clock at the very latest. Instead the ships were tacking about in apparent confusion. Now we will have a closer look at this fleet. When the war started, the Americans were well aware that naval operations would play a strong, and probably, a decisive role in the struggle. They quickly converted merchantmen into warships, and by the beginning of 1776 a sizeable fleet was ready for duty. Commodore Esek Hopkins was put in command and his first and most urgent operation was to seize the military stores in New Providence. The

Commodore Esek Hopkins.
Commander-in-chief of the American fleet 1776

Americans were very short of powder and in December 1775 George Washington had written that 'our want of powder is inconceivable'. Thus, on 17 February 1776, Hopkins put to sea with the first American fleet consisting of eight warships and set a course for New Providence.

Two of the vessels collided in stormy weather. The remaining six ships assembled at Hole in the Wall, Abaco, where, on the same day that Dorsett reported to the Governor, two Bahamian sloops were captured and their captains impressed as pilots. Hopkins then conceived a most ingenious use for the local vessels. Aboard these and aboard one of his own sloops, the *Providence*, he placed 220 marines and 50 sailors. The three sloops, with the marines and sailors hidden below deck, would sail into the harbour without arousing suspicion, and before Nassauvians could organize resistance, the fort and town would have been taken.

The Americans Attack

At first, everything seemed to go splendidly. Most of the fleet remained out of sight and the three sloops moved on ahead. But as they got close to the bar, and were preparing to enter the harbour, the air was suddenly shattered by the roar of cannon fire. We can imagine the panic which gripped the marines and sailors, crammed like sardines in a tin, in the dark, stuffy holds of the sloops. The officers in charge quickly decided that it would be sheer suicide to cross the bar and altered course to rejoin the fleet.

Back at Fort Nassau, Governor Browne had no idea what had been achieved by his alarm cannon with their noisy, but harmless, blank charges. He was worriedly surveying the wreckage which had been caused by the mere discharges. Three guns had been used to fire the alarm, and two of these had dismounted, their rotten carriages collapsing under the shock of recoil. Even more serious was the erosion and the frightful cracks in the masonry of the north-west bastion. This looked straight on to the bar and its guns were essential in preventing an enemy coming from that direction. If the Americans had known all this, they might have stood off and watched the fort disintegrate under the stress of its own discharging cannon. But Commodore Hopkins did not know this and believing his ruse to be discovered, he discarded his bold and swift plan in favour of a safer and more tedious one. They would attack Fort Montagu from the land.

About two miles north-east of Fort Montagu is a good anchorage called Hanover Sound. The entrance, though only two hundred yards wide, presents no problem to local seamen when the weather is right. It was into this Sound that the American fleet was brought to anchor, under the guidance of the impressed Bahamian pilots. About 270 marines and sailors were put ashore at a place called Fox Hill Creek. Thus the focus of activity was suddenly shifted from west to east and the urgent matter of putting Fort Montagu into a proper state of defence was carried out between nine and ten o'clock in the morning.

Fort Montagu Abandoned

The New Providence militia consisted of 300 men between the ages of fifteen and sixty but this number could not be relied on, for many were at sea. On this day the Governor could muster only 150 but not all these were properly armed. A Lieutenant Burke, with about sixty men, was sent eastward to meet the advancing enemy. Some time later, another armed party set out from Fort Nassau, with the Governor and members of Council in the lead. Near Fort Montagu, they were met by Burke's men in full retreat. Having sighted the 270 Americans they had been sent to engage, they quickly favoured discretion over valour and were returning to Nassau to protect their families and property. Governor Browne then ordered the guns of Fort Montagu to be spiked and a general retreat to Fort Nassau. This was a critical decision, for if resistance was to be attempted it had to be done there and then. The guns of Fort Montagu could have been trained on a narrow path along which the Americans had to pass and the militiamen in ambush could have had a telling effect. But the decision to spike the guns left not only Fort Montagu but the entire town open to the invaders.

Governor Browne was anxious to know the intentions of the Americans and later the same day Lieutenant Burke was sent to enquire. He reported a fully armed force of about 250 to 300 and that the invaders had come to seize the gunpowder. At 8.00 p.m. the Governor, Council and inhabitants of Nassau agreed that resistance would be useless and that the powder should be sent away. Chambers who was still waiting with his fast sloop the *Mississippi Packet* threw overboard his cargo of wood to make room for the powder and left at 2.00 a.m. for St Augustine, Florida. The Americans must have known the gunpowder was being shipped out but they could do nothing. The larger American ships were bottled up in Hanover Sound and the smaller ones were even farther in behind Athol Island. No pilot in the world could have brought them out through those reef-strewn waters on that stormy Sunday night.

American Occupation

Hopkins issued a manifesto 'To the Gentlemen, Freemen, and Inhabitants of the Island of New Providence' stating that the Americans had come only to take away the gunpowder and military stores and that there would be no harm to persons and property so long as they were unopposed. Fort Nassau was occupied on Monday morning, and the Governor taken prisoner. The Americans spent two weeks in Nassau in the leisurely business of loading the loot. A considerable amount of war material was found, including twenty-four barrels of gunpowder which had been left, apparently, as a peace offering. But Hopkins must have been considerably annoyed at the much larger quantity which had slipped through his hands.

It is reported that the Americans had an enjoyable stay in Nassau. The officers were entertained by some of the principal inhabitants and Bay Street was taken over by the marines and sailors who went on a two week spree of indulgence in rum, women and song. Before the fleet got home, several of the men died and, on arrival in port, one hundred and forty had to be admitted to hospital. This illness was blamed on excessive drinking but some Bahamians still maintain it was *obeah* that brought them down. More likely, it was one of the contagious fevers.

Captain Rathbun

New Providence had been almost defenceless before Hopkins arrived; after he left, it was virtually wide open. A small quantity of military stores and powder subsequently obtained afforded little sense of security. It became clear to the Americans that the island could easily be taken any time there was reason to take it. The enticement for the next raid was, however, quite different from that of the first. The British brig *Mary* had been damaged, by running on a reef, and had come into harbour for repairs under the guns of Fort Nassau. What protection they could have afforded was never to be tested, but they looked murderous enough. Captain Rathbun, who had been a lieutenant on the *Providence* during Hopkins' invasion of New Providence, heard of the plight of the *Mary* and made for Nassau with the object of taking her as a prize. Rathbun dropped anchor outside Nassau harbour about midnight 27 January 1778. He knew he would have to deal with Fort Nassau first.

If anyone in the harbour or onshore had noticed the *Providence* that night, he would have thought nothing of it. The war sloop was disguised as a trading vessel and it was customary for ships arriving during the dark hours to wait for daylight to cross the bar.

Under cover of darkness, twenty-eight men were ferried ashore about a mile west of Fort Nassau. Equipped with arms and a scaling ladder, the party picked its way eastward along the shore. John Trevett, who had also been involved in the previous invasion, was in charge of the shore party and he recalled that during the American occupation a picket had been removed from the fort's palisades, probably to facilitate the loading of the war material.

To his great delight, it had not been replaced, and through the fourteen inch gap in the fence he led his men. There was no difficulty at all in taking the fort which was manned only by two sentries. Through the rest of the night the Americans shouted the customary half-hourly reassurance 'All is well'. And watchmen on ships in the harbour responded 'All is well'. Nassauvians were astounded, on waking that morning, to see the American flag flying from Fort Nassau and its guns pointing menacingly at the town.

A north-wester had blown in during the night and Rathbun was compelled to put out to sea. Therefore, he could not enter the harbour at daybreak and give aid to Trevett, as planned. This left the twenty-eight Americans in the fort in a very critical situation. If the Government and people of Nassau had known there were only twenty-eight men there, there might have been trouble but Trevett spread the word that he had well over two hundred with him. Furthermore, he threatened to open fire on the town if he were attacked.

The Gayton

Late in the afternoon, a British privateer, the *Gayton,* not knowing what had taken place, was seen approaching the bar. The Americans concealed all signs of their presence, with the object of surprising her after she had entered the harbour. But a group of Nassauvians, seeing the ruse, went over the bar in small boats and warned her off. Several plans to attack the Americans came to nothing. The *Gayton,* on her way to attack at sea, ran aground and about 200 armed citizens who crowded the fort were deterred from action by renewed threats that the town would be cannonaded.

Rathbun decided to take as prizes the *Mary* and two other vessels. Two schooners, for which he had no prize crews, were burnt, after their cargoes had been removed. Gunpowder and military stores were loaded on to the ships. What was not wanted was destroyed. On the third day, the Americans sailed away.

We look back on these military activities with much admiration for the humaneness with which they were carried out. They were bloodless operations. On both occasions, the American leaders exhibited remarkable restraint. The fact that the Americans came with no grievances to redress, probably accounts for the fact that they left no wounds for time to heal.

12

Conquest and Reconquest

Montford Browne returned from what he called his 'loathesome captivity' in 1778 to learn that the Americans had raided New Providence once again. But he took little interest in this. His mind was preoccupied with vindicating his honour with respect to the first invasion which was not an easy thing to do. It is difficult to say what should be thought about this Governor who had certain knowledge of the invasion a week before it happened and waited until the enemy was in sight, before giving consideration to a course of action. Of even greater interest to us, however, is the behaviour of the Bahamian people during those days of crisis. Browne declared that he had been 'deserted by all the Inhabitants in the defence of the Place, and that they were all Rebels'.

Governor Browne under Attack

A joint committee of the Council and Assembly replied to this accusation with bitter resentment. If Browne knew of traitors, it pointed out, why did he not bring them to trial, and if guilty let them suffer the fate which traitors deserve.

The Inhabitants in general [wrote the Committee] did their duty and followed your Excellency with a determined spirit to have Engaged and defeated the Enemy, had your Excellency thought proper to have led them on to the Attack, and had you not retreated and abandoned Fort Montagu, and thereby left their Houses, Property and Families to the ravage of the Enemy.

Let us consider again two incidents which took place during Rathbun's occupation. When the British privateer was sailing into a trap set by the Americans, which would have resulted in her capture or destruction, a large number of the townspeople 'men, women and children ran to the hills behind the town waving hats, coats and aprons' to warn the *Gayton* away. On the second day of this occupation, about two hundred men voluntarily armed themselves and crowded in on Fort Nassau with the intention of storming it. They dispersed only when Rathbun threatened to open fire with the eighteen pounders and reduce the town to rubble. These reactions can hardly be interpreted as evidence of welcome. It seems quite clear that those who co-operated with the invaders were, in the main, Americans with rebel sympathies. Some of these were engaged in business activities in Nassau and some were crewmen of American vessels which had been taken as prizes by British privateers.

From this distance we can hardly expect to know all the factors which contributed to the lack of resistance. But most assuredly the unprepared, unenergetic and indecisive Governor Browne was chief among them. There is nothing to suggest that the rank and file of Nassauvians did not resent the invaders or that they had not the courage or the willingness to defend their island home. The lack of leadership was the crippling thing. By every quarter of the people Browne was condemned for his miserable performance during the Hopkins' invasion, and for his attempts to place the blame on others. Complaints of severest censure, forwarded to the Home Government, finally resulted in his being removed from office.

By the time John Maxwell arrived in 1780 to take up the duties of Governor, both France and Spain, seeking revenge for their defeat in 1763, had allied with the Americans. Rumours were rife, and Maxwell did his best to shore up defences against the day the impending storm would break upon him. Every local man fit to bear arms was pressed into the militia. A number of invalids, that is to say soldiers who were not fit for front line duty, were brought in from America. Two shiploads of military supplies were asked for and received from the British in New York.

Spanish Invasion and Occupation

When the invasion fleet did appear on 6 May 1782, however, it made Maxwell's precautions seem ludicrous. Never had Nassau-vians seen anything like it. It must have seemed that all the ships in Christendom were descending on their little island. Estimates of the total number ran as high as eighty-two. Beside American and Spanish warships, there were forty transport vessels. The personnel numbered more than 5000, including 1500 soldiers. The Commander-in-Chief of the expedition was His Excellency Don Juan Manuel de Cargigal, Governor of Havana.

There could be only one result to this massive confrontation. Governor Maxwell took the only responsible course he could take. He capitulated. It was obvious that this was no ordinary retaliatory raid. The Spaniards had come to conquer the Bahamas, once and for all.

The terms of surrender were not severe. In fact the Spaniards were surprisingly generous, considering their long-standing enmity for the Bahamian people. The Governor and all British troops were allowed to depart with their families and possessions. Local inhabitants who chose not to leave were assured that their real and personal properties would not be molested, and that they would be left to the enjoyment of their own religion and all their former rights and privileges. At the end of eighteen months those remaining would be obliged to swear allegiance to his Catholic Majesty.

There was no chance in the world that the occupation could be a settled arrangement. The great disparity in the status of the two groups was itself a bar to harmony. Six hundred Spaniards

remained in permanent garrison and these soldiers, quite naturally, took on the superior airs of masters. The 2500 Nassauvians,
deprived of all say in their affairs, endured their inferior position
with sullen resentment. The additional barriers of race, language,
religion and culture helped to produce an endless flow of irritating
and inflammatory incidents.

The capitulation terms were broken with increasing frequency,
and in many respects. Before many months, everyone was seen to
belong to one of two camps, either the oppressors or the oppressed.
It was humiliating for Bahamians to have to live under the harsh
rule of a nation for which they had never felt anything but
intense hatred and fear. That the Americans had helped to bring
this about added greatly to the embitterment. But the most
galling aspect of the miserable situation was that certain residents
who were rebel sympathizers had assisted, and were assisting,
the foreign masters of their country.

Some Nassauvians escaped to Florida or to other Bahamian
islands. The remainder of those in New Providence, the great
majority, could only pray for deliverance.

Colonel Andrew Deveaux

In North America, the war had taken a very bad turn for the
British and the end was in sight. But there were still many gallant
men* who were anxious to strike a blow for the Empire in which
they believed. And a Loyalist, Colonel Andrew Deveaux of the
South Carolina militia, was one of these. At the age of eighteen he
had first experienced military service and, during the next few
years, he proved himself to be a born commander. His restless
and daring nature led him on to accomplish feats which seemed
impossible to lesser men. Operating with small and highly mobile
forces, he wrought havoc on the enemy out of all proportion to
the numbers of his troops.

Exiled in St Augustine, Florida, he heard from Bahamian
refugees of the sufferings of Nassauvians under the Spanish yoke
and he resolved to do something about it. He rounded up some

* See Chapter 13.

Colonel Andrew Deveaux

of his old comrades in arms and he fired them with his own
enthusiasm for the enterprise. Out of his own pocket he provided
his sixty-five volunteers with arms, uniforms and provisions.

Six small vessels were engaged for transport. These were more
than were necessary, but Deveaux hoped to pick up some additional volunteers when he reached the Bahamas. Two privateers
of twenty-six and fifteen guns and two smaller vessels comprised

the armed escort. The fleet set sail on 30 March 1783, and five days later arrived at Hole in the Wall, Abaco.

Deveaux stationed some of his ships at strategic points so that a watch could be kept on all sea lanes leading to New Providence. He then sailed to Harbour Island to recruit additional men and sent a Captain McKenzie to Eleuthera to do the same. An ever-lasting tribute to Harbour Island and Eleuthera is that 170 men volunteered. This represented almost every male who was fit to fire a gun. Two days were spent in making soldiers of these fishermen and farmers. The two islands also contributed about fifty small fishing boats which were to play a part in Deveaux's stratagem.

Deveaux's Attack on Nassau

All units of the fleet rendezvoused at Egg Island on 9 April where final preparations were made for a descent on New Providence at daybreak the next morning. The Spaniards had moored two galleys near the Eastern harbour entrance to reinforce the defence afforded by Fort Montagu and Deveaux's plan was to attack ships and fort simultaneously. One hundred and fifty men landed, probably in the vicinity of Dick's Point, and stole quietly toward the fort. They were seen, however, by sentries on duty and the unsuspecting Spanish garrison was thrown into confusion.

As far as they could see, a mighty army was about to fall upon them. Deveaux had formed his men into what he called 'divisions', with wide spaces between the groups, to give the illusion of large numbers. The fleet was well within sight of Fort Montagu and rapidly rowing back and forth were the Harbour Island fishing boats looking for all the world as if they were putting hundreds and thousands of men ashore.

The Spaniards hastily spiked the cannon and retreated to the west. At Fort Montagu, the British detected the smell of burning powder and forced a prisoner to reveal the source. A train of powder leading to the magazine had been lighted and if it had not been discovered Fort Montagu would have been blown to bits in a few minutes.

Three lusty cheers from Deveaux and his men on top of the

fort were answered from the harbour where the marine section under Major Archibald Taylor had also done its job well. The two galleys were in their possession. Notwithstanding this auspicious beginning, Deveaux's job had just commenced. There were 600 Spanish soldiers to be met with yet, and Fort Nassau had to be overcome.

To the east of the town, in an area called the White-Grounds, the Spaniards formed a line of defence. Deveaux brought some of his cannon ashore and for two days an artillery duel rumbled on without much damage to either side. But by 13 April the British were in an excellent position. All the area east of Nassau, including Fort Montagu, was in their hands and they held Society Hill which commanded both the town and Fort Nassau. The bulk of Deveaux's force was deployed on the White-Grounds, but he led the Spaniards to believe that this was merely a picket line. Many widely separated areas were occupied by a few men. And from each of these encampments the troubled enemy heard a continuous outpouring of warlike sounds which gave the impression that the woods to the east and south of the town were alive with men.

A final imaginative touch was gained by introducing to the Spanish Governor two Indian chiefs of the 'Cherokee and Choctaw' tribes, dressed up in war regalia. These chiefs told the Governor that their braves, hidden in the woods, were on the warpath, awaiting only the order to take Spanish scalps.

The Governor, thereupon, asked for a truce of twenty-four hours so that he might consider the terms of surrender presented by Deveaux. The truce was granted, but during the night the enemy used the time to improve his military position. The guns of Fort Nassau, which always pointed seaward, were turned around and at daylight a furious cannonade of Society Hill was commenced.

Deveaux responded by hauling seven cannon to the top of the hill and threatened to blast the fort to pieces. Fort Nassau was thereby made untenable and had to be abandoned. The loss of this stronghold was decisive and, on the morning of 17 April, the Governor surrendered. When Deveaux hauled down the Spanish flag it marked the last time that a foreign banner was to fly over the Bahamian capital as a symbol of dominion.

Spanish Surrender

It was quite a shock to the Spaniards when they saw the army which had conquered them. Of a total of 220 men, only 150 were equipped with muskets. By the articles of capitulation, the Spanish garrison of 600 soldiers was allowed to return to Havana. Don Antonio Claraco Sanz, the Governor, and five of his chief officers were detained as hostages until those Bahamians who were in Cuban dungeons were repatriated.

Nassauvians went wild with joy at their deliverance. They could hardly find words to express the gratitude they felt toward Deveaux. It is an interesting twist of history, that a short time before the recapture of New Providence, the entire Bahamas had been restored to Britain by the Treaty of Versailles. This fact, however, does nothing to diminish the splendid achievement of Deveaux and the gallant Harbour Islanders and Eleutherans who assisted him. A contemporary writer considered it 'an enterprise, perhaps, without a parallel in the modern history of war'.

13
The United Empire Loyalists

Population growth in the Bahamas had been very slow. In 134 years the inhabitants had increased from the original seventy to only 4000. But during the three years after 1782 newcomers were to stream into the islands in such numbers as to seem a veritable human flood.

We may look on the middle of 1783 as a dividing line. For many years thereafter, those who were here before that were known as the 'old inhabitants', and those who arrived after, the 'new inhabitants'. The population in 1782 stood as follows with blacks and whites approximately equal in number.

New Providence	2750
Harbour Island	500
Eleuthera	450
Long Island, Exuma and Cat Island	250
Total	3950

Not included in the table are the Turks Islands, then an uncertain appendage of the Bahamas, which had a permanent and seasonal population of nearly a thousand Bermudians working the salt ponds there.

We cannot leave these old inhabitants without expressing the highest admiration for their resourcefulness, courage and tenacity. All too often, the fruits of years of toil were destroyed in a few hours by the violence of nature or of man. Just as frequently they set to work to build again, and to try again. The destiny of the country, however, was soon to be taken over by the 'new inhabitants' and we will now see how they fared.

The Loyalists in America

When referring to the Revolutionary War, we think of the contestants as being British and American. The actual situation was much more complicated, for the people of the colonies were themselves divided. On one side were the Rebels or Whigs who wanted political separation from Britain, and on the other side were the Loyalists or Tories, who stood for a United Empire.

The treatment afforded the unfortunate Tories remains one of the most sordid chapters of American history. All sorts of malicious indignities were inflicted upon them in the name of patriotism. Tarring and feathering was a favourite sport of the mobs throughout the war. After the Declaration of Independence in 1776 each state enacted laws designating them as traitors. Thousands were deprived of their civil rights, debarred from earning a livelihood, robbed of their possessions, imprisoned, and finally banished from the land of their birth. Thousands of others left voluntarily to seek the protection of the British flag.

Because of proximity and climate, East Florida became the preferred asylum for southern Loyalists. This was an old Spanish colony which had been ceded to Britain after the Seven Years War. It was looked upon as a military outpost during Spanish rule and after two decades of British sovereignty the population was hardly more than that of the Bahamas. It had not joined the other colonies in revolt; in fact, throughout the war the inhabitants had shown no enthusiasm for the rebel cause. The harassed Tories of Georgia and the Carolinas saw that great empty space as a nearby, safe land of refuge. As their prospects deteriorated, they began to remove there by the hundreds. And when the British army abandoned their home states they poured into Florida in thousands.

Many of these Loyalists had owned sizeable estates, or were otherwise citizens of consequence in their communities. In Florida, and especially in St Augustine, they set about making new lives for themselves. They acquired land, built houses, developed plantations, and engaged in businesses and the professions.

The colony being British, they hoped to regain a sense of security and some semblance of their former fortunes. The Governor was informed that it was the King's wish that Florida should become a 'secure assylum for loyalists from the refractory colonists'. But fate had yet another blow in store for these wretched people. The Treaty of Versailles which restored the Bahamas to Britain also restored Florida to Spain. British residents were given eighteen months to settle their affairs and get out.

Arrival of the Loyalists

In June 1783 the first batch of Loyalists arrived in Nassau from St Augustine. In charge of operations was Brigadier-General Archibald McArthur, and few men would have envied his job. It must be remembered that the great majority of these refugees were close to destitute. Many of them were to be recompensed for their losses by the British Government later, but for the moment only a few such as the Rolles and Kelsalls who went to Exuma could afford to charter vessels and provide for themselves on arrival.

McArthur had to supply transportation which was itself a formidable undertaking. But when the Loyalists and their slaves were put ashore in Nassau the real problems began. Shelter had to be provided where no shelter existed. Army tents and lean-tos of ships' sails, palmetto thatch, rough lumber or anything else that could be found, sprouted up all around the town. Almost every mouthful of food for this increasing mass of people had to be imported. Sometimes vessels bringing these precious cargoes were wrecked. When this happened, some of the refugees were reduced to near-starving conditions.

All through 1784 the exodus from Florida continued. But toward the end of that year the Governor gave notice that the last transport vessel would leave on 1 March 1785. Florida supplied by far the greatest number of immigrants, but some came from other places on the continent including a thousand or more from New York. The exact number of refugees who came to the Bahamas will never be known. Estimates range between 5000 and 7000 Loyalists and slaves.

By June 1788, the population of the colony had more than doubled and stood at approximately 9300. The Negroes, for the first time, had taken a strong numerical lead and comprised about two-thirds of the total inhabitants. A relatively small number of Loyalists were able to work their way into government service, the professions, businesses and the trades. But it was in agriculture that they made their great impact on the colony.

Sir Guy Carleton

Sir Guy Carleton, Commander-in-Chief of British forces in America suggested to the Home Government that escheated and ungranted land in the Bahamas should be parcelled out free of cost to the Loyalists. This proposal was adopted and on 10 September 1784, Lieutenant-Governor Powell was instructed to proceed accordingly. But the British Government did not own the Bahamian land. The Lords Proprietors still retained title to the real estate by virtue of their 1670 grant. Woodes Rogers and his successors had consistently urged that something be done about that, but nothing was done. Now, it was most urgent that something be done.

As soon as agreement could be reached with the majority of the Proprietors, the land was freed. Final completion of the transaction was to take some years. A sum of £7850 was voted by the House of Commons in June 1784 'to perfect the purchase of the Bahama Islands'. Two years later, an additional sum of £6356 was authorized. On 20 March 1787, all proprietary rights were surrendered to the King; £12,000 was paid for the entire archipelago which was surely a good bargain.

Upon application, forty acres of Bahamian land were allowed

to each head of a family. In addition, twenty acres were allowed for every white or black man, woman or child in a family. Loyalists were exempted from all charges connected with the grants and from the annual quit rents of two shillings per 100 acres, for ten years.

The Bahamas experienced a land-rush such as had not been seen before and has not been seen since. Loyalists scoured the islands in search of suitable acreage. The Governor and his Council were deluged with applications. Plantation huts were put together with great rapidity since everything necessary for their construction was at hand. Masses of timber were available for window and door frames, plates and rafters. Loose rock, which abounded everywhere, was used for the walls and these stones were cemented together and smoothly finished with white lime made by burning the same Bahama rock. Palmetto leaves, never far to seek, made cool and rain-proof roofs.

The slaves proved to be very skilful at this type of building. In a very short time, accommodation was provided for all who were to be a part of plantation life, including a manor house for the owner or his manager. Sir Guy Carleton had caused several surveys to be made, all of which pointed out the scarcity of soil. Nevertheless, there was evidence that a variety of tropical and sub-tropical crops might be successfully cultivated.

Cotton Plantations

Most exciting to the new inhabitants was the prospect of cotton. Lieutenant John Wilson, sent out by Sir Guy Carleton to report on the islands, was most optimistic about the possibilities of growing this commercially important fibre. Toward the end of 1783 on the island of Exuma he noted that

. . . there are cotton trees now growing . . . which were planted by a Mr La Rush who died about eighteen years ago. Although the trees have been entirely neglected since his death, being now intermixed with weeds, shrubs and bushes, which have spontaneously sprung up amongst them, yet they flourish in a surprising manner and yield a great quantity of cotton every year.

A cotton plantation

The planters could hardly wait to get their seeds into the ground. Coaxed by a warm sun, these quickly germinated and a virgin soil pushed the young and vigorous plants to a marvellous height and breadth in a few months. And what hopeful excitement must have taken possession of the planters as they watched the profusion of bolls develop to maturity and then split to expose their precious, white fluff to the pickers' fingers.

For the first few years after the crops began to come in, planters were handsomely rewarded for their industry. Wilson reported that they 'all succeeded, and from being very poor, have in a few years become wealthy'. Five years after the first Loyalists arrived, there were 128 large plantations employing ten or more slaves, scattered throughout Bahamas. And, of course, there were many smaller farms attended by fewer slaves.

Land values soared to peaks which in some areas have not been surpassed until recent times. A tract in the Caicos Islands was sold, a year after being granted, for £9450 and was subsequently resold for £70,000. A grantee considered £20,000 too little for a Long Island property. This is something to think about when it is remembered that only £12,000 had been paid to the Proprietors for the entire Bahamas a short time before.

Cotton became a sort of 'white-gold' which dominated all Bahamian economic thinking, far more than wrecking or privateering had ever done. At long last, Bahamians thought the touchstone of a peaceful, sound and enduring economy had been found. In 1773 and 1774, Bahamian exports to Britain amounted to little more than £5000. In 1786 and 1787 they were valued at close to £59,000. Cotton made most of the difference. Nearly a million pounds of it were coming in from the fields every year. Six square-rigged vessels were seen in Nassau harbour at one time loading cotton for England. But just as prosperity was looking its brightest, the first disaster struck.

Failure of the Cotton Plantations

The Governor, Lord Dunmore, addressed the Legislature at the opening of a new session, on Thursday, 5 February 1789.

Knowing [he said] how necessary your presence was on Your Plantations after the very pernicious visitation you have had from that destructive insect the Worm, I delayed calling you together so long as the Public Business of the country would permit . . .

The destructive worm, of which Lord Dunmore spoke, was the chenille. The little, hairy, harmless-looking fellow had destroyed much of the last crop and no one knew what, if anything, could be done about him. To make matters worse, another pest appeared, the red bug, which was capable of ruinous staining of the fibre. These two together brought dismay to the planters who just a short time before had been buoyant with dazzling success.

Over the next few years there was a considerable lessening of damage to the fields, but the pests returned in greater numbers in 1794, and once more the crops were largely destroyed. Whether the planters might have found some way of overcoming the pests will never be known, for about this time they recognized the symptoms of an even more incurable problem; the nutrients of the shallow Bahamian soil were giving out. By the year 1800 it was evident to all that the cotton plantations would fail.

McKinnen, after visiting some of the abandoned plantations in 1803, penned a remarkably accurate observation: '. . . although nature [he wrote] in all of . . . (the islands) . . . spontaneously brings forth many vegetables both curious and beautiful, she has hitherto refused to resign herself to continued cultivation.'

The Planters Depart

It is distressing to trace the decay of the plantations. Cotton did not die a sudden death. It lost its pre-eminence, but it continued to be one of many things upon which the owners depended in trying to make something of their estates. Salt-making, wood-cutting, livestock raising, truck farming and even wrecking; all played a part in the desperate effort to stave off disaster. But the sheer difficulty of making ends meet was too much for the planters. One by one, they quitted their land and quitted the Bahamas. By the early 1830's most of them were gone.

The abolition of slavery seemed only to hasten the departure of the remainder. L. D. Powles, author of *Land of the Pink Pearl,* looked back over forty-seven years of post-emancipation history to remark: 'Ever since the emancipation of slaves . . . the colony has been gradually going to the bad. One by one the old planters left the country, until at the present time there is scarcely a representative of them left . . .' Those who were still alive had grown old and weary, worn out by time, troubles and toil.

There is pathos [wrote Dr Thelma Peters] in the death of the last Loyalist, Burton Williams, who had taken his slaves to Trinidad in the 1820's but who returned to live out his last years at Watling's Island (San Salvador) where he had gone first as a youth. Foreseeing that there would be no tools left with which to dig his grave when he died, he had it dug ahead of time, out of the limestone ridge. His foresight was wise, for when this once energetic and rich man died at an advanced age, a Negro servant had only to shovel away the light leaf mould from the waiting grave, and to do this he used the only tool that was left, . . . a sharpened barrel stave.

Because of their greater numbers, their better education and their initial burst of energy, the Loyalists soon dominated the social, political and economic life of the colony. As they saw it, the Bahamas had not made much progress because of the indolence and ignorance of the 'old inhabitants' and, understandably, they looked on these people with disdain. Derisively, they called them 'conchs' after the lowly molluscs which formed an important part of their diet.

It is an ironic epilogue that every island which the Loyalists tackled alone was abandoned by themselves or by their offspring. Their descendants were to carry on in fair numbers only in those islands with a body of 'old inhabitants' and they were able to do this only by adopting the economic ways of the despised conchs.

Legacy of the Loyalists

But the contribution of the Loyalists to the Bahamas should not be underestimated. Many fine families in the nation today still uphold the resolute character of their forbears who came here

Remains of a plantation house, Cat Island

Loyalist tomb, Exuma

one hundred and ninety years ago. And the Bahamas would be much the poorer without them. It should be noted also that the slaves of the plantations had a much better start, after emancipation, than the free blacks from captured slave ships.* Nearly all the settlements comprised of the latter failed, but the plantation Negroes made a success of their little villages, almost without exception, because of the skills and the discipline taught them by the Loyalists.

The architecture of the capital city was enhanced by the fine houses which the Loyalists built and by the majestic simplicity of the public edifices which they raised. Education was elevated to a new level of importance, a library was opened, and the first Bahamian newspaper was published. The courts were infused with a greater dignity and sense of justice, and the Legislature conducted its affairs with a gravity and decorum unknown before.

Their plantation houses are all ruins now and scattered through the islands are hidden and weathered tombs, marking all that remains of those who died here. But the intangible assets which they brought with them still remain and these constitute an enduring monument to a remarkable group of men and women.

* See Chapter 14, p. 129.

14
Out of Bondage

Slavery is much older than man's recorded history. In the New World it had existed long before Columbus. But under Spanish rule the Lucayans and Tainos died off so rapidly that, by about 1510, the Spaniards were forced to consider the importation of African slaves. They had seen these people in Spain, where the Portuguese had been selling them for many years, and they were so impressed by their physical strength and longevity that they considered one African to be worth four Indians.

The Slave Trade

The African slave traffic started as a trickle but soon developed into a flood, first to Haiti and other West Indian islands and then in 1619 the first slaves were taken to English North America to be sold in Virginia. The unfortunates were drawn mainly from that fertile area of West Africa, south of the Sahara which fronts the Bight of Benin, formerly called the Slave Coast, and now Nigeria, Dahomey, Togo and Ghana.

The African, fated to be a slave, faced three major hazards. Since no man surrenders his freedom voluntarily, first of all he had to be captured. This was undertaken by African chiefs, some of whom made quite a lucrative business out of bartering their captives for European goods. Many of those who were set upon died of wounds received during their desperate resistance, and many others died in the stockades where they were kept for disposal.

The next hazard was the sea voyage. European purchasers treated the distraught captives only slightly better than cargo. Stacked between decks with barely an inch of unoccupied space, with no sanitary conditions and with just enough food to maintain life, the wonder is not that so many died but that so many survived the voyage.

In the New World the captives were sold off as cattle were sold and they became the legal property of those who bought them. Then came a period which was politely called 'seasoning'. The Negro had to adapt himself to rendering strict obedience to a strange people, to living in a strange land with strange customs, to learning a new language, and to performing enforced and unaccustomed toil. Probably not more than half of those who were taken in West Africa survived to become settled and productive slaves across the ocean. But this dreadful waste of human life had no effect on the men who profited from the slave trade or on those who profited from slave labour.

Slavery in the Bahamas

By the time the Eleutherian Adventurers came to the Bahamas in 1648 slavery was well established to the north and south. The only conditions necessary to bring it to the Bahamas were the demand, and a moral acceptance of the system. The constitution of the Eleutherian Adventurers does not mention slavery and we have reason to believe they were opposed to it. Their *Articles and Orders* do mention some Lucayans who had been 'sold at certain Caribe Islands', and expresses the agreed intention of 'redeeming' them and returning them 'to the places from which they were taken'.

The Vendue House where everything was sold including slaves

The man who drowned when the *William* was wrecked* was
a Negro, and there may have been others among Sayle's group.
We do not know. But soon after the first settlement was established
the authorities of Bermuda banished all their free Negroes and
some troublesome slaves to Eleuthera. Thus, the first blacks
to arrive in the Bahamas came as free men and women. And
through the years Eleuthera was to live up fairly well to its name
of Freedom. As late as 1788, the 310 'people of colour' living there
were 'mostly free'.

In New Providence events took a different turn. Slavery
was introduced there almost from the very beginning by the
farmers who tried to establish plantations. But nothing much
came of farming in those days, at least nothing that required large
numbers of field hands. In fact, throughout the proprietary period,
the sea was a stronger attraction to the settlers than the land.

Woodes Rogers made determined efforts to improve agriculture

* See Chapter 5, p. 43.

and this created a greater demand for slaves than ever before. For the first time, regular slavers found it profitable to stop at Nassau with their human merchandise.

This ended when the European and West Indian farmers left the Bahamas. And the series of wars which followed favoured the more lucrative business of privateering. Yet there continued to be some demand, for during that period of affluence the ownership of slaves became fashionable. Apart from those needed to care for small farms, some were used as domestic servants; some were put to work producing salt or as construction labourers; and some were sent to sea on wrecking and privateering vessels.

Those coming into the Bahamas, however, were only a fraction of the enormous numbers which were flowing into the sugar islands of the West Indies. And, with the exception noted during Rogers' time, the local requirements prior to 1783 were supplied mainly by pirates, privateers and wreckers. Slaves were always looked upon as valuable booty and when brought to Nassau, they were either sold to trading vessels from abroad or to local residents.

Before the loyalist influx there were probably not more than a thousand slaves in the Bahamas. But that number was largely increased by the 4000 or more brought in by these political refugees. The amount of land which could be obtained and the amount of cotton which could be grown was directly proportionate to the number of slaves owned. Early success, therefore, led plantation owners to undertake expansion, and additional slaves were brought in annually until 1804 when the last arrivals were recorded.

In the Bahamas today, consciousness of racial distinctions has almost totally disappeared among the blacks, and, because of intermarriage, it would take a well-trained anthropologist to link any great number of them to their ancestral tribes. During slavery, however, the distinctions were obvious. Apart from physical differences, many spoke their native languages, followed their own tribal customs and took pride in their particular race. The Yoruba, Congo, Ibo, Mandingo, Fulani, Hausa and other tribes were all represented among Bahamian blacks. Apart from the Negroes, there were some Indian slaves brought in from North America. But they were a small minority who had no great or lasting effect on our history.

A Festival in slavery days

Treatment of Slaves in the Bahamas

Contemporary travellers who were qualified to make comparisons were in general agreement that slaves were treated far better in the Bahamas than elsewhere in the West Indies. But it is a difficult matter to deal with because, however they were treated, they were still slaves. On the plantations, which were not large in comparison with other places, the owner or his agent supervised the daily chores. The paid overseer with his long whip was not seen in the Bahamas. Every plantation slave family had its own plot of land on which vegetables and fruit were grown for home use. Deprivation was rare and starvation unknown. This is in striking contrast to the thousands who starved to death on some of the sugar islands.

Visitors to the Bahamas were amazed at the spontaneous song and laughter which always accompanied their labours. An English missionary who visited the Bahamas in 1801 said he

. . . was highly gratified by the cheerfulness with which the negroes went through their daily tasks . . . upon seeing and contemplating their situation both in a temporal and spiritual light (he) would rather be a slave in the Bahamas than a poor free cottager in England.

James Stephen, a staunch abolitionist, noted a few years later, that the provisions and stock raised on the plantations did not provide the remuneration received by planters in other colonies, 'but to slaves the effects were ease, plenty, health and the preservation and increase of their numbers, all in a degree, quite beyond example in any other part of the West Indies'. In enumerating all the benefits the Bahamian slaves enjoyed, he reflected, quite sadly, that they were deprived of the 'infinitely greater one, and the hope of all—Freedom'. This was the crux of the matter. Good treatment of slaves was commendable but insignificant compared to the immense evil of the system itself.

Pressure for Reform

For a long time the horrors of the slave trade were known only to a relative few. People in England believed that it was a kindness to remove the Africans from their 'barbarous' surroundings and transport them to plantations across the ocean where they could enjoy the blessings of 'civilization'. But some inquisitive minds, not believing this, began to investigate the dark crimes connected with that trade and in a number of pamphlets brought them to the attention of the British people and Parliament. The British began to feel responsible for this terrible business, for it was their seamen and financiers who had been foremost in promoting it. After some years of consideration, Parliament in 1807 passed a law abolishing the trade as far as British ships and ports were concerned. This had no direct effect on the Bahamas because, as we have seen, the importation of slaves had ceased by 1804. But it had an indirect effect which we will look into later.

About this time, the African Institution was formed in England. Its main objectives were to persuade other countries to abolish the slave trade, to see that the English laws prohibiting it were effective, and to promote better conditions for those already enslaved in British colonies. The Institution had a powerful voice in Parliament in William Wilberforce. The Anti-slavery forces next advocated a periodic registration of all slaves in British colonies. This, they reasoned, would reveal any unlawful importation of new slaves.

Parliament, in agreeing to this, decided to leave the actual legislation to the colonies which would have to enforce the law. The matter was pressed by successive Governors, and strongly resisted by the Bahamas Assembly which expressed the view that neither the African Institution nor the British Government should interfere with local conditions in a colony of which they knew nothing. The registration, they pointed out, would be expensive to undertake owing to the scattered nature of the islands, and it would serve no useful purpose since no slaves were being imported into the Bahamas anyway. After five years of wrangling, the bill was passed by the Legislature in 1821. The first registration (1822) showed a slave population of 10,808 spread over seventeen islands and island groups.

Parliament then proceeded to its next objective, the betterment of the conditions of slavery. The recommendations sent to the colonies are too voluminous to be stated, even briefly. The

Assembly which represented the interests of slave-owners objected again to British intrusion in local affairs. They argued that Britain had encouraged the Loyalists to establish plantations in the Bahamas with the use of slave labour, and they had no right to interfere with an institution they had sanctioned.

But the British Government continued to press the matter and, in 1824, a new slave code was adopted which, with amendments in 1826 and 1829, took care of many of the recommended reforms. During the latter year, a new Governor arrived, Sir James Carmichael Smyth, who was a known abolitionist. He was relentless in advocating further reforms; and even took money out of his own pocket to help those in distress. Smyth greatly alarmed the Assembly and the slave-owners, and they petitioned for his recall. But the British Government replied that it fully endorsed the attitude and actions of the Governor.

Abolition of Slavery

In fact, the Government was being subjected to increasing pressure from an aroused British public which was exasperated by the way the colonists resisted every reform which was proposed to them. As a result of this pressure, in August 1833, the Abolition of Slavery Act became law. Governor Smyth had finished his term and Lieutenant Governor Balfour issued proclamations to both slaves and masters informing them that on the last day of July 1834, slavery would come to an end.

As the great day approached, the fear among whites was that the slaves, intoxicated as it were by the long awaited changes in their lives, might resort to great mischief. But Balfour did his job well. Proclamations were issued urging both blacks and whites to remain orderly. The clergy of all denominations toured the islands explaining to the slaves that they should expect no sudden and dramatic changes, that emancipation was but the first step in their rise to freedom, and that for some years yet they would have to serve as apprentices to their former masters. As a result, one of the most momentous days in our history, 1 August 1834, passed quietly by. Compensation paid by the Imperial Government to slave owners averaged £12 14s 4¾d for each slave.

Apprenticeship was a transition between slavery and freedom. The emancipated slaves were bound to work for their former masters for a fixed number of hours a week in return for land-use, clothing and other allowances. The apprentices kept the same houses in which they had lived as slaves. In the beginning, they retained much the same relationships to their former masters but the new terms 'employers' and 'apprentices' soon generated new ideas. Voluntary agreements between the two groups became increasingly popular. Sometimes regular wages were paid for their labour; and sometimes time off and land to work were substituted for food and clothing. All agreements were supervised by special magistrates to ensure that they were equitable. The system was designed to last six years for farm workers and four years for others. But the Assembly decided that all should be released at the same time. Thus, on 1 August 1838, the former slaves became legally free to command their own lives.

Settlement of Free Negroes

Briefly, we have to consider yet another group of Negroes, those who were brought to the Bahamas from slave ships captured at sea. The total number landed at Nassau between 1808 and 1838 was probably about 3000. They were technically free but totally incapable of looking after themselves in a strange land. Government therefore was obliged to assume responsibility for them. And it was quite a problem to fit these Africans into Bahamian life.

Sir James Carmichael Smyth conceived the idea of using ungranted Crown land where they might be settled. He reasoned that with farming and fishing and with what local industries they might develop, they could become self supporting. In New Providence, the villages of Headquarters (now Grant's Town), Adelaide and Carmichael were founded for this purpose.

Smyth also settled some on Highborne Cay in the Exumas. But it was his successor, Colebrooke, who greatly expanded the experiment as far as the Out Islands were concerned. Free settlements were set up at many islands, including San Salvador, Rum Cay, Ragged Island and Long Island. None of these except Headquarters, was very successful; some were quickly abandoned and others could carry on for some years only with government help. These Negroes were hardly fitted to make their own way in isolated communities. They had no common language, and they did not possess that ingrained knowledge which is essential to wrest a living from the Bahamian soil and sea.

It was found that the best way for them to learn the English language, become adapted to Bahamian life and eventually self supporting, was to place them as indentured servants for a number of years. In 1838, however, when the apprentices were released, the feeling against any form of involuntary servitude was so strong in Britain that the Governor was instructed to cancel all outstanding indentures. As a consequence, in the fall of that same year, all bonded Africans were given their liberty.

There were mighty problems ahead for the Bahamas, but from 1839 onward they were faced by a people who were all free.

15
The Wrecking Industry

For centuries 'Land ho!' has been a welcome sound to the home-ward bound, and 'Thar she blows!' has thrilled the hearts of many a whaling crew. But it is doubtful if these two cries taken together ever summoned up the sheer joy and intense excitement which 'Wrack Ashore!' has stirred in Bahamian breasts. Since 1648, there have been Bahamians ready and anxious to salvage ships and cargoes wrecked on the rocks and reefs of the shallow sea. The men who engaged in this business called themselves 'Wrackers' or 'Wreckers', and they were known to others as 'Wreckers'.

The Adventurers

The Eleutherian Adventurers were conscious of the value of wrecks even before they came to the Bahamas. Their *Articles and Orders* laid down strict rules for disposing of salvage and sharing of proceeds.

Whatsoever ordinance can be recovered from any wraks, shall be wholly employed for the use of the publick, and serve for the fortification of the Plantation. That all other wraks which shall be recovered upon, or near the Islands, or upon or near any the adjacent Islands . . . shall be delivered into the Custody of two such persons, Merchants or Agents for the said company as shall be yearly chosen . . . and the Wraks . . . shall be made fit for sale . . . and sold for the best price and advantage . . .

It then goes on to stipulate that the wreckers were to receive one third of the net proceeds.

Before many years the Adventurers had blossomed into expert wreckers. Unfortunately, only a fragmentary account of one voyage has come down to us. On 2 August 1657, a Bermudian wrecker by the name of Richard Richardson arrived at Eleuthera 'where the Inhabitants did live, at Captain Saile's house, and one Curtis by name which was in the house made us welcome. . . .' Richardson, after quarrelling with some of his crew took up abode in Preacher's Cave, where the Adventurers first sheltered.

News was soon received of a wreck ashore near 'Jeames Mans Iland'. So the Bermudians in their vessel and the Eleutherians in Sayle's shallop set out on the voyage in consort.

. . . and so we went downe, and got that voyage about 80 lb. a share, beside a share of silver that weighed about 1400 pieces of eight. And so when we came up we came at Spanish Well and there we shared the money.

We have seen how the increasing number of wrecks in the Bahamas attracted Bermudian seamen to New Providence. John Oldmixon, writing of this island during the proprietary period said

As for Wrecks the People of Providence, Harbour-Island and Eleuthera, dealt in them as it is said the good Men of Sussex do: All that came ashore was Prize, and if a Sailor had, by better Luck than the rest, got ashore as well as his Wreck, he was not sure of getting off again as well. This perhaps is Scandal, but it is most notorious, that the Inhabitants looked upon every thing they could get out of a Cast-away Ship as their own, and were not at any Trouble to enquire after the owners.

Wreckers at work

The Loyalists

Immediately before the Loyalists started up their plantations, exports to Britain were comprised almost entirely of wreck goods. The great flurry of activity connected with cotton drew attention away from wrecking but when cotton-growing fell on hard times the Loyalists were drawn to wrecking too.

The vessels which had been built to carry farm produce to Nassau, and supplies and provisions back to the islands, became increasingly idle with the decline of the plantations. To put them to profitable use the owners frequently sent them out on wrecking voyages. They were manned partly or entirely by slaves. This was invaluable training, for when these people were freed many of them were already quite skilful at the wrecking business.

There is something special about 'the wrecking days' to Bahamian minds. Privateering had been carried on mainly by foreign ships with foreign crews. Pirates were entirely foreign. Plantation agriculture had been based on slave labour. But when wrecking developed into the main industry of the colony, it was an all Bahamian enterprise and all Bahamians who took part in it were free.

Since the 1660's there had been vessels in the Bahamas engaged primarily in wrecking. But over the years the majority of Bahamian men had looked on wrecking as a second calling. At the joyous cry of 'Wrack Ashore!' the farmer dropped his hoe, the fisherman his net, the carpenter his saw and all who could get on board a vessel went wrecking. On returning, they again took up their customary occupations and waited expectantly for the next wreck.

The Wrecking Era

The long period of peace after 1815 favoured a general increase in trade. Furthermore, the United States of America was beginning to be conscious of its destiny as a great trading nation. Merchants were calling for vessels faster than its burgeoning shipyards could launch them. Much of American trade was with the West Indies and Caribbean and Gulf ports. The Bahamas with

Woodes Rogers and family at Fort Nassau

Unloading cotton at Nassau

Nassau

Freeport, Grand Bahama

Independence Day, Clifford Park

its shallow sea and millions of reefs stood athwart these routes. As would be expected, the cry 'Wrack Ashore!' was heard with increasing frequency.

Local shipyards began building vessels specifically for the wrecking business. Speed was an essential ingredient of design for not only was there a large area to be watched, but the first vessel at a wreck had certain advantages over those which arrived later.

By 1856, there were 302 ships licensed to engage in salvage and out of a population of 27,000, 2679 Bahamians held individual wrecking licences. If we consider that there were about 13,000 males and that less than fifty per cent of these were fit for vigorous occupations, then we arrive at the astonishing conclusion that nearly one half of the able-bodied men of the colony were engaged in wrecking.

Apart from vessels and men, there are other statistics to show the importance of the wrecking industry. As far as the Government was concerned, wreck goods were regarded as regular imports on which duty had to be paid. In 1856, wreck goods amounted to £96,304 or more than fifty per cent of total imports. As for exports, considerably more than two-thirds of these were comprised of wreck goods during the 1850's. The variety of articles shipped abroad would have led an unknowing observer to believe that the Bahama Islands were dotted with factories.

Profits of Wrecking

All salvaged goods were required by law to be brought to Nassau and disposed of by auction at the Vendue House. But it should be noted that there were certain items such as clocks, barometers, steering wheels, and chests of drawers, which wreckers looked upon as trophies of the adventure and which they seldom surrendered. And there were other items of immediate use to the seamen and their families, chiefly tackle, food and clothing, which were frequently hidden from the authorities. As a rule, customs officials closed their eyes to this sort of thing.

Of the bulk of salvage which went through legitimate channels, the Government put in a prior claim for fifteen per cent customs

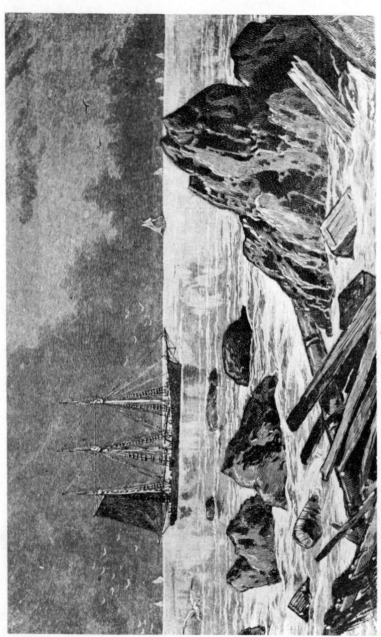

The schooner Galvanic. Queen of the Bahamian wrecking fleet

duties to be paid at the time of sale. On goods unclaimed by owners the Vice Admiralty Court took thirty per cent and the Governor ten per cent. On all goods, warehousemen, commission agents and labourers received approximately fourteen per cent. The wreckers were allowed forty to sixty per cent of the net value, the actual percentage depending on a number of variables. What was left went to the owners and this was usually very little.

Apart from this immediate division of the spoils, the wrecking industry provided employment for those who built the vessels and those who rigged them and kept them in repair. Food, clothing and almost every article of domestic and industrial use flooded the country at costs far less than if they had been regular imports. Lawyers benefited from the necessary legal work involved in drawing up papers, adjusting claims and appearing in court. But the merchants received the lion's share through the lucrative business of trading in salvaged goods.

On the surface, the forty to sixty per cent of the net proceeds paid to the wreckers would seem large. And that is perhaps why they are often pictured as semi-pirates who roamed the Bahama Sea gathering great wealth from the misfortunes of others. But in the best of years the average received by an ordinary seaman was little more than £20. Governor Rawson compared their calling to a lottery 'in which the blanks far exceed the prizes, and in which the prizes too often bring only a redemption from debts incurred during the unprofitable wasted months of vain expectation'.

Both owners of wreck goods and government officials were incensed by what they considered to be unnecessary destruction and waste, especially the practice of breaking open containers and spilling the contents. It was said that ruined cargo and littered decks were more remindful of a 'sordid scramble for plunder' than true salving. But most of the wreckers' vessels were small and the conditions of the wrecks and the vagaries of the weather usually allowed but a short time for salvage. The remuneration received depended on the value of the goods salvaged and not on size or weight. Therefore, the wreckers wisely loaded their vessels with the most valuable merchandise and discarded the rest.

Nassau about 1840

No doubt the wreckers had a good idea of where their interests lay. Daniel McKinnen recorded an interesting conversation he had with one of them at sea.

Q. What success in cruising?
A. Middling—but middling.
Q. We have seen very few wreckers to the eastward—are there many to the westward?
A. We lay with forty sail four months along Floriday shore.
Q. Forty sail? Then certainly you must have had many opportunities of being essentially serviceable to vessels passing the Gulf stream, by directing them to keep off from places of danger, with which you made it your business to become acquainted?

A. Not much of that—they went on generally in the night.

Q. But then you might have afforded them timely notice, by making beacons on shore, or showing your lights?

A. No, no [laughing]: we always put them out for a better chance by night.

Q. But would there not have been more humanity in showing them their danger?

A. I did not go there for humanity: I went racking.

In fairness to McKinnen we do believe that he asked these questions with tongue in cheek, and that he enjoyed the humour of the conversation as much as did the wrecker.

Now we will turn our attention to the serious charge of collusion. Briefly, this was an agreement between unscrupulous wreckers and even more unscrupulous captains, whereby the latter would purposely run their ships on to reefs for a share in the spoils. That some of this went on, there can be no doubt.

Dr James Wright, who studied the matter, was convinced that collusion came about because there were just too many wreckers. Consequently, some of them gave a helping hand to the navigational hazards provided by nature. We do believe that these were relatively few, and their criminal acts should not be held against the main body of wreckers who were essentially honest people.

Wrecking Stories

The stories that can be told about the wreckers would entertain an audience for forty days and forty nights. That there was a strong sense of fair play among them, and that wrecking permeated every strata of society is illustrated by the following incident. In a wrecking town, the morning church service had begun on a Sunday when from outside there rose the cry: 'Wreck ashore!' Immediately there was a movement toward the doors. The minister, with complete understanding of the situation, commanded: 'Keep your seats please. We will have one minute of prayer for the success of this voyage, and then we will all start fair.' After beseeching the blessings of the Lord, there was a hasty rush to the seashore and the wrecking vessels, with the minister in the lead.

There was a kerosene wreck near Harbour Island which was looked upon as a blessing, for kerosene, or paraffin, was the fuel used for lamps and cooking stoves. Much to the dismay of the wreckers, the arm of the law appeared in the persons of a magistrate and a uniformed policeman. They informed the wreckers that every single five gallon tin had to be surrendered to the authorities. By chance, a wrecker passed up a tin that was leaking, and it was handed back. It had no salvage value. With great glee he took the precious liquid home and filled his stove and all his lamps. After that, no one knew why there should be so many leaking tins, no one, that is, except the wreckers who then considered a hammer and a nail to be essential parts of their equipment.

Lighthouses

Bahamian wreckers looked upon the erection of lighthouses with dismay. After all, they reasoned, the Lord put the reef there and he made the wind to blow and the sea to rage. Lighthouses were the works of man and, all things considered, they preferred to be on the side of the Lord.

Nowhere were lighthouse builders more frustrated than those who went to Elbow Cay. The people of Hope Town placed every obstacle they could think of in the way. They refused to supply fresh water to the construction crew, and at night they sank the vessels loaded with building material. But the work went on to completion. A few years after it began to function, lightning struck the tower one night and the inhabitants were convinced that Providence had intervened on their behalf. The next night, however, the light shone forth as bright as ever, to their bitter disappointment.

Without the Bahamian wreckers, hundreds of thousands of pounds' worth of imperilled merchandise which was saved, would have been swallowed up forever by the sea. And this merchandise proved to be a great boon to the Bahamian people. There were many to say that far too little of the proceeds found its way to the rightful owners of the goods. But we must remember that except for the efforts of the wreckers the owners would have received nothing.

The Wreckers as Lifesavers

Between 1845 and 1870, more than 300 ships came to grief on the reefs and shoals of the Bahama Sea. The crews of these, totalling thousands of men, frequently had but one hope of salvation, the wreckers. Time after time we read of loss of life through shipwreck and how it would have been much greater except for the exertions of the wreckers. An American report dated 30 June 1860, speaks of several wrecks near Abaco.

Of the loss of life [it states] we have no account but this is believed to be small owing to the exertion of the wreckers, who are always on the

*Medal for courage in saving lives awarded to Captain Robert Sands of Abaco (1853)
by the Royal National Institution for the Preservation of Life from Shipwreck*

look out for their prey, and have, I understand, frequently saved life
at the risk of their own . . .

James Wright pointed out that the wreckers performed many
acts of daring in the midst of difficulties and dangers.

They not uncommonly forgot self, sustained personal injuries and
material losses and sometimes failed to recover anything to indemnify
themselves. Of course they were out to make money, but that did not
prevent them from rescuing endangered human beings before they
turned to saving property.

In 1853, Captain Robert Sands of Abaco was awarded the silver
medal of the Royal National Institution for the Preservation of
Life from Shipwreck and the Queen's commendation for courage
and generosity shown at a wreck.

Further proof of generosity and compassion was demonstrated
when a slave ship grounded near the same island in 1860. The
captain offered a substantial sum of money to the wreckers if
they would help him get his human cargo of 289 souls to Cuba
where they were to be sold into slavery. This bribe was stead-
fastly refused and the wreckers saw to it that the captives were
brought to Nassau and freedom.

During the first quarter of the nineteenth century, Bahamian
wreckers did quite well among the Florida reefs and keys. Salvage
from there, as from other places, was brought to Nassau for disposal. In 1825, however, a United States law decreed that goods
from wrecks in that area had to be brought to an American port
of entry. Many Bahamian wreckers thereupon settled at Key
West. Although lost to the Bahamas, they were mainly responsible
for the rise to importance of that island as a wrecking centre.

In the early 1860's, a far graver event in American history had
a more profound effect on Bahamian wreckers. The great Civil
War had broken out. The Administrator of the Bahama Islands,
C. R. Nesbitt, reported in 1862 that 'the interruption of commerce . . . and the blockade of the Southern States have paralized
the avocation of wreckers'.

16

Breaching the Blockade

When George Washington declared the Revolutionary War at an end on 19 April 1783 the thirteen former British colonies, bonded into one nation, began their march through history. The affairs of the Bahamas were destined to be influenced by every major event involving that young and vigorous republic. Governor Maxwell resumed his post after the islands were returned to Britain in 1783. Both he and his successor, James Powell, had their hands full in coping with the thousands of Loyalists and slaves who came to the Bahamas after England's defeat.

Lord Dunmore who arrived as Governor in 1787 inherited a host of internal problems which he did little to resolve but he did turn his attention to the matter of defence. He had been Governor of Virginia at the start of the revolution and perhaps the sting of defeat was still fresh in his mind. With great energy and at great cost, he set to work to make New Providence stronger than it had ever been before. His most important works, Forts Charlotte and Fincastle, still stand as testaments to their robust construction.

France declared war on England in 1793 and, except for a

short respite at the turn of the century, the conflict continued on land and sea for many years. After Napoleon's hope of conquering England was blasted by Lord Nelson, the French directed their energies to ruining English sea-trade. England, in turn, declared a blockade of European ports under French control.

This greatly annoyed the United States whose merchant seamen were enjoying a thriving commerce with both sides. America's anger reached boiling point, however, when England took to searching her ships for British deserters and, on 1 June 1812, she declared war. Immediately the Bahamian people were alerted to the possibility of invasion, for they had not forgotten the events of 1776, 1778 and 1781.

Defence of the Bahamas

The colony, however, was not as defensively weak as it had been during the revolution. Apart from Dunmore's powerful forts, the Second West Indian Regiment was in garrison. Furthermore, a number of ships of the Royal Navy were on continuous patrol of the neighbourhood. Loyalist spirit dominated the Bahamas and a surge of patriotism swept the colony. There quickly developed a determination to do everything possible to escape the indignities and hardships of another military occupation. The militia in New Providence was completely reorganized into companies of Infantry, Field Artillery, Marine Artillery and Dragoons, comprising about 500 men.

Harbour Island was able to raise three companies of militia. Crooked Island had its own Crooked Island Artillery and a Battalion Company. Exuma and Long Island each boasted a company. Throughout the Bahamas there was excitement and great vigilance. Drills and military exercises were carried out daily and strict discipline prevailed everywhere. Never before had the islands known such intensity of preparedness and alertness.

As time went by no regular American naval vessels came to Bahamian waters, although American privateers were seen frequently. These caused great havoc to British shipping and kept the Bahamas in a state of alarm. Bahamians, never ones to miss a chance, sent out their own privateers. Perhaps it was in retaliation that American privateers plundered and partially burnt the little town of Spanish Wells, and raided Marine Farm, Crooked Island.

As far as the Bahamas was concerned, the War of 1812 turned out to be more of a privateering war than anything else. And, as happened whenever trade with the United States was interrupted, many people suffered from shortages of goods and provisions, and extremely high prices. Out Islanders suffered more than Nassauvians who were able to get fairly regular supplies from captured ships. The war which lasted two and a half years was unsatisfactory all round. From the American point of view it showed up some regional differences of opinion which argued ill for the future of the union.

Internal Differences in America

The South and West had favoured the conflict, but the North which stood to suffer from the interruption of trade opposed it vehemently and when it did come lent little support. Nevertheless, the union held together and went on to experience enormous growth in area, population and wealth. By the 1850's, however, some serious stresses again became evident. Doubts as to the workability, or even the desirability of the union, led many Americans to pledge their loyalties first to their home states and, secondly, to their own geographical areas.

The theory was put forth by a number of prominent politicians that a state could secede from the union if it so wished. As they saw it, each state had voluntarily joined the union, and therefore any state had the right to voluntarily leave the union. This was a course of action which became increasingly appealing to some southern states, whose great fear was domination by the more populous North. Differences in economies, life styles and attitudes between North and South resulted in heated disagreements on national policy.

Of special significance was the question of slavery which the North was anxious to see abolished. To Southerners, this thought was anathema. Abolition, they contended, would ruin their economy and completely destroy their way of life. When Abraham

Lincoln was elected President in 1860 without winning a single southern state, it was obvious that a gaping fissure had opened along the Mason–Dixon Line, the boundary line separating the slave states from the free states, the South from the North. South Carolina seceded right away, and six other states followed soon after.

Lincoln considered these activities to be acts of open rebellion; the seceding states were exercising powers they did not have, he maintained. He was resolved to hold the union together by all necessary means, including military force. The seceding states were equally resolved to maintain their sovereignty, and they banded together as the Confederate States of America. Obviously only a spark was needed to plunge the country into bloody civil war.

The American Civil War

On 12 April 1861, the Confederate cannon opened fire on Union-held Fort Sumter, in Charleston harbour. This was the first shot of a most unequal contest. The North was overwhelmingly superior in men, money and industrial capacity. The South, with its agricultural economy, had to rely on imports for almost every manufactured article needed to carry on the war or even to survive. Having judged this to be the Achilles' heel of the rebellion, Abraham Lincoln on 19 April 1861, proclaimed a sea blockade of the Confederacy. When extended a short time later, the coast involved ran from Cape Henry in Virginia southward around the Florida peninsula and then westward to the Mexican border, a distance of 4000 miles.

In the early days, it was referred to as a 'paper blockade', and was the cause of much amusement. Ships belonging to the South and those of foreign nations went in and out of supposedly blockaded ports with the greatest of ease. The first vessel to arrive in the Bahamas from one of these ports was the *Prince of Wales*, a Confederate schooner of seventy-four tons and a crew of five. She entered Nassau harbour on 5 December 1861, with a load of cotton.

During 1862 and into 1863, little Bahamian sloops and schoon-

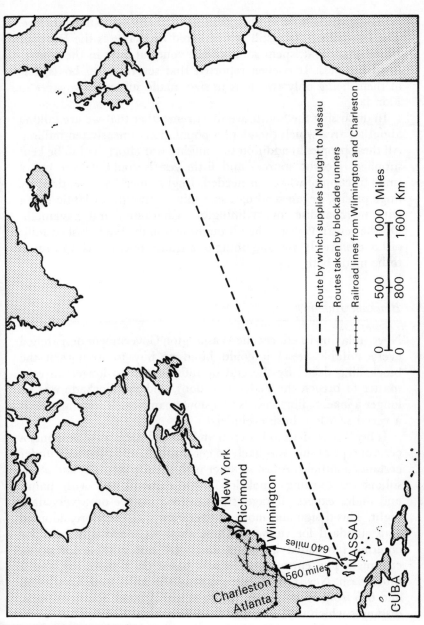

Routes of the blockade runners during the American Civil War

ers made voyages far more profitable than any ever known before. The fast-sailing *Dart*, still remembered by many as the Harbour Island mail boat, spent some of her youthful days in the contraband business. It is even reported that several open boats, one of them being only two tons in size, made successful voyages to Florida.

In discussing the South, we must remember that we are talking about an area which then had a population of nearly ten million. All these people, in addition to a mighty war effort, had to be kept supplied. Nearby sources and little vessels could deliver but a small fraction of what was needed. English merchants, enticed by huge profits, began sending steamships across the Atlantic laden with merchandise for Wilmington, Charleston and Savannah. On the return voyage, they brought cotton for the famished mills of Lancashire. It was something of a trader's dream with fortunes to be made both ways.

Blockade Running

Never relaxing its efforts, the Washington Government despatched every suitable vessel it could build or buy to strengthen the blockading fleets. By the end of 1862 it was no longer an easy matter to breach the Federal cordons, and the blockade was no longer a joke. Sailing vessels and slow steam vessels were finding it a very hazardous business indeed.

It became evident to Federals and Confederates alike that only a certain type of ship was likely to get through, and then only under certain conditions. A fast steamer with shallow draught and a low silhouette, burning smokeless coal, camouflaged with paint, and under expert pilotage, stood a good chance on a very dark night. This design and mode of operation was, therefore, adopted as a standard for runners. These ships were specially built for entering blockaded harbours and were not suitable for ocean crossings. The entire concept was based on a short run and a quick dash. New Providence was only 560 miles from Charleston and 640 from Wilmington, the principal Atlantic southern ports, distances which took no more than forty-eight hours. Thus it was that Nassau became important as a trans-shipping port where

Blockade runners in Nassau harbour

The Royal Victoria Hotel

goods from ocean steamers were transferred to blockade runners, and *vice versa*. And it was then that the Bahamas experienced a boom far surpassing anything in its previous history. More cotton was seen in Nassau in those days than the Bahamian plantations ever produced.

Boom on Bay Street

An eye witness described the Nassau water-front as follows

Cotton, cotton, everywhere! Blockade runners discharging it into lighters, piled high upon the wharves and merchant vessels, chiefly under the British flag, loading with it. Here and there in the crowded harbour might be seen a low, long, rakish-looking, lead-coloured steamer with short masts and a convex forecastle deck extending nearly as far aft as the waist, and placed there to enable her to be forced through and not over a heavy head sea. These were the genuine blockade runners, built for speed: and some of them survived all the desperate hazards of the war.

In Nassau, money flowed like water, labouring wages more than doubled in the urgent business of building warehouses, and moving goods. Out Island people streamed into the capital to claim their share of this seemingly inexhaustible wealth. Often, there was no place to live, but who cared? Workers slept on porches, in sheds, on the street and between bales of cotton. Their pockets were filled with money and that was the important thing.

English and American businessmen took over Bay Street and the harbour front. Shops and warehouses sprouted up as fast as they could be built. And they were all filled to the ceiling before the last nail was driven. Fortunes, which ordinarily could not be accumulated in a lifetime, were made in a few weeks. Quinine, which could be bought in Nassau for $10 was worth $400 in Charleston. An investor who bought $100 worth of cotton in Wilmington would receive $1000 for the same weight in England.

Captains, pilots and sailors of the blockade runners found it impossible to spend, or even squander, all the money they made.

A captain received £1000 for a week's round trip. In addition to this, he was allowed to bring ten bales of cotton on his own account, which normally yielded a similar sum. Pilots received £750, with the right to bring five bales. An ordinary seaman would walk ashore after a voyage with £60 in his pockets. The new Royal Victoria Hotel, built at a cost of £26,000, was the centre of business and social activities. There, on the cool verandahs and patios, daring captains and pilots, eager buyers and sellers, Confederate officers and agents, and Federal spies, would talk over the news, arrange deals, throw dice, eat their sumptuous meals and drink champagne.

The Government Treasury had never been in such a healthy state. Many public works were undertaken and a public debt of £47,786 was completely wiped out. Annual imports reached a peak of £5,346,000 and exports £4,677,000, figures that were beyond imagination before the Civil War.

While the majority of blockade running captains were attracted by the money and the excitement, there were genuine southern patriots who risked their lives for their country without thought of reward. Famous among them was Captain J. Wilkinson who had been an officer in the U.S. Navy, and who had successfully breached the blockade more than twenty times. On his last trip, he was about to enter Wilmington when he realized that it was in Federal hands. He then tried for Charleston Harbour, but that too was blocked off. With his full cargo, which was intended to succour the dying South, he turned his ship

. . . again, and for the last time . . . for Nassau. As we turned away from land [he wrote] our hearts sank within us, as the conviction forced itself upon us that the cause for which so much blood had been shed, and so many sacrifices cheerfully made, and miseries endured, was about to perish.

The last blockade runner to come to Nassau was the steamer *Imogene*. She crossed the bar with a cargo of cotton, from far off Galveston, on 10 May 1865. It was all over. The blockade runners left the harbour, the agents barred their office doors and went home, the shops were closed, the warehouses emptied, and the splendid Royal Victoria Hotel was soon untenanted.

Depression and Hurricane

A contemporary observer remarked that the Bahamas was rich one day and poor the next. 'Ruin', he said, 'fell in an hour'. Perhaps it did not happen all that quickly, but in a matter of weeks or months the colony had slumped, once again, into economic depression.

The following year, a devastating hurricane added to the miseries and the problems. It came along almost a century before the practice of naming these whirling monsters was adopted and, normally, it would have gone into the records simply as the hurricane of September/October 1866. But the severity of this storm was such that it received the distinction of a name, 'The Great Bahama Hurricane'. For many years afterwards, Bahamians were accustomed to speak of 'the year of the hurricane'.

Individual hurricanes which strike the Bahamas normally affect only a particular section of the archipelago, leaving the rest of the islands relatively unscathed. But this particular storm swept the entire chain. Early on 30 September a mighty wind descended on the Turks and Caicos Islands. Moving north-westerly in a wide and destructive course the 'eye', with a diameter of twenty-three miles, was over Nassau between 7.20 and 8.50 p.m. the next day.

At Harbour Island, the largest Out Island settlement, there was hardly a house undamaged. Farm crops were entirely destroyed and every vessel was either sunk, driven ashore or wrecked. A deputation of three, including the Methodist Minister, was sent to Nassau to plead for help. The Governor told them they had to rely on themselves for assistance. No wonder he replied in this manner, for he was preoccupied with his own ravaged capital where 601 houses were destroyed and an equal number badly damaged. More than a thousand people were homeless. The devastating hurricane had changed the normally placid Nassau harbour into a raging, frenzied torrent which swept everything before it. Of more than 200 vessels in the harbour only one remained intact. Even the dead were affected by the disaster. An old cemetery on the western seashore was washed out and bones and skulls littered the beach.

A writer who talked with eye witnesses a few years later reported

The ocean rolled completely over Hog Island into the harbour in surges so enormous that the crest was even with the gallery of the lighthouse, sixty feet above the sea. Houses and forests went down before the wind like reeds; many which withstood its force when it blew from the north-east collapsed when it shifted to the south-west. In twenty-four hours the city was like a town sacked and burned by the enemy . . .

At Rum Cay, not a house remained undamaged, and the greater part of an abundant salt crop was washed away. On a plantation at Long Island, the sea water came in on the land to a depth of fifteen feet. The only refuge for the people was the upper floor of the old manor-house which fortunately, did not crumble. All the livestock was drowned, the fresh water wells polluted, and agricultural crops buried under silt. Throughout the islands there were many injuries and deaths. Especially tragic was the fate of crews of vessels which were caught in unsheltered areas. For weeks after the storm, bodies which escaped the sharks were being found where they had washed ashore along the coasts.

The collapse of blockade running had produced an awful slump, and then the hurricane had come along to smash what was left of Bahamian economic life.

17
Sea and Soil

After the American Civil War and the resumption of normal trade, it appeared that wrecking would regain its former importance. In 1865, the last year of blockade running, only £28,000 of wrecked goods were salvaged, but the following year the figure jumped to £108,000. In 1870 it soared to £154,000, an all-time high. The remark was made that 'so long as ships sailed the ocean and Bahama reefs stood in their way there would be wrecks'. But the very next year a decline began which was never reversed, and by the end of the century the wrecking industry was all but dead.

Many factors were responsible for this. Steam was taking over from sail; better qualified captains and officers were employed; and insurance companies were demanding greater seaworthiness of ships. A network of lighthouses built by the Imperial Government, and the availability of more reliable charts also contributed greatly to safer navigation and fewer wrecks.

During the thirty years from 1870 to 1900, while the wrecking industry was dwindling away, the population of the Bahamas rose from 39,000 to 53,000. With an ever-increasing number of mouths to be fed, Bahamians were obliged to turn once more to local industries to see what could be harvested from their own soil and sea.

Sponges

In 1870, when wrecking was at its peak, we note that £14,000 worth of sponges were taken from the Bahamian sea-bed. This was less than one-tenth of the value of salvaged goods, but the future looked promising for this young industry as sponges were in growing demand abroad and they were abundant on the Bahama banks. By 1896, when wrecked goods were valued at only £2000, sponge products had climbed to £81,000. Sponging had taken the place of wrecking as the chief maritime industry of the Bahamian people.

The sponge is an animal which anchors itself to the sea-floor. Its porous and elastic skeleton which retains the name of the animal has found wide use since antiquity, and Bahamians had used it for generations. It took a shipwrecked Frenchman, however, to see the commercial possibilities of the sponge. He made the first overseas shipment in 1841. And by the end of the century, the industry had grown tremendously.

A creature of the shallow banks, the sponge grew most abundantly in that large underwater area to the south-west of Andros known as 'the mud'. Great quantities were also found on the Little Bahama Bank, west of Abaco. Other sponging grounds of significance were the Exuma sound, the Bight of Acklins and the Bimini Bank.

The essentials for gathering sponges, Bahamian fashion, are a dinghy, two men, a waterglass, and a pair of hooks. One man, standing on the stern sheets, sculls the boat while the other, seated forward, scans the sea-bottom through the waterglass. On sighting a marketable sponge, a signal brings the dinghy to a stop. The iron hooks on the end of a long pole are then lowered, the sponge dexterously wrenched from its attachment and brought into the boat.

Many of these small boats operated from settlements or temporary camps to which they would return at night. But a far greater number were attached to sloops or schooners which allowed greater mobility. Thus, depending on the type of operation, at the end of a day the sponges would be thrown on a vessel's deck, or on dry land, to die. Next, they would be put into a fenced-in area of sea-water called a kraal, so that the decomposing tissue might be partially washed out. Final cleaning was done by alternate beating and washing and then the sponges were put in the sun to dry.

After a voyage of about six weeks, the catch would be brought to Nassau. Depending on the weather, the size of the vessel, the number of dinghies and crew members, ability of the men, and luck, the catch would vary from 5000 to 15,000. The sponges would be sorted according to kind: wool, velvet, reef, hardhead, yellow and grass and placed in the Sponge Exchange for sale.

Sale was by sealed tender, which seems to have been a very good method. Expert buyers would look over the lots, estimate the weight and quality, and place their bids. They were so good at this that often the difference between the bids was very small. Theoretically, the money received was shared between owners of the vessel and crew according to custom or agreement. In practice, those merchants owning both sponging vessels and supply houses would insist that a part of each seaman's share be taken in provisions. This 'truck system', obviously, was open to other abuses and was resented by the seamen who had no option but to go along with it.

After making seven voyages during a year, a sponger would receive up to $300. Those employed in preparing sponges for export earned fifty to seventy-five cents for a ten hour day. Even with the 'truck system' this was better than wrecking had been and better than anything else in sight in those days.

Of course, sponging lacked much of the excitement and the thrill of adventure which was attached to wrecking. But even so old timers, who as young men went 'on the mud', look back on their voyaging years with deep nostalgia. They will talk on and on about the amusing incidents and the good humoured banter which lightened their labours and filled their leisure hours. They speak too of other things; of shrieking winds and raging seas, and ships and shipmates lost forever. Most tragic of all memories is the 1899 hurricane, still etched in the minds of a few who witnessed it as boys. First came the east wind which blew the water off the mud as far as the eye could see. The vessels settled on the bottom and careened over and during the calm of the 'eye' some crews walked on to the mud and lit fires and cooked their meals among the sponges. Then came the west wind bringing with it a thunderous wall of water. Like so many toy boats, the vessels were rolled over and over, and three hundred men were drowned.

Sponging was a great boon to shipbuilding. More boats were launched than at the height of the wrecking industry. Early in the present century, 587 sloops and schooners of from one to forty-three tons burthen, with their 2517 dinghies, were kept busy in the sponging business. Apart from these, 291 open boats operated from Out Island settlements. Over 5000 men and boys were engaged in gathering at sea and 258 men and women were employed in sorting, clipping and packing on shore. But the money earned benefited every class and found its way into almost every Bahamian pocket.

Citrus Fruits

To consider again agricultural pursuits, although the soil is thin, it is fertile for a time and the climate so conducive to growth that agriculture has always been, and still remains, a perennial attraction. Throughout the centuries, vast areas of uncultivated land have exerted an irresistible appeal which has lured many an investor to his ruin.

We have seen how both the Eleutherian Adventurers and the Lords Proprietors were unable to make a successful plantation colony of the Bahamas. We noted too that Woodes Rogers had great hopes in this respect and that his European farmers had made great strides for some years. Then came the Loyalists with the greatest and most promising of all agricultural ventures which also ended in failure.

Now we will consider some other products of the Bahamian soil which provided employment and benefited the economy toward the end of the last century. Citrus growing had been carried on locally for hundreds of years. And Bahamians who first tried to make a living from farming found citrus to be the most reliable and often the most profitable crop. The trees grow well in 'black loam' which is the commonest soil of the Bahamas, especially when planted in holes and depressions where it has accumulated to some depth.

The perennial problem facing Bahamians has been to find sufficient local products which could be sold abroad to pay for essential imports. Citrus was for a long time a dependable standby and as far back as two centuries ago, the colony was able to export 12,000 lemons, 347,350 limes, and 46,500 oranges in a year.

When Bahamian wreckers began to settle in Key West in the 1820's and 1830's, they took citrus seeds with them to establish the kind of gardens to which they were accustomed. Being much like the Bahamas in soil and climate, the Florida Keys were equally resistant to intensive cultivation and presented no real competitive threat. The United States had bought Florida from Spain in 1819, and there followed a period of cotton growing on the mainland similar to that which took place in the Bahamas. After the Civil War and the so-called 'reconstruction period', however, the northern part of the state was opened up to fruit growing on a large scale. Great citrus orchards were established and Bahamian growers found it difficult to find a market.

Nature intervened on the side of the Bahamas during the winter of 1894-5. The people of Florida still refer to the frost invasion of that year as the 'Great Freeze'. Their citrus groves were largely destroyed and some of the growers moved to the Bahamas where the menace of frost is unknown. This stimulated a great revival of the industry, locally. More citrus fruit were shipped abroad than would seem possible today. From 1870 to 1900, an annual average of nearly 3,000,000 oranges were sent to American markets. Toward the end of the century, grapefruit gained popularity and 300,000 of these were exported in 1900.

Pineapples

The pineapple was introduced into the colony by the Palatinates and has remained a local favourite ever since. From the time

*First cargo of pineapples
shipped from the Bahamas
to England in 1844*

of Woodes Rogers, pineapples have been shipped abroad. The number exported in 1772 was 6000 dozen. In 1842, the first shipment was made to England where the exotic fruit brought as much as eight shillings each. By 1876, the cultivation had greatly increased and 300,000 dozen were sent that year to London, New York and Baltimore.

The pineapple plant produces a single fruit and then dies. Propagation is by suckers or 'slips', which require eighteen months to crop. Areas of 'red loam', which is considered to be the oldest and most fertile of Bahamian soils, is the only local land that has been found suitable for its cultivation. But, even so, only about three crops can be obtained before the soil nutrients begin to fail. Large quantities of fertilizer help to a degree, but will not prolong the usefulness of the soil for more than a few seasons. The only satisfactory solution for the farmer is to move to a new area which has not been cultivated for fifteen to twenty years. Under these conditions 'red land', which is relatively scarce, was at a premium as farmers tried to produce more and more pineapples.

There was no way that the scattered crops could be collected together and loaded on large steamers. Consequently, small sailing vessels were employed. These, with their shallow draughts and small capacities, could be brought close to land in the vicinity of the growing areas, and be fully loaded from a single plantation or a single island. Not infrequently the vessels were delayed by adverse weather so that the cargo rotted. But small fortunes were made when the fruit arrived at its destination in prime condition to find a good market.

Canning was introduced to take care of the poorer or surplus fruit and that which ripened between shipments. Beginning in 1876, factories were established at Harbour Island, Eleuthera, Abaco and New Providence. In 1900, the astonishing quantity of 7,000,000 dozen pineapples were exported, plus 37,000 cases of canned fruit.

Sisal

But of all the agricultural pursuits which came to maturity after blockade running and wrecking, nothing inspired so much hope as sisal. A Newfoundlander, Sir Ambrose Shea, came to the Bahamas as Governor in 1887, and he immediately became excited about the economic possibilities of the fibre contained in the leaves of *agave rigida sisilana*.

Forty-two years before that, the plant had been introduced into the Bahamas from Yucatan by the then Colonial Secretary, C. R. Nesbitt. He had fibre extracted from the long green leaves and sent to England for assessment. A favourable report was received, and over the years several unsuccessful efforts were made to establish an industry. The statistics were impressive. The hardy plant will live for fourteen years, grow like a weed and produce thousands of offspring. From the fourth year onward a semi-annual cutting of leaves would yield from one-half to a ton of fibre for each acre under cultivation.

It is little wonder that Governor Shea looked on sisal as a sort of magic plant which would completely transform the Bahamian economy. He travelled to Canada, Newfoundland and England to spread the gospel among potential investors. The Governor was a good salesman and the proposition he outlined was almost an irresistible one. There was plenty of land available and plenty of labourers. Tracts of Crown Land would cost only sixteen shillings an acre and after four years an annual profit of £10 could be expected from each acre planted out. As if this were not sufficient, a bounty of £4 10s was offered for each ton of fibre exported during the first seven years. In addition, to prevent a glut on the market, only 100,000 acres of land would be sold to investors during the first ten years. Within a year the entire 100,000 acres had been taken up. And the general satisfaction and prospects were such that many of the investors agreed to forego the bounty offered by the Government.

Concern was felt for Bahamians who owned no land and who preferred to grow their own sisal rather than work for a wage on the large plantations. Each head of family, in this category, was granted ten acres at the old price of five shillings per acre, to be paid for from proceeds of the first harvest. These grants were independent of the 100,000 acre limit. Soon, sisal was growing everywhere. Almost everyone who had a patch of land was planting sisal. Within a few years fourteen mills were at work on the hard green leaves, separating the valuable fibre from the useless pulp.

Baled sisal ready to be shipped abroad

The amounts invested were huge. One English company put £150,000 into several plantations. The Chamberlain family staked £50,000 in a plantation at Andros. But these outlays were small when compared to the anticipated returns. For example, Mr Joseph Chamberlain, the future Secretary of State for the Colonies, might have calculated that with 5000 of his 7000 acres planted out, he would recover his outlay in five years, at the first cuttings, and that each year thereafter he would receive returns almost equal to his capital investment. His actual estimate of a thirty per cent annual return must have seemed very conservative. Sisal was indeed a dazzling prospect. It rapidly overtook citrus and pineapples and quickly climbed to second place, just behind sponging, in economic importance.

The End of the Agricultural Boom

Toward the end of the nineteenth century, it appeared that the Bahamian people were emerging from economic turbulence and insecurity, and could look forward, in the new century, to stable and sustained progress. But this hope was short-lived. The 'Great Freeze' of 1894–5 convinced the railroad and hotel tycoon Henry Flagler that he should push his Florida rails farther south. The first train rolled into the little town of Miami in 1896 and Florida once again presented severe competition. California also got into the citrus business.

To protect its own farmers, the United States imposed a duty of one cent a pound on imports, which placed Bahamian growers at an additional disadvantage. Those who struggled on with their oranges and grapefruit could expect a market only when, occasionally, the Florida production was severely diminished by frost.

Pineapples present much the same story. The overworked red soil became less productive, and the 7,000,000 dozen harvested in 1900 were never to be equalled again. Jamaica, Cuba, Florida and Hawaii all went into pineapple growing and some of their larger, improved varieties were more than a match for the little Bahamian 'scarlet'. A United States duty of $7·00 per thousand was more than the local industry could bear. With increasing frequency, loaded vessels arrived at American ports to find a

Neville Chamberlain when manager of Andros Fibre Company

poor market and, often, hardly enough money could be cleared to pay this impost.

Sisal proved the most disappointing of all, because so much hope had been attached to it. The Chamberlain experience was typical of many others. Joseph Chamberlain had sent his son, Neville, later to be Prime Minister of Great Britain, to supervise his Andros Fibre Company. Planting began in 1892 and by April 1895, 6000 acres of former pine and scrub had been brought into cultivation.

. . . you ought to see the place [wrote an eye-witness] new houses springing up by the dozen everywhere, fine roads in all directions . . . railway being laid down 7 miles into the forest, and a long jetty stretching out into the deep water.

In 1896, when the first plants were four years old and should have shown long and dark-green leaves, ready for cutting, Neville Chamberlain noted that they were yellowish and stunted 'as bad as can be'. He wrote to his father, 'I no longer see any chance of making the investment pay'. Even sisal would not grow in rock.

Plantation owners soon discovered that they could not compete with growers in Mexico where the plants grew more luxuriantly, and labour was cheaper. All the large plantations failed. The closure of the Andros Fibre Company resulted in 800 people being put out of work. Throughout the Bahamas, thousands of others who had become accustomed to a daily wage were likewise affected, and those who were not attracted to sponging could see nothing before them but a return to the subsistence they had known before.

Emigration to Miami

But just as they were falling on hard times, the Bahamian people heard some exciting news. Wonderful things were going on in Miami, and there was a great demand for labour there. Flagler's railroad was bringing in Northerners by the thousands, all anxious to stake a claim in southern Florida, with its gentle climate. A remarkable building boom was on, and any Bahamian who wanted a job could find it.

Bahamians left their home islands by the scores and hundreds and came to Nassau to find passage across the Gulf Stream. Vessels, whose names linger only in a few memories now, the schooner *Sarah E. Douglas* and the motor vessel *Frances C* among them, went over the bar, trip after trip, so crowded with people that there was barely standing room on their decks. Records are scant but perhaps ten to twelve thousand Bahamians emigrated during the first two decades of this century. One Bahamian in every five left home. This migration, in reverse, was twice the number that came to the Bahamas during the Loyalist influx.

18

War and Whisky

In 1892, a telegraphic cable was laid between Jupiter, Florida and New Providence. Sir Ambrose Shea, the Governor, who had launched the sisal industry, sent and received the first messages to demonstrate to Nassauvians that they were no longer dependent entirely on incoming ships for news of the outside world. In 1913 this was superseded by a wireless system which brought to the Bahamas news of the outbreak of the First World War in 1914.

Crowds milled about the government bulletin board to catch every scrap of information as soon as it was posted. Newspapers were quickly bought up as sellers moved along the streets shouting: 'Extra! Extra! Latest War News!' Sponge and sisal merchants were informed by telegram that the markets of the world had collapsed in the face of a possible global upheaval and the resulting uncertainty.

On 7 August, three days after Britain entered the war, the Legislature was called into special session. The Governor, Mr Haddon-Smith, informed members that a bill would be introduced to legalize the issuing of necessary proclamations. He spoke of the blow to trade, the probability of hard times for Bahamians, and the possible necessity of relief measures. And he requested the Legislature to authorize the Governor-in-Council to provide what relief might be required.

Bahamian Contribution

That same evening, a public meeting was held in Rawson Square. The Governor pointed out that imported food might soon become scarce, and that Bahamians should exercise economy and do all they could to make the colony self-sufficient. A War Relief Committee was formed under the chairmanship of the Speaker of the House of Assembly. The first job this Committee set itself was to undertake a monetary collection. Voluntary contributions came from the well-to-do and the not so well-to-do. Gold sovereigns were mixed with widows' mites. Many workers gave a day's pay; children gave their pennies and half-pennies. Before the end of the year £3000 had been sent to London.

The Governor, writing to the Secretary of State, said

The majority of the inhabitants of these Islands are poor. Many by contributing, I am sure, have not only denied themselves luxuries, but in many cases, the necessaries of life, but to have refunded their offerings would have given pain. There have been instances of seamstresses and market women earning a few shillings a week insisting on giving either three or two shillings. There have been other instances of people who had buried gold which they would not have unearthed except in dire need, but to be one of the subscribers to the War Fund they have dug up their hidden treasure; this has been the case in the Out Islands and accounts for many of the contributions of £1. 0. 6d. which is the (present) exchange of the American $5 gold piece.

The National Chapter of the Bahamas of the Imperial Order Daughters of the Empire, formed in 1901, and the Bahamas Red Cross Guild, formed in 1915, were vigorous throughout the war in raising money, in shipping foodstuffs to England and in supplying many thousands of garments to the British Red Cross.

A group of young girls formed the Bahamian League of the

Cross of Geneva, which collected money to help the Belgians
and others, and sent gifts to Bahamian soldiers serving overseas.
A Flag Day was organized by *The Tribune* on behalf of the
Bahamas Contingent and the *Guardian* organized a Belgian Relief
Fund. A Ladies Committee dedicated itself to helping men of the
West India Regiment, and The St Andrew Society and the Nassau
Chamber of Commerce both gave generously to deserving causes.

Bahamian Volunteers

The economic gloom came to be overshadowed by a buoyant
spirit of patriotism, the likes of which had not been known since
the war of 1812. Many Bahamians were anxious to get into the
actual fighting and, after undergoing preliminary training, the
first group of selected volunteers turned out on the Eastern Parade
for all the town to see. The Governor's wife presented them with a
silken flag bearing the colony's Coat of Arms. The flag was

First Bahamas contingent leaving to join the British West India Regiment in
1915 *(The schooner* Zellers *was lent by the Honourable Horace Myers to take
the contingent to Jamaica. He later received the M.B.E. and was presented by
the Bahamas Legislature with a piece of plate).*

attached to an historic staff which had once carried the colours of the old Bahama Militia. On 1 September 1915 this first contingent known as the 'Gallant Thirty' sailed. They were followed by a second contingent of 105 men in November 1915 and, in the following May, by a third contingent of eighty-seven men.

Altogether, 486 volunteers departed officially to become a part of the British West India Regiment. Other Bahamians joined the regular British, Canadian or American forces, making a grand total of about 700 men. Of those who enlisted in the colony, six were killed in action, three died from wounds and twenty-eight died from other causes.

The cost to the Treasury of recruiting, equipping and despatching Bahamian volunteers was £27,621. Expenditure for a Home Defence Force amounted to £8655. To these two items must be added other contributions made by the Government, which collectively totalled £47,292. Voluntary contributions from the people amounted to £10,316. The economy of the colony did not suffer as much as had been anticipated. Exports to European markets were adversely affected, but those to the United States held up well. In fact some products forged ahead of pre-war years. For example during 1917 sponge sales at the local Exchange totalled £152,000, exceeding the best previous year, 1913, by £53,000. And sisal did better still, bringing in £181,700.

Government revenue, in 1913, amounted to a little more than £100,000. But that was an exceptional year, being more than £23,000 greater than the average of the preceding five years. During the war years it hovered between £77,000 and £90,000, which compared most favourably with pre-war receipts. However, there were annual deficits due chiefly to expenses connected with the contingents. These were met by loans which increased the public debt from £43,000 to £69,000.

On the labour side, Bahamians found their customary employment in fishing and farming, sisal growing and sponging. The American government had recruited 2500 Bahamian labourers in the summer of 1918 in connection with the construction of a new port at Charleston, South Carolina. When the war ended, this construction work ceased and these men returned to the Bahamas.

Effects of War in the Bahamas

During the war, no hostile act was committed on Bahamian land or sea. The nearest incident occurred on 6 August 1914 when the German cruiser *Karlsruhe*, coaling at sea, 120 miles north-east of San Salvador, was sighted by *H.M.S. Suffolk*. The *Karlsruhe* was the speedier of the two and got away but, in her haste, her boats were left behind. One of these, an excellent thirty foot motor launch drifted into Hope Town, Abaco. At an Admiralty sale it was bought by an American and was used for some years after as a ferry between Nassau and the Porcupine Club at Hog Island.

About the beginning of 1916, there were rumours that German submarines had been seen in the Gulf Stream, close to the western islands of the Bahamas. Consequently, in June 1916, the Governor asked the Assembly to approve the creation of a Volunteer Force for home defence. Members, thinking of the cost of such a force, promptly labelled it the 'Home Expense Force' and rejected it by a large majority. The Governor then called for volunteers under the powers granted him by the Proclamations Act of 1914, and the force of nearly 200 came into being in December.

Additional precautions were taken. Lighthouses in the Nassau vicinity were put out; houses in New Providence, ships in harbour, and motor vehicles were required not to show bright lights; a patrol boat was placed on duty and a 4·7 inch gun was mounted to command the harbour entrance. These restrictions which caused annoyance to tourists, residents and local vessels were considerably eased after the United States entered the war and put ships to watch for submarines in the area. Apart from those who went overseas, and those of the south-eastern islands,* the Bahamian people, in general, suffered little distress because of the war.

Bootlegging

In the United States after the Civil War, Temperance had come to mean abstinence when applied to alcoholic beverages. Temper-

* See Chapter 20.

ance organizations sprang up all over the country and some of these found their way to the Bahamas. In Nassau, around the turn of the century, there were many men and women who 'took the pledge' not to drink spiritous liquors. And at Harbour Island the young women of the Temperance group would gather at night to sing 'The lips that touch whiskey will never touch mine.'

The power of the Temperance movement was shown when the Eighteenth Amendment to the United States Constitution was ratified by the required number of States and after 15 January 1920 it became a Federal offence to manufacture, sell, transport, export or import intoxicating liquors. The Temperance movement had not done so well in the Bahamas. No restrictive laws had been passed or even proposed. Thus, the colony was well placed to become an important centre for the trans-shipment of contraband, as it had been during the Civil War.

English and Scottish liquor manufacturers who had become

Cases and barrels of whisky on Nassau waterfront

accustomed to small orders from the Bahamas were soon shipping vast quantities. The steamers which brought it, too large for Nassau harbour, anchored off the bar or other nearby anchorages, and the cargo had to be taken ashore by lighters. Warehouses were built all along the waterfront as in blockade running days, to accommodate the flood of cases and barrels.

Getting this liquor into the United States during Prohibition was called 'bootlegging' or 'rum-running'. In the beginning, a number of Bahamians tried this but, in general, the Bahamian share of the trade was to operate supply depots and make the liquor available as close as possible to United States territory. Americans took it from there and performed the actual smuggling.

Many American vessels came direct to Nassau for their supplies, flying another flag of course. The American Consul and agents of the American Revenue Service kept a close watch on the harbour and this made it necessary for them to anchor to the east, out of sight, where they were loaded by small local vessels. After receiving their cargo, they, and ships from other places, made their way to 'Rum Row'. This was an area of open water four or five miles off the coast of New Jersey which constituted a great liquor shopping centre in international waters. As many as one hundred vessels were seen at anchor there at any one time.

As darkness fell, business commenced. Little power boats would come out to make their purchases and vanish again into the night. And each ship would stay there until her cargo was sold out. Profit was normally reckoned at 100 per cent. It cost the merchants about twenty dollars to put a case of whisky on sale at 'Rum Row', and this same case was sold to the smugglers for forty dollars.

It was, however, an uncomfortable and hazardous anchorage. A contemporary writer said that the life

. . . would be intolerable for most men. The small schooners are comfortless and toss like corks. They are often swarming with cockroaches, and the crew lie in the row—often for months at a time—either stewing in fierce, merciless heat, or shivering in Arctic winds which freeze the spray and rain until the ship is covered with icicles.

Lawlessness was common and even piracy was not unknown, for there was no law out there.

Gun Cay, Cat Cay, Bimini and West End, Grand Bahama, are all within sixty miles of the Florida coast. As soon as rum-running started, it became evident that stores of liquor in that area would be most convenient for American buyers. Stocks brought from Nassau were established in vessels at anchor, on barges in harbours and in warehouses on land, and business began on a 'cash and carry' basis.

At a distance offshore were the sturdy ships of the U.S. Coast Guard, about seventy-five feet in length and capable of fourteen knots. Their quarry were craft of a different breed. Averaging about thirty-five feet in length, they were lightly built and equipped with powerful engines. On a smooth sea, and travelling light, some of them would attain speeds up to fifty knots. At sundown, it was a thrilling sight to see fifty or sixty of them in Bimini harbour, lined up bow to stern, engines roaring, waiting the opportunity to slip by the ever-watchful Coast Guard.

Usually these power boats carried about 300 sacks of whisky or gin, containing six quarts each. The cost at Bimini or other nearby places was $12 to $14 per sack. Smuggled ashore in Florida the same sack brought $100 to $120. Each boat had a two man crew, a captain who received $1000 a trip, and a mate who was paid $500. Frequently, two round trips would be made between dusk and dawn.

The smugglers developed a remarkably efficient organization. On lonely beaches and inlets along the sparsely populated Florida east coast the receivers, by pre-arrangement, would be ready. From over the dark sea their ears would detect the characteristic roar of high-speed engines. A signal from a flashlight would indicate whether 'the coast was clear'. If Coast Guard vessels or Revenue Officers were about, the craft would quickly move on to a second or even a third rendezvous. With the stern of the vessel brought as close as possible to the beach, the shore party would form a human chain along which the sacks were passed from boat to waiting van. Twenty minutes only were allowed for unloading.

During daylight, little sea-planes would operate. After passing the blue-black water of the Gulf Stream and the Florida east coast, they would alight on some sequestered stretch of water in the lonely Everglades. Their cargoes were small, twelve to fifteen sacks. But for each trip the pilot and plane were paid $500, and some of them made as many as five round trips a day.

Boomtime Again

Thus, the liquor continued to flow year after year in enormous quantities from Nassau to parched American throats. In 1917, before United States Prohibition, 38,000 gallons were imported into the Bahamas. By 1922, the quantity had increased thirty-five times over and stood at 1,340,000 gallons. There were regular liquor merchants in Nassau who imported and exported, advertised their products, and communicated with buyers by coded telegrams. A larger number invested their money and received their dividends in secret, and an even larger number, many of whom had 'taken the pledge', found that they could profit by some indirect connection with the trade, without too much torture to their consciences.

They all made money, a few becoming millionaires in a very short time. Ordinary labourers, who otherwise were lucky to earn a dollar a day, were paid six times as much for handling liquor. And if they worked at loading the American-bound vessels gratuities often exceeded their pay.

The Lucerne Hotel on Frederick Street became the headquarters for men of the rum-running business as the Royal Victoria had been for those of the blockade running business. To that emporium came a steady stream of Americans to drink their booze, play dice for $50 a throw, and arrange their deals. Many of these were considered to be dangerous back home, and even criminals. Under the same roof slept members of rival gangs who, if they met in the United States, would greet each other with bullets. But the burly Commandant of Police made his inspection tour of the premises every evening, advising one and all to keep their weapons out of sight, and that there would be no gun play in Nassau. And there was none.

The American Consul, instructed by his Government to do everything possible to suppress the trade, could only report, month after month, its flourishing condition. From every imported case and barrel of liquor, the Bahamas Government exacted a duty. At one time this amounted to twenty-four shillings a case, but because of fears that such a high tariff would place the colony in an unfavourable trading position, it was reduced to its former value of twelve shillings. One hundred thousand pounds in revenue seemed to be the best that the colony could hope for during the ten years preceding Prohibition. Often, the revenue was considerably less than this.

The year ending 31 March 1920, showed an almost unbelievable upswing. The revenue exceeded expenditure by £95,000, a sum greater than the original total estimate of receipts. This surplus was more than enough to wipe out the public debt of £69,000. Two years later, the revenue rose to £471,000 and in another year to £853,000. Of this latter figure, £716,000 represented import duty on liquor. At that time, the Treasury surplus, despite unprecedented expenditure, had climbed to £265,000.

Effects on Nassau

During the prosperity of the Prohibition era Nassau saw great improvements in public utilities and in visitor accommodation and amenities. An electricity plant put in service in 1909 was greatly enlarged and improved. A city water supply and a sewerage system were installed. The harbour was dredged to a depth of twenty-five feet, and the Prince George Wharf was built. Ten-year contracts were signed and subsidies paid for a year-round steamer service from New York and a winter service from Miami.

The Government provided a loan of £430,000 for building the New Colonial Hotel in 1922, and £15,000 for the construction of a golf course. A few years later, £150,000 was loaned to a local company towards the erection of the Fort Montagu Hotel. In 1920 a gambling casino was opened at the Bahamian Club on West Bay Street—a foreshadow of things to come.

During the middle twenties a great land boom developed in Southern Florida; thousands of building lots were sold, sight unseen, many of them under water. Some of this boom spilled over to New Providence. Large estates, especially to the west of Nassau, were bought up by American speculators and subdivisions like Westward Villas, The Grove Estate and Treasure

Trove were laid out. Even Rose Island, rechristened 'Nassau Isle', was reputed to be in for a bright future of residential development.

Treasury revenue which reached £852,573 in 1922–3, dropped the following year by £300,000, and it was feared that the bubble had burst.

But the liquor boom was just getting into its stride. From 1926 to 1930, receipts topped the million pounds mark each year and did not show an appreciable decline until 1931. A year after the repeal of the Prohibition Amendment, they slumped to £276,000.

The End of an Era

In the beginning, the bootleggers had considered it great sport to play hide and seek with the Coast Guard, whose few clumsy vessels they could easily outrun and out-manoeuvre. This service, dedicated to aiding vessels in distress and saving lives at sea, was ill-prepared at first to cope with the fast and determined rum-runners. Soon, however, the number of ships and men was greatly increased. A vessel was positioned to watch each and every ship anchored at 'Rum Row', and shore patrols were kept informed of every activity by wireless telegraph. As many as twenty-one vessels patrolled the Miami–Fort Lauderdale area. The fast runners from the north-western Bahamas faced a virtual blockade.

In agreement with other countries, the United States extended its territorial waters from three miles to twelve. Runners which managed to get through the blockade cordon were confronted with small well-armed picket boats as speedy as their own, and often considered themselves lucky to get back out again. Thirsty Americans were compelled to depend more and more on their own moonshine whisky and bath-tub gin, as the era approached its end. National Prohibition was repealed in 1933.

19
Hard Times

The liquor boom was not the only thing to occupy Bahamians during the 1920's. In March 1926, a burglary, singular in the history of the colony, was perpetrated. Within a few hundred feet of the Central Police Station, the Currency Commission's vault was blown open and the colony's reserves of bullion carried off.

Hurricanes Again

Later that same year, the islands were left reeling from the vicious onslaught of three hurricanes, a record number for any single year within living memory. Another tropical storm came along in 1928, and the next year the capital was ravaged by the severest 'blow' since 1866. This disturbance drifted across the Atlantic and seemed destined to pass comfortably to the north of our islands. On 24 September, however, it curved to the south-west, came straight through the North-east Providence Channel, increased enormously in intensity, and slammed into New Providence the next day.

For three days and three nights this monster squatted over the capital island. When it finally moved on, there was hardly a leaf left on a tree and the city was a shambles. During the ordeal, hundreds of families were forced to seek safe shelter when their own houses began to disintegrate. As a result, many of the sturdier residences were crammed with weeping and frightened neighbours who had lost all their possessions and were fearful for their lives. With every gust of wind striking home like a battering ram, and with water pouring in everywhere, hour after hour, day after day, the terror and anxiety were almost too much for human nervous systems to endure. After it was over, the inhabitants walked out into the streets in a bewildered daze, looking and feeling as if they had been through the fringes of Hades.

Wall Street Crash

During the fall of that year, while Bahamians were busy repairing the damage wrought by the hurricane, the Americans were grappling with a disaster of an altogether different nature. The stock market, after climbing to dizzy heights, suddenly crashed with awful consequences. Investments which had been worth fortunes were suddenly worth little more than the paper which denoted them. It soon became evident that the stock market crash was but the beginning of a general economic collapse. Banks and businesses failed in unprecedented numbers; many people lost their savings, their farms and their homes. And most depressing of all was that thousands of Americans, unable to find employment, were forced to stand in breadlines in order to survive. Everywhere, there developed a paralysis of confidence and even of hope. This depression, which reached its depth in 1932, affected much of the world. Our main concern is how it affected the Bahamas.

Bahamian Poverty

First, we must understand that poverty was the Bahamian

norm. Most of the islands had known peaks of prosperity but never plateaux. Things like certain and steady employment, large savings, investments in stocks and bank mortgages were unknown to the great majority of the Bahamian people. In short, they could fall from no great height because they had not climbed very far. Next, we must understand the meaning of poverty in the local sense of the word. Traditionally, this has meant a scarcity of money and of those things which can be acquired only with money. In modern, urban societies this takes in everything. But the Bahamian people, who were thinly scattered over a large archipelago, needed not a penny to obtain the bare essentials of life. All the materials for an adequate shelter were provided by nature, almost on the spot. The soil, always reluctant to produce abundant crops, seldom failed to provide all that a family needed, and with little exertion on the part of the farmer. From the bounteous sea, close-by everywhere, a boy in a few hours could gather sufficient nutritious protein to feed his household for a week.

Thus, there was no starvation in the Bahamas and there were no breadlines. Just as nature had seemingly set a limit above which Bahamians could not climb, so had it provided a base line below which they could not sink. At least that is the way it was, in general, up to the 1930's.

The human mind is such that it always fixes its sights on better things. A man, who smokes his home-grown tobacco in a clay pipe, yearns for a briar and a sweet aromatic blend. The housewife is anxious to put aside potatoes in favour of wheat flour for the daily bread. A father with no education is conscious of his disadvantage and he makes an effort to send his children to school. All these things we confidently call progress, and all these things call for money. If Bahamians were to progress, therefore, they had to find some sound and enduring means of earning money. That had been the problem since 1648.

After 1920, the population which had remained static for twenty years, began to rise again. Ten years later, it stood at 60,000. No longer were there outlets for employment abroad. United States immigration restrictions prevented Bahamians from working in that country, and the stevedore and contract labour business of the south-eastern islands, which we will discuss later, had dried up. Bahamians were confined to the Bahamas, so to speak, and whatever could be made of their lives had to be made at home.

Sisal

After the failure of the large plantations, the machinery which had been used to clean the sisal leaves was either sold elsewhere or left to rust away. But the sisal plant, when it can send its roots into favourable soil, is like a weed, difficult to eradicate. Furthermore, it is self-propagating. Thus, sisal remained in many areas as a perennial part of the landscape, always there, needing no attention and ready to harvest whenever there was a market. Mr Neville Chamberlain had sent some samples of his sisal to New York for appraisal. The report he received was that it was inferior to the Mexican product in both length and pliability. This was bad enough but later on when sisal growing became a peasant industry and when the leaves were retted in sea water and hand cleaned, the local product was even more inferior.

Bahama hemp, as it was sometimes called, could be sold in America only when conditions were disturbed in Mexico, or when there was an unusually large demand. During the First World War we saw that sisal did sell well, and even surpassed sponges as a money-earner for a time. This was due chiefly to the activities of the Mexican bandit chieftain Pancho Villa. In the United States, Bahamian sisal was used mainly as binder twine for grain harvests. Encrusted with salt, it rusted the machinery which twisted it and when put to use, mice attracted by the salt, gnawed through the fibre, leaving the sheaves to fall apart. Americans, undoubtedly, were glad to be rid of both Pancho Villa and Bahama hemp.

Since its introduction, sisal had been made into rope for local use by a simple hand-cranked apparatus. This was loosely twisted and had not the strength of the machine-made product. After the war, a group of Nassau businessmen, headed by Mr Herbert McKinney of the firm of John S. George and Co., conceived the idea that a regular rope-walk might be economically feasible. The large number of vessels which comprised the sponging fleet, together with the fishing and trading vessels, required a fair quantity of rope to keep them going. The machinery, bought in New York, was properly installed and put into operation. It was soon realised, however, that even if local sisal could have been obtained free of cost, it still would have been impossible to make rope cheaper than that imported from far away England. The English were getting their sisal from vast African plantations and they knew the secrets of mass production. The sisal industry limped along during the 1930's, sometimes bringing a few dollars to families who badly needed them. During the Second World War there was an encouraging flicker of new life but it was dead a few years later.

Tomatoes

As sisal declined in importance, its place in the economy was taken by tomatoes. This vegetable, first introduced in 1875, grows beautifully under the cool, dewy nights and sunny days of Bahamian winter. Four years after introduction 8130 boxes were sent to the United States. Because it ripens quickly and is easily damaged in handling, it was a risky product to ship abroad in the sailing schooners of the day. Growers preferred the tougher and slower ripening pineapples and oranges.

Soon after the First World War, and the common use of motor driven vessels, it was found that if properly graded and packed, tomatoes could be shipped to the New York market and reach the consumer in good condition. In 1923 they had an export value of more than £39,000, second only to sponges. Tomato growing was the new and exciting industry of the 1920's. It is remarkable to reflect on the great quantities of these vegetables which were grown in the rocky Bahamian soil. The turnover on labour and investment was quick, 120 days from planting to reaping. Many packing houses were established and these were beehives of activity during harvest time when wrapping and crating went on day and night.

A number of American buyers came to the Bahamas to exercise a great deal of control over the industry. To farmers who needed it, they provided money for seeds and fertilizer. The buyers also took care of all expenses connected with packing, shipping and marketing. At the end of each season, accounts were settled between buyers and growers. This kind of arrangement was necessary for many farmers to be able to operate, but it produced frequent dissatisfaction as indicated by the contemporary ditty

> Mr Buyer say: Yer work for me
> An' yer money yer'll never see
> Bye, bye, blackbird.

The truth is, for the majority of farmers, tomatoes were something of a lottery, like the wrecking business. Sometimes they did well and sometimes the season was a total loss. But Bahamians have never turned their backs on a gamble. Some local growers went in for it on a fairly large scale, did their own packing and shipping and took care of their own expenses. In seasons when good crops coincided with good markets their rewards were substantial.

The industry was dealt a severe blow when, in 1929, the American Government imposed an import duty of 1½ cents a pound to protect the Florida growers. Thereafter, it was impossible to ship profitably to the United States.

After the imposition of the American tariff, arrangements were negotiated for selling to Canada. This was a much smaller market, for whereas during the season it had been common to ship 70,000–80,000 bushels per week to New York, the Canadian market could absorb no more than 15,000 bushels. Consequently, the acreage under cultivation had to be severely reduced, and the industry shrank. Furthermore, as time went by, Bahamian tomatoes met increasingly stiff competition even in the limited Canadian market from both Florida and Mexico. The industry struggled along until about 1950 when it finally expired. Today, tomatoes are grown only for local consumption.

Sponging

In all this catalogue of failure there remained one successful enterprise. Sponging, with its thousands of men on the mud, went on and on while other industries fell by the wayside. Actually up to 1925 it must have seemed that sponge-fishing would endure forever and get better and better. At that time, the income earned by sponge fishermen soared to £200,000, and a local song, 'Sponger Money Never Done', commemorated both the durability and prosperity.

The series of severe hurricanes, which began in 1926, did much damage to the sponge beds, but apart from this there developed unmistakable evidence of overfishing. Quite naturally this was a

Sponging vessels in port

matter of serious concern, because the sponge industry meant so much to the country. By 1932, the fishermen were finding it difficult to make a living, and vessel owners and outfitters were sometimes losing money. It was then that hope was revived through what came to be called 'cultivation'. It was demonstrated that a grown sponge could be cut into a large number of pieces and that each piece would survive and grow to maturity if secured to a stone and placed on the sea-bed.

Many people went in for cultivation, some planting hundreds of thousands of sponges. But at least four years were required between planting and reaping. In the meantime the natural beds on which many thousands of people relied were being depleted.

The Imperial Government decided to lend a hand by sending out a scientific team to enquire into the industry with the object of promoting conservation and continued productivity. This project called the 'Sponge Fisheries Investigations', headed by the capable Dr F. G. Walton-Smith was well under way when toward the end of 1938 disaster struck. A deadly malady started among sponges in the south-eastern Bahamas, and in a short time spread throughout the archipelago. Within a few months after the first fatalities were observed, well over ninety per cent of Bahamian sponges were dead. With the object of leaving the few surviving animals as stock to see what, if any, regeneration would occur the beds were closed to fishing.

Some regeneration did occur and many years later the beds were opened experimentally for a short time and a very limited catch. One of the former leading sponge merchants experienced great delight to be back again at the business which had occupied his youthful days. With great pride he offered a string of sponges to his married daughter. She declined the offer and explained that she now preferred artificial sponges in her kitchen; they were so clean and neatly made and came in such beautiful colours. This suggests that even if the industry had not been destroyed suddenly by agents below the sea, it was doomed to be strangled slowly by others above the sea. Nevertheless the sudden collapse of such a large and stable industry was a staggering blow to thousands of Bahamians who had depended on it for a livelihood.

During the latter years of the 1930's the Bahamas, or most

of it, was enveloped in dense economic gloom. It seemed that both man and nature had contrived to destroy every prospect of success. In New Providence men, who were prepared to sell their labour for a few shillings a day, walked the streets on the lookout for jobs that were seldom found. The relatively few young men and women who finished high school found mainly frustration in their search for employment. Produce of the farms was brought to the Nassau market to rot unsold, and fishermen frequently earned insufficient to pay for food consumed during their voyages.

During those dark days, soon to be made darker by a world-wide conflict, there shone two dim lights of encouragement. In 1936, the long-dead salt industry was revived at Inagua, and in 1937 the colony experienced the best tourist season in history with 34,351 arrivals.

20

The South-Eastern Bahamas

During the 1930's, there was a revival of the salt industry which had once been of great importance to the Bahamas. This revival turns our attention to the south-eastern islands which, historically, have played a dominant role in the production of salt.

Geography

Geographically, the area is separated from the rest of the Bahamas by the Crooked Island Passage and is comprised mainly of the Crooked Island Group, Mayaguana, the Inaguas, and the Turks and Caicos Islands. Old timers, of necessity, had to be alert to the slightest advantage in making their way through a difficult world. Those who thought of salt and who cast their eyes on the Bahamas quickly noted that the south-eastern islands were a little drier, a little warmer and the trade winds blowing over them were more regular. In short, they were better suited for making salt.

Another geographical feature to consider is that the group

straddles the famous Windward Passage, an important maritime highway. This, too, has had an important bearing on the history of some of these islands.

A traditional disadvantage is the distance from New Providence, the capital. Small sailing vessels, which have been the only means of communication and transportation until recent years, often take a long time to make the voyage. A week or more for a one way trip is not unusual. Under normally crowded conditions, passengers become fatigued and sick, livestock half-starved and farm produce spoiled. Thus, it is not surprising that these islands, having advantages and disadvantages of their own, have not always followed the mainstream of Bahamian history.

First Salt Making

After the Lucayans, the first people to take an interest in settling the area were the Bermudians. As early as 1668, they started making salt at the Turks Islands, and soon they were producing it in great quantities, despite French and Spanish interference. This product became the most important commodity of their trade, and it was looked upon as being vital to the economic welfare of Bermuda.

Because its people were the first to settle there, and because it was they who had developed the one and only industry, Bermuda laid claim to the Turks Islands. Bermudians maintained that the Bahamas did not really need the Turks Islands as it had many others on which salt could be produced. But the Bermudians needed them very much for, as one of them pointed out, ' . . . they have no other resources whatever, their whole dependence being on Salt, Cedar and Sailors'. Notwithstanding these arguments, the Lords Proprietors, anxious to get their hands on the salt export duty, insisted that the Turks Islands were as much a part of their grant as any other islands of the Bahamas.

The situation really became heated during Haskett's time, at the beginning of the eighteenth century. This Governor seized several Bermudian vessels for not paying the tax and boasted that even though he had 'never hanged a Bermudian', he 'would

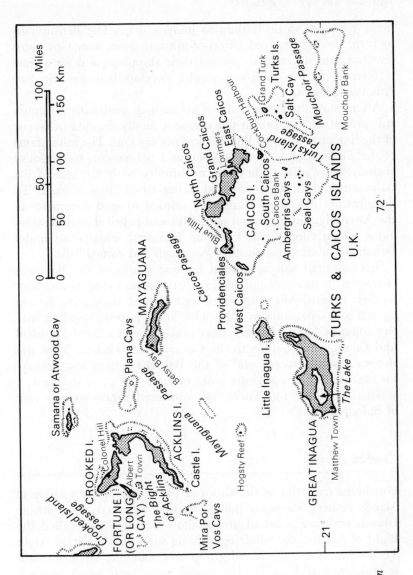

*South-Eastern
Bahamas*

make no more to do it than to hang a dog'. The Bermudians in turn, having received letters-of-marque from their Governor, sent out armed vessels to protect their shipping; and for a time it seemed that a mini-war might develop between the two Atlantic colonies.

After more than a century of wrangling, and with Bermuda still protesting, the British Government finally decided in favour of the Bahamas in 1803. But this was not the end. The inhabitants of the Turks Islands, both seasonal and permanent, were almost entirely Bermudian. They felt no affinity with the rest of the Bahamas and strongly resented being ruled from Nassau. To demonstrate this, for a while they refused to send a member to the Assembly. But it was not sentiment and political consideration alone which riled them. From an economic standpoint, under Bahamian administration, they lost much and gained little.

Tax on their salt accounted for one fourth of the Bahamas Government revenue, and precious little of this found its way back to their islands. After prolonged agitation on their part, Britain agreed to a separation in 1848. The Turks Islands, together with the adjacent Caicos Islands, were placed under a local President and Council, responsible to the Governor of Jamaica. Thus was the most south-eastern end of the Bahamas chain lost perhaps for ever. From an economic point of view it was, at the time, a serious blow, for the Turks had produced ninety-six per cent of Bahamian salt.

Crooked Island

On the eastern edge of the Crooked Island Passage is a group of islands bearing the same name. Acklins, Crooked and Fortune Islands embrace a broad and shallow bay which is called the Bight of Acklins, the whole resembling somewhat a Pacific Atoll. To the Lucayans, the island group was Saomete, but Columbus re-christened it Isabella. He would have been much pleased, however, with a later name, 'The Fragrant Islands', for he wrote that 'When I arrived here . . . there came from the land the scent of flowers or trees, so delicious and sweet, that it was the most delightful thing in the world.'

Crooked Island was settled by the Loyalists soon after 1783, and before the end of the century there were forty plantations with a total of a thousand slaves, working three thousand acres of land planted out in cotton. We already know about the difficulties of the plantations. A few planters tried their luck on Acklins Island with no better results. By 1803, the estates were mostly deserted. The planters who remained and who, perhaps, had not the resources to leave the colony and try elsewhere, looked to the salt ponds of uninhabited Fortune Island for relief, and it was they who started the salt industry there. One planter with forty slaves was able to rake 35,000 bushels in a season.

Great Inagua

But it was Great Inagua, the most southern island of the Bahamas, which was destined to become the great salt producing area of the colony, in succession to the Turks Islands. The Lucayans called this island Babeque, but it came to be known as Heneagua or Heneaga, by the English some time before modern settlement. This was probably a corruption of two Spanish words, *lleno* (full) and *agua* (water). A more descriptive name could hardly be found, for salt water lakes and ponds comprise much of the interior.

Around the middle of the eighteenth century, the French showed a great deal of interest in Inagua because of its strategic position. Cattle were put ashore and signs erected, proclaiming it to be a possession of the French King. But nothing came of this.

Legend has it that Henri Christophe, later to be King of Haiti, built a retreat there around 1800. Foundation stones, reputed to be the ruins of his castle, can still be seen near North-East Point. This is an intriguing story and it is a great pity that Daniel McKinnen, who toured the area in 1803, and who had an ear for interesting facts, seems to have heard nothing about it. McKinnen did hear that there was, at that time, one solitary inhabitant on the island; not Christophe, but a 'fugitive outlaw from Long Island accused of having committed there a wanton murder on his innocent slaves'. He heard further that 'some few families . . . were on the point of removing this year to Heneaga'. They were attracted by the salt ponds.

By 1848, the year the Turks and Caicos Islands were lost, there were 172 people on the island. Their settlement on the sheltered west coast was named Matthew Town in honour of Governor George B. Matthew. Salt ponds, a mile or so away, were being worked and the product sold to calling ships.

The next year, the Heneagua Salt Pond Company, the first joint stock company to be floated in the Bahamas, was formed to develop the salt industry in a big way. Extensive pans were created. Windmill-driven pumps were installed to maintain the brine at proper levels. Iron rails were laid from the salinas to the sea. And, over these rails, mule-drawn trams carted the salt to a specially built storage house in Matthew Town. An interesting feature of this Salt House, which still stands, is that the arched entrances are decorated with bricks recovered from the submerged ruins of Port Royal, Jamaica.

In good seasons a million and a half bushels were produced, and sold. Prices soared during the American Civil War and by 1871, the population had increased to 1120, and Inagua was being spoken of as the 'El Dorado' of the Bahamas.

Thereafter the increasing production of mined salt in North America caused a decline in prices, and when the United States imposed a protective tariff of six per cent it was no longer possible to ship to that country at a profit. The death of the salt industry was a serious blow to Inagua. Soon, however, there was something else in the wind which gave new impetus to a people who were economically becalmed.

Stevedores

During the latter part of the nineteenth century, there was an upsurge of development activity in Mexico and Central America. This called for the importation of large quantities of material and many labourers. Loaded ships passing by Inagua found it convenient to stop there to engage stevedores and contract workers. In 1902 alone, 143 steam, and 85 sailing vessels dropped anchor at the Inagua roadstead to take on 2880 workers. This was many times the number of able men in Matthew Town. Thus, it became a centre to which Bahamians of other islands were drawn by the hundreds. It was a magic port from which one could go to distant places, and earn money. Its fine houses, broad streets, carriage traffic, and bustling commerce all combined to produce a throbbing, booming atmosphere.

From there, workers departed to stevedore on ships of the Hamburg–American Line and the Royal Netherlands Line, or to work as contract labourers on the Panama Canal, the Mexican Railways and the mahogany industries of Central America. After their stint, they returned first to Inagua to throw a party, primed with 'Key' gin and barrelled beer, and then to drift back to their former life styles, a little richer and a little wiser.

This same type of employment and prosperity was enjoyed by the Crooked Island group. In one year alone ninety-five ships of the Atlas Company and the Pacific Mail Steamship Company called at Fortune Island to engage more than 2000 labourers.

Depression and Revival

It is often said that the shot which killed Archduke Ferdinand was heard round the world. Most assuredly it was heard in the south-eastern Bahamas. For the outbreak of the First World War put a dead stop to the stevedoring and migrant labour business on which the people depended for their daily bread. Proud and prosperous inhabitants of these islands were quickly reduced to beggars and it became necessary for the Government to send them food from Nassau.

There were hopes that after the war there might be a revival of this type of employment, and when ships began to call again it looked as if the days of prosperity would surely return. These optimistic signs, however, were short-lived. Those who went to Inagua in the early 1930's, were struck by the overpowering desolation of the town and its people. Residences and business houses alike were untenanted and falling into decay. Much of the population had left, and those who remained could see no hope for the island.

Then, in 1936, there came three New Englanders, the Erickson

Brothers. They had come to revive the old salt industry, and soon an industrial hum dispelled the quiet of Matthew Town. Mechanized tractors, diesel-powered pumps and giant lorries were imported to do the work which had once been done by hand rakes, windmills and mule-drawn trams.

The following year a disturbance occurred which threatened to wreck everything. It started off as a personality clash between a few Americans and a few Inaguans. Underlying, perhaps, was a resentment felt by some of the natives toward the new arrivals who were about to dominate the economic life of the island. Arguments soon progressed to fistfights and court cases. Two young brothers of Matthew Town, dissatisfied with the justice they had received, armed themselves with shot guns and went on a rampage of terror. One man was shot dead and several wounded; a number of buildings were fired, and the government wireless communications equipment destroyed. With arson and murder hanging over their heads, the two brothers fled to Haiti, but sanctuary was denied them. They were returned to the Bahamas and in Nassau they were tried and hanged. Nothing daunted, the Ericksons carried on and, within a few years, Inaguan salt was once again flowing to world markets. Mechanization and ingenuity had overcome both competition and tariffs.

Soon there was full employment, and it became necessary to bring in Turks Islanders to help produce the yearly harvest of 50,000 tons. Great expansion of the salt works took place during the 1960's after control was acquired by the Morton Salt Company. In recent years the pans have yielded over a million tons annually and the solar evaporation plant there is the second largest in the world.

Wrecking

We cannot leave Inagua and the Crooked Island group without noting their role in the wrecking industry. The fact that the Bahamian eastern wrecking fleet was headquartered at Albert Town contributed much to the bygone prosperity of Fortune Island, and was probably responsible for its name.

The large number of ships passing by, strong currents and an abundance of reefs, all combined to guarantee a good supply of wrecks and wreck goods, especially before lighthouses came along. Commander Langton-Jones, in his delightful little book *Silent Sentinels*, tells how eagerly the Inaguans jumped to the cry of 'Wreck Ashore!' While building the lighthouse,

> time and again, trouble arose with the contractors and labourers . . . as these men would absent themselves in a body leaving not even a boy on the site, while they went to see what loot could be obtained from some unfortunate vessel . . . The same applied to the eight hundred labourers at one time employed in the local salt industry; not a man of whom would remain at work the minute a vessel in distress was reported!

General Post Office

An interesting bit of history, of which Crooked Islanders are proud, is that their island once accommodated 'The General Post Office of the Bahamas'. At Pitt's Town, the monthly packet, on her return from Jamaica to England, would deliver and take on mail, passengers and freight. A small local schooner was engaged to complete the service by plying between Crooked Island and Nassau. This went on until steamships replaced sailing vessels in the carrying of mail.

Mayaguana

Mayaguana, one of the few of our islands to retain its Lucayan name, is the most eastern of all the islands under the jurisdiction of the Bahamas Government, and is virtually unknown to any but its own people. The island, though thickly wooded and comparatively well suited to agriculture, did not attract the Loyalists. Up to the year 1812, it was still uninhabited. It was some time after, that people from the Turks Islands began to settle there, and there are some who say that the physical features of the present inhabitants reflect this ancestry.

All of the old industries, which brought some prosperity to

other parts of the Bahamas, passed Mayaguana by. And neither has Mayaguana nor any other of the south-eastern islands benefited directly from the post-war Bahamian prosperity based on tourism. Except for the salt works at Inagua, there is little going on anywhere in the area.

21

Second World War

Communications with the outside world and within the colony were much better in 1939 than they had been in 1918. Not only was the Nassau Wireless Station greatly improved but, beginning with Governor's Harbour, Eleuthera, in 1920, telegraph stations had been installed at most of the major islands. Governor Sir Bede Clifford had made the first radio broadcast from Nassau in 1932, and five years later Radio Station ZNS commenced regular programmes. Many houses were equipped with their own radio receivers, and in a number of isolated settlements community receivers were in operation.

Thus, the great majority of Bahamians were able to keep abreast of the dramatic events taking place in Europe which culminated in Britain's declaration of war on Germany on 3 September 1939. When the dimensions of this conflict and its similarity to the one of a generation before, were realized, it was called the Second World War.

As had been the custom for hundreds of years, whenever there was fear of enemy action, a local Volunteer Defence Force was organized. In fact, recruitment started the very day that Britain entered the war. The Bahamas Volunteer Defence Force was soon able to muster four companies, totalling close to 500 men, who came from all parts of the Bahamas. Night and day they were on guard at vulnerable points throughout New Providence. These were not idle exercises for, as the war progressed, enemy submarines began operating close to the Bahamas and even in the deep water channels passing through the archipelago. The possibility of saboteurs being put ashore from these U-boats was considered a real threat.

Duke of Windsor as Governor

The Honourable Charles Dundas had arrived in November 1937 as the colony's Governor and, at the time, there was nothing to suggest that he would not hold the post for the usual period of five years. But back in England, since the start of the war, the British Government had been faced with the vexatious problem of what to do with the Duke of Windsor.

This man, who had abdicated his Kingship 'for the woman I love', had quitted England and taken up residence, first in France, then in Spain and finally in Portugal. Rumours were rampant that the Germans were trying to persuade him to collaborate with them, that he might be kidnapped by them, or that he might even be murdered by them. Above all, the Government wanted him out of Europe and either back in England, or in some country far removed from the area of conflict. England, he might have preferred, but the difficulty there was that the Royal Family had made it plain that his wife would not be recognized by them. This was a situation which the Duke refused to accept and, as an alternative, he consented to be sent to the Bahamas as Governor.

News that the Duke of Windsor was to be their Governor was almost unbelievable to the Bahamian people. That a man who had been head of a mighty Empire of hundreds of millions was to rule an impoverished colony of 65,000 people was indeed close to incredulous. But it was all true enough. Governor Dundas departed, and on 17 August 1940, the Duke and Duchess of Windsor arrived in Nassau.

H.R.H. the Duke of Windsor and his Government House office staff, 1945. L. to R. Bridget Maura (Mrs David Knowles), Joan Brown (Mrs Paul Albury), Capt. Gerald Dugdale, H.R.H. the Duke of Windsor, Lt.-Col. F. A. Wanklyn, M.C., Mrs Lois Chipman, Major Gray Phillips, M.C., Marette Butler (Mrs P. Holden)

By that time, Germany was master of Europe and the Battle of Britain had commenced. The aim of the Nazi rulers was to terrorize and starve Britain into submission. As bombs rained on English ports and cities, German submarines were taking a heavy toll of ships which were bringing in the supplies needed for survival.

Submarine Warfare

Bahamians were awakened to the grim realities and horrors of submarine warfare in October 1940 when two young British seamen, whose names were Widdicombe and Tapscott, were found on an Eleutheran beach more dead than alive. Their ship, the *Anglo-Saxon*, had been torpedoed, by a German naval craft, about 800 miles south of the Azores. The crew then took to the eighteen foot jolly-boat and sailed their craft westerly with the trade winds over 3000 miles of ocean, dropping overboard the dead as they succumbed. After seventy interminable days of exposure and starvation, the two hardy survivors, looking like bronzed and shrunken mummies, reached Eleuthera. Their epic voyage in an open boat rivals that of the celebrated Captain Bligh 151 years before.

The men were taken care of by the Bahamas Branch of the British Red Cross, which had been formed on 16 November of the previous year. Throughout the war, this worthy organization made itself responsible for the welfare of about 250 sailors who were brought into Nassau after their ships had been sent to the bottom by German U-boats.

British resources which were already desperately strained by the mammoth effort of fighting the Battle of Britain, now had to contend with the submarine menace. Some useful help was received from the United States which, although at this time technically neutral, was, nevertheless, sympathetic to the Allied cause. In September 1940, fifty First World War vintage destroyers were given to Britain in exchange for ninety-nine year leases on a number of bases from Newfoundland to Trinidad. These bases included two in the Bahamas, one at Great Exuma Island and one at Man-o-War Cay, Abaco.

Employment Problems

The Duke and his Government were anxious to increase the self-sufficiency of the Bahamas and provide employment for its people. Bahamians were encouraged to grow whatever produce could be grown and to raise whatever livestock could be raised. A lack of jobs was not nearly so serious in the Out Islands, where the people were always close to the sea and soil, as it was in New Providence. In the capital island at that time were nearly 30,000 people, close to half the population of the colony. The majority of these had come to depend on urban employment. They had neither the knowledge nor the inclination, the boats nor the land, to enable them to switch to fishing and farming.

Fortunately, the seasonal tourist industry held up for the first two years of the war, that is to say before America's entry into the conflict. Fortunately too, a substantial amount of employment was provided through development projects undertaken by two very wealthy men then residing in the colony, Sir Harry Oakes, who had made a fortune from Canadian gold mines, and Mr Axel Wenner-Gren, a titan of Swedish industry.

Several hundreds of jobs were also created by the activities of the War Materials Committee. The objective of this Committee, formed in June 1940, was to supply Britain with any local materials or products which might help in the prosecution of the war. Under the energetic chairmanship of Mr Etienne Dupuch (now Sir Etienne), editor of *The Tribune,* it started off by collecting scrap metal. The islands of the Bahamas were combed for every bit of metal which could be found. Old cars and old vessels were dismembered by acetylene torches. Labourers with machetes cut their way through tangled bushes to find the cannon of ancient fortifications and to uncover once again the rusting engines and iron rails that were relics of the cotton, salt and sisal industries. Soon the metal, all cut and sorted, reached mountainous proportions and was finding its way to Britain by shiploads to be converted into machines of war.

Next, the Committee turned its attention to food. A canning factory owned by Mr W. C. B. Johnson was put at the disposal of the committee and operated by him to preserve the surplus fruit from Bahamian orchards. This provided additional jobs and was of significant help to farmers. Of all the colonial Empire, only the Rhodesias exceeded the Bahamas in food gifts to Britain. This is only a small insight into the vigorous and wide-ranging activities of this Committee. Everything imaginable from gold jewellery to sisal and honey was collected in aid of the great cause.

United States Enters the War

On a December morning of 1941, the Japanese, in a surprise bombing raid on Pearl Harbour, did great damage to American military might centred on Hawaii, and the United States was drawn into the war. The local tourist industry immediately collapsed and the serious unemployment situation suddenly became critical.

Three months later, the Montagu Hotel was reopened to accommodate an entirely new type of guest. Bahamians soon learned that the wiry and agile young men in khaki who moved in there were members of the Queen's Own Cameron Highlanders, who had gone through the hell of Dunkirk. That a company of this crack regiment should be sent to Nassau was a sure sign that something important was in the wind.

The 'Project'

Great quantities of construction equipment and building material began to arrive; and it soon became known that a large installation was to be built in New Providence by Lend-Lease arrangement, and in connection with the training of airmen. Under supervision of the U.S. Army Engineering Department, an American firm, Pleasantville, Incorporated, began work on 20 May 1942.

This was one of a number of bases to be built in the West Indies and elsewhere, and the Anglo-American agreement was that workers would be paid at local prevailing rates. Six years before, the Bahamas House of Assembly had passed an act establishing a minimum wage of four shillings per day. Prior to that, it had ranged between one and three shillings. Two sites were involved; one adjacent to Grant's Town, where Sir Harry Oakes had already developed a small landing field, and the other in the Pine Barrens near the western end of the island. They were called Main Field and Satellite Field, respectively, and collectively they were called 'The Project'.

Considering the demoralizing lack of employment existing at the time, it was thought to be a godsend by both Government and labour that suddenly two to three thousand jobs should be available. Yet, before a month had passed, New Providence was shaken by a destructive and bloody riot. What the Bahamians received as pay was small when compared to that paid to Americans on the job. Furthermore, the Americans let it be known that they thought the Bahamian wage ridiculously low and that they were certain the contractors would pay more if they were allowed to do so.

His Royal Highness, the Governor, was to say later, 'I wish to explain that the decision to pay local rates of wages for work on this and similar projects was made in accordance with a high policy far beyond the power of this Government to control.' Perhaps this should have been said sooner, for in the minds of the workers the Bahamas Government was the only obstacle to better wages and better life.

On Monday morning, 1 June, some hundreds of labourers, many carrying machetes, sticks or clubs, marched into town and gathered in the vicinity of the public buildings. There, they were addressed by a few officials and others who urged peaceful behaviour. In the meantime, other demonstrators were surging up Bay Street from the west. One of these took a bottle from a parked Coca Cola van and hurled it through the glass window of a shop. That set off a general *melee* of window smashing and looting. The riot had commenced.

In a few hours, Bay Street was a shambles, but before noon it had been cleared of rioters by the police, with the assistance of some of the Cameron Highlanders. The rioters then moved over the hill and went to work in Grant's Town. A number of barrooms were looted, and this naturally resulted in a worsening of the situation. After relatively peaceful conditions were restored, the soldiers and police withdrew. But that same afternoon the mob reformed and attacked the Grant's Town police station. The four men on duty were forced to flee.

The Riot Act was read and a curfew was imposed that same day, prohibiting any person not a member of the armed forces or police from being out of doors between 8 p.m. and 6 a.m. The Volunteer Defence Force was of great help in enforcing this. An attempt was made on Tuesday, 2 June, to break into a grocery store in Grant's Town, and some damage was done to a pharmacy on Shirley Street. Apart from the firing of some government vehicles, these two incidents were the last of the disturbance. On 8 June the curfew was revoked.

During the disturbance and curfew period ten men were hit by gun fire: three were shot dead, two died of wounds and the others recovered. A number of minor wounds caused mainly by stones, sticks and glass bottles were suffered by others including members of the police and military forces. His Royal Highness, the Governor, announced at the end of June that, with some difficulty, he had been able to get the daily wage of unskilled workers raised from four shillings to five shillings a day. In addition, there would be a free meal on the site. The labourers, who had returned to work right after the disturbance, carried on, with apparent contentment, until the project was finished.

Hardly had the riot rubble been cleared away when an area of the Nassau business section became engulfed in flames. On 28 June the disastrous fire started in a small store on Bay Street, swept on to George Street, and before it could be brought under control the oldest business block in the city had been destroyed. Nassauvians still relate how the Duke of Windsor, smudged with soot and soaked to the skin, struggled with the fire hoses, side by side with hundreds of other volunteers.

Bahamas Battalion

Throughout the war, Bahamians left home to join regular British, Canadian or American forces. Nevertheless, there was a desire that some distinct Bahamian unit should be organized for active duty. As a result, the Bahamas Defence Company, North Caribbean Force, was formed in October 1942. Later, it was named the Bahamas Battalion. Like the Volunteer Defence Force, its 300 recruits came from all over the Bahamas. A contingent of this Battalion, under the command of Lieutenant Wenzel Granger, which left home in May 1944, saw service in Italy and Egypt.

Training for Coastal Command

To return to the bases in New Providence, before the construction crew could move out, the staff and trainees were moving in, for

Officers of Bahamas Battalion second world war. Back row L. to R. Lt. David Smith, Lt. William Pemberton, Lt. Augustus Roberts. Front row L. to R. Capt. Reney (substituting as Adjutant for Capt. George Lightbourn, then in Jamaica), Major D'Arcy Rutherford, Commanding Officer, and Lt. Wenzel Granger.

this was a desperately urgent business. Allied ships were being sent to the bottom by the score, and the survival of Britain depended on a sufficient number getting through. A large measure of hope resided in that arm of the R.A.F. called Coastal Command. Its planes, operating from a number of bases, were providing an increasingly effective umbrella of protection for convoys as they plodded across the Atlantic Ocean.

There was no doubting the ability of the United States, the greatest industrial nation on earth, to produce as many thousands of bombers as were needed. The urgent matter was that crews should be trained and ready to fly them as they came off the assembly lines.

The climate of the Bahamas was thought to be ideal for training airmen for Coastal Command service, and that is why the complex built in New Providence was one of the largest in the Empire. The thousands of trainees who came here were not new to aeroplanes and the sky. Already familiar with single-engined aircraft, the 'conversion courses' at Main and Satellite Fields were designed to acquaint them with the intricacies of two-engined Mitchells and four-engined Liberators. An idea of the magnitude of the operation can be gained from the fact that more than 3000 officers and men were on permanent staff. No. 111 Operational Training Unit, as it was called, turned out over 5000 trained airmen, constituting more than 600 crews. As they finished their courses, they left the Bahamas taking their aircraft with them, to join Coastal Command squadrons in Britain, the Azores and Iceland.

While all this training was going on, there were other 'pilots of the purple twilight' winging their way in and out of New Providence. Aircraft were brought to Nassau by American crews almost hot off the production lines. Here, they were taken over by crews of No. 113 Wing, Transport Command, and flown by a southern route to the military aerodromes of North Africa, the Middle and Far East. During the war, more than 2000 aircraft passed through Satellite (Windsor) Field on their way to distant battle zones.

All this aerial activity was bound to result in casualties. Hardly a week passed without the news of a fatal crash. In a well-kept R.A.F. cemetery lie the bones and ashes of fifty-one of the more than eighty young men who died so far from home and whose bodies were recovered. More than a hundred and fifty others went to watery graves in the Bahama Sea.

Frogman Training

Along the shores of Salt Cay, near New Providence, one would occasionally glimpse odd looking creatures coming out of the sea. They were men in strange underwater garb, which gave them a striking resemblance to giant frogs and they were called frogmen. The exercises they were engaged in were a part of the training of the Sea Reconnaissance Unit which later prepared the way for the crossing of the Irrawaddy river in Burma by the British 14th Army. The work of this small and gallant band has been highly praised by the Supreme Allied Commander, S.E. Asia, Admiral Mountbatten.

New Providence, in those days, took on all the aspects of a military encampment. Along Bay Street, airmen in blue from many nations jostled each other. The thoroughfare was additionally crowded with white-suited sailors of allied warships, soldiers in khaki, and arm-banded military police. Nowhere to be seen were the rich and idle who once came to soak in the sea and worship the sun. The corridors of some of the hotels now resounded to the steady thump of service boots.

The leisure hours of these thousands of men were considerably brightened by the commendable efforts of the local branch of the Imperial Order Daughters of the Empire. Canteens were set up and many social events were organized to provide welcome diversion from the regimentation of military life.

Murder of Sir Harry Oakes

An event occurred in the summer of 1943 which diverted the attention of Nassauvians from the war. Early in the morning of 8 July, Sir Harry Oakes was found dead in bed. The condition of both bed and body made it immediately obvious that he had been the victim of savage murder. A shock wave of horror surged through New Providence, for Sir Harry had been looked upon as a great benefactor of the Bahamas. After taking up residence in New Providence in the 1930's he had immediately launched a number of enterprises upon which he spent fortunes, and which did much to beautify the island, improve its facilities and relieve the unemployment situation. In 1939, he resigned his seat in the House of Assembly, which he had won the year before, to become a member of the Legislative Council.

Realizing that world attention would be focused on the tragedy, the Duke of Windsor assumed supreme responsibility for the investigation. Two detectives were flown in from Miami and they carried on their work while rumours flew fast and wild. On the following afternoon, 9 July, Alfred de Marigny, who was married to Sir Harry's elder daughter Nancy, was charged with the murder. A special jury was empanelled and for twenty-two days the sensational trial vied with the momentous events of the Second World War for space in the world press. The accused was acquitted and the murder remains unsolved. Over the years, the macabre slaying and the subsequent trial have never failed to provoke animated discussion and, from time to time, in a newspaper article or a book some writer purports to reveal the long sought 'truth'.

Bahamian War Effort

By the early part of 1944, all North Africa had been conquered, and the Allies were fighting their way up the Italian peninsula. This news, cheering as it was, did not obscure the fact that the great and decisive battles were yet to come.

The cost of the war to Britain was staggering, and there was comparatively little the impoverished Bahamas could do to help. Nevertheless, there was a determination throughout to do whatever could be done, for this was seen to be a global clash between the forces of tyranny and those of freedom, and the lives of Bahamians were bound to be affected by the outcome. Soon after the conflict started, the Legislature voted an outright gift to the British Government of £20,000. A loan of £250,000 from the colony's reserves was authorized in 1940, and a further loan of an equal sum to be funded by local subscription was approved a few years later. A number of committees and organizations donated cash gifts for specific purposes and made generous donations of food and clothing to the war distressed of many nations.

Seventeen Bahamian men left home to work in the munitions factories of the United Kingdom. Between two and three hundred men and women of Bahamian birth saw service in the armed forces of Britain, Canada and the United States. Fourteen men lost their lives while on active service.

The 6 June 1944, was a day when free men, the world over, held their breath. The greatest invasion armada in history set out from England to strike at Fortress Europa. A foothold was gained and tenaciously held. As the bridgehead was steadily enlarged, and as the mighty Allied armies began to roll back the vaunted legions of Nazi Germany, there developed a confident feeling that the end was in sight. But many bloody battles were to be fought, many men were to die, and nearly a year was to go by before the armies of the British Commonwealth and America met with their Russian allies in Berlin.

22

New Providence and Tourism

After the Second World War, the greatest field of employment open to Bahamians was not in their own country but in the United States. Actually, this opportunity opened up soon after America's entry into the war. The young men of that nation who were conscripted into the armed forces and drawn to the factories, seriously depleted the manpower upon which the farms depended. To maintain a high level of vital food production, it became necessary to recruit labourers from outside the country.

Employment in the United States

As far as Bahamians, and especially the people of New Providence, were concerned this was a timely deliverance from a depressing situation. For after the abrupt end of tourism, and after work on the bases had finished, there was precious little employment at home.

The exodus began in 1943 and went on for more than twenty-three years. It was thought prudent by the Bahamas Government

not to have more than 5000 people away at any one time. Therefore a system of rotation was introduced. Some stayed for a
season, or for one or two years, and when they returned others
were sent in their stead. Later, those who had gone before were
given another chance. Plane loads of men, and some women,
were continually departing and arriving. Workers were drawn
from all over the Bahamas so as to spread the benefits as widely
as possible. They were employed in many States mostly as farm
labourers but some found jobs in factories.

As it turned out, when this demand began to decrease, workers
were finding increasing job opportunities at home. There was a
trailing off rather than an abrupt end. In 1966 less than 200
Bahamians went to America as contract workers. But this is
getting ahead of our story and we will return now to consider
other post-war developments and especially tourism which was
to be so important to the Bahamas.

Investment in the Bahamas

After the Labour Party came to power in 1945, there was a flight
of capital from the United Kingdom because of taxation fears.
Much of the capital which flowed into the Bahamas was invested
in properties. Real estate prices soared to heights undreamed
of before. A Bay Street property was sold by its Bahamian owner
for £70,000, which was a fortune he never expected to see. A
year later, it was sold again for £150,000, and a few years after
that for £300,000. Frequently these properties were immediately
leased to their former owners at unbelievably low rates. In this
way, many businessmen found the capital they needed for
expansion.

With the influx of English capital, wage earners, who had
struggled to build family homes costing £1000 to £3000, found
eager buyers at £8000, £10,000 and even £15,000. Some made
more money in a single transaction than they would have
saved in a lifetime, and some rebuilt and resold several times
over. Thus did money from the United Kingdom stimulate
business activity, the building industry and the economy in
general.

Tourism

Hence, during the immediate post-war years, the economy rested on a tripod of English investment, employment in the United States, and the tourist industry, which had almost regained its pre-war level. The difficulty was that this was seen to be a very shaky foundation and there were great fears that it might fall apart at any moment. Expectations were that both the inflow of capital and the labour market would soon dry up and tourism was looked upon, at the time, as an unstable industry which might suffer from any one of a number of causes. After all, a bombing raid on far away Pearl Harbour had resulted in crushing it just a few years before. As an example of what could happen in the future, some politicians pointed out that a local outbreak of malaria or yellow fever would instantly stop travel to the Bahamas. It was foolish, one of them said, to depend on an industry which was subject to the chance of a mosquito bite.

Others became convinced that even though tourism was no cure-all, it was the best thing in sight at the time; in fact, about the only promising thing for the future. Foremost among these was Mr Stafford Sands (now Sir Stafford) an able lawyer and politician whose mental energy and ability to get things done was something of a legend, even then. A delegation called on the Acting Governor, Mr Derek Evans, in 1950, and urged that Sir Stafford be made Chairman of the Development Board. Mr Evans agreed, and tourism commenced a climb which is still going on and which seems to have no peak. It has become the most successful industry the Bahamas has ever known.

The First Tourists

The word 'tourist' came into use around 1800 to describe one who makes a tour for pleasure. Such an exercise was looked upon as almost sinful by Americans of the eighteenth century and, to a lesser extent, the nineteenth century. To their minds, beset with a strong puritanical streak, touring was akin to drinking. The pleasurable aspects of either could be tolerated if its primary aim was to benefit the health, but never for unqualified enjoyment.

Thus, the first tourists to the Bahamas were 'invalids'. And in trying to set a date for the beginning of tourism, we can begin by saying that no invalid, in his right mind, would have come to New Providence before 1718, or until after both the filthy town and the cut-throats who harboured there, had been cleaned up by Woodes Rogers. Therefore, we can say with some certainty that tourism began in the 1720's or about 250 years ago.

As early as 1740, Nassau had gained some reputation as a health resort. Peter Henry Bruce, the military engineer who arrived that year to fortify the island, had this to say:

The Bahama islands enjoy the most serene and the most temperate air in all America, the heat of the sun being greatly allayed by refreshing breezes from the east; and the earth and air are cooled by constant dews which fall in the night, and by gentle showers which fall in their proper seasons; so that as they are free from the sultry heats of our other settlements; they are as little affected with frost, snow, hail, or the north-west winds, which prove so fatal both to men and plants in our other colonies; it is therefore no wonder the sick and afflicted inhabitants of those climates fly hither for relief, being sure to find a cure here.

In North America, as pointed out by Bruce, the cold winters were found to be debilitating to the frail and sick. Those who felt a little bilious or a little consumptive and who also were a little wealthy, were advised by their doctors to seek a change of air. And no air was considered to be more agreeable to comfort and health than that of the Bahamas during the cooler months.

The profitable privateering of the mid-eighteenth century had resulted in great improvements to Nassau. It was further improved by the Loyalists a little later. Beautiful and substantial houses with high ceilings and wide verandahs were built on the hills behind the city. These fine houses surrounded by flower gardens and fruit orchards looked to the north on a seascape of incredible beauty. With every sense pleasurably stimulated, it is little wonder that invalids who were guests of these mansions soon experienced a return of health and vigour. Daniel McKinnen who visited Nassau in 1803 observed that 'the general aspect of the place has something in it fresh and lively . . . a town as well built as any I saw in the West Indies'. The recent improvements to the metropolis, he went on to say, 'if persisted in, must soon render it highly attractive and ornamental'.

It was neither a quick nor an easy matter to get to New Providence in those days. Travel by either land or sea was slow and uncomfortable. Furthermore, the invalid had to find accommodation in a private home. It was not until the 1840's that Nassau could boast of four good boarding houses, which provided rooms and meals for eight shillings and sixpence per day.

The behaviour of some of the visitors cast a suspicious light on the degree of their illnesses. They swam in the sparkling sea several times a day, rode horseback for hours on end, drank copious quantities of wine and brandy, went on all day 'marooning' parties to nearby islands and danced till dawn. It became obvious to some of the leading men of Nassau that 'treatment' like this was bound to become attractive to an ever-increasing number of 'invalids'. But they also realized that nothing much would come of the tourist business until good transportation and suitable accommodation were provided.

Steamship Service

Consequently, an Act passed by the Legislature in 1851 offered an annual bounty of £1000 to any person or company who would provide a 'good substantial and efficient' steamship service between New York and Nassau. It was no easy matter for the Government to raise this subsidy. The duty on imported goods was increased from five to ten per cent in order to provide the additional revenue required. If it fell short, the Receiver-General was authorized to make up the deficiency by means of a loan.

Though well advertised among ship operators in both England and the United States, the subsidy did not prove sufficiently attractive. In fact, it was only after it was increased to £3000 (the additional £2000 being paid by the Imperial Government), that a contract could be signed for a monthly service with Mr Samuel Cunard. The first ship, a paddle-wheel steamer named the *Karnak*, took five days to make the first voyage from New York to Nassau in 1859. This was the first deliberate effort by the Government to increase the number of visitors to Nassau and it must,

Cunard Line. S.S. Corsica *which provided one of the first steamship services between New York and Nassau.*

therefore, be looked upon as the foundation stone of a substantial tourist industry.

Royal Victoria Hotel

The Government then proceeded to build a hotel. Today, it is almost impossible to understand the magnitude of this enterprise. But when one remembers the difficulty in raising the £1000 steamship subsidy, some idea is gained of how enormous must have seemed the £25,000 needed for a hotel. Construction of the Royal Victoria Hotel began in 1859, and by the time it was completed in 1861 the American Civil War was under way. Revenue derived from blockade running, proved more than sufficient to wipe out the huge public debt incurred in building it and, perhaps, saved the Government from acute financial embarrassment.

Tourism, during the post Civil War years, attained the status of a small, but important, industry. Surgeon Major Bacot writing in 1869 said:

For many years the islands have been visited during winter months by invalids from America, unable to withstand the bitter frosts of the mainland. . . . There is no doubt whatever, that the climate is (in Nassau) during the winter months simply delightful; . . . there is scarcely a day on which the new comer cannot take his walk or drive, or enjoy a sail upon the quiet waters of the harbour, with a summer breeze to fan, and a blue sky to smile on him, and yet he is but four days distant by steamer from New York, where at this very time, the snow is falling, the day is dark and gloomy, and the only air to be breathed, is the stove-heated atmosphere, within the fast closed doors . . . Whether it be climate [he continued] or the partial exemption from the struggle for gold, or as M'Kinnon said that the genius of the first inhabitants, the innocent and light hearted Lucayans still lingers about the Bahamas, nowhere will a stranger find more amiable friends, or a kinder welcome than at New Providence.

The season of 1870 was very successful with the Royal Victoria filled to capacity. And in 1873, Nassau had its best tourist season up to that time with nearly five hundred arrivals.

Twentieth Century Tourism

Toward the end of the nineteenth century, the great tycoon Henry M. Flagler, having brought the Florida East Coast Railway to Miami, turned his attention on Nassau. He was a man who did things on a grand scale and he was the first foreign investor to plough a substantial sum of money into the field of Bahamian tourism. As a start, he bought the Royal Victoria Hotel which, under several lessees, had not done too well and which the Government was happy to sell. Next, he entered into an agreement with the Government to construct a large hotel on the site of the old Fort Nassau and Parade Grounds. This structure, the largest the Bahamas had ever known, built of Georgia pine and named the Colonial, opened in 1900; and in the same year a Miami–Nassau winter steamship service was commenced.

There was no longer any talk of invalids. The splendid facilities of the Royal Victoria and Colonial Hotels were for the rich who could afford to be idle for all, or part of, the winter. This type of visitor, and a four month season, set a pattern for the tourist

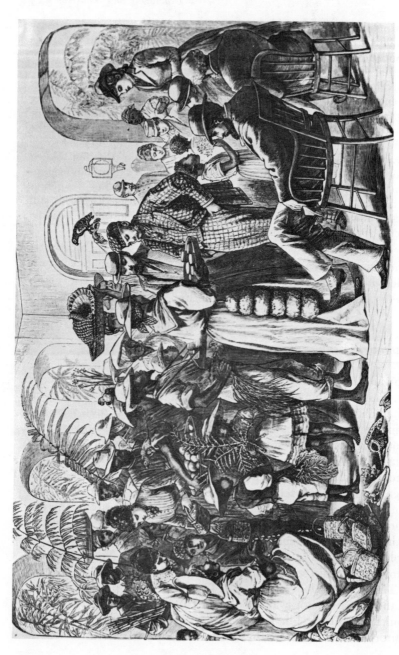

Pedlars selling curiosities in the portico of the Royal Victoria Hotel 1878

industry which remained unchanged for the next fifty years or until Sir Stafford Sands entered the scene to change it dramatically. During that half century Nassau was transformed from a fishing village into a modern city.

When the Colonial Hotel went up in flames in 1922, the the industry would have been in severe straits except for the buoyant revenues of the Prohibition era. The Government was able to purchase the site and lend a large sum to the Bahamas Hotel Company for the construction of a fireproof building. The New Colonial Hotel, which still stands, was completed in less than eight months and opened for business in February 1923. Later, as noted before, the Government advanced another large sum to a local company to assist in building the Fort Montagu Hotel, three miles east of Rawson Square. An interesting sidelight is that some members of the Assembly objected to this project, asserting that visitors would be reluctant to stay so far out of town. During the 1930's, several small hotels were built and the visitor total of over 34,000 in 1937 exceeded the population of the island for the first time. Helping to bring in this large number of people was Pan American Airways which in 1929 had commenced a sea-plane service between Miami and Nassau. In 1941, this airline switched to land planes, making use of the small airport built by Sir Harry Oakes a few years before.

When visitors started to come again after the war, the statistics were not very encouraging. The 32,000, who arrived in 1949, were actually 2000 less than those of twelve years before. But when Sir Stafford took over in 1950, an impressive forty per cent increase signalled his first year of control. The Development Board, under his chairmanship, had two broad aims: to increase the number of visitors and to make tourism a year-round business. Conditions were favourable to both these objectives. An increasing number of Americans possessed the desire as well as the means to tour; large and dependable aircraft made travel inexpensive, swift and comfortable; and, of great importance, air conditioning had come to the Bahamas. This remarkable invention which removed the dread of summer heat, was the chief factor in making year-round tourism possible. It is important to note that the first large post-war hotel, the Emerald Beach, which opened in 1954 was temperature controlled and designed for continuous operation.

An early Sikorsky sea plane—the type which pioneered the Miami–Nassau service of Pan American World Airways.

Modern Transportation

As the 1950's rolled on larger planes were flying into New Providence, and soon to come were the fast, screaming jets. Oakes Airfield, adjacent to residential areas and bounded by the Blue Hills to the south, was a patently unsuitable site for the development of a large and noisy 'Jet-port'. The decision was made to move to Windsor Field, the old Satellite Field of wartime days, which in ten years had been reclaimed by pine barren vegetation. A splendid new International Airport was opened there on 1 November 1957, under very inauspicious circumstances.

Taxi-cab owner-drivers, roused to fury by the announcement that tour cars would be used for the transportation of passengers, placed their vehicles across the roads leading to the terminal and effectively closed the airport for thirty-six hours. After negotiations and arbitration failed to settle the dispute, the whole matter erupted again on 12 January and soon developed into a general strike. During the nineteen days that this went on, all tourist facilities were closed down. There were many who felt that some lasting damage might result from this unpleasant interruption but, before many months had passed, visitors were flowing through the airport as if the strike had never occurred.

Cruise ships lying off the bar, just outside the harbour, have long been the subject matter of many a Bahamian postcard. The prettiness of the scene, however, was not so much appreciated by passengers who had to ride the small and crowded tenders to and fro, nor by captains who were unable to make use of port facilities. Those in authority had long realized that a deepwater harbour, capable of accommodating the largest liners, would be a significant asset to the tourist industry.

With tourism and revenues booming during the 1960's, it was decided to proceed with this twenty million dollar undertaking. The project was finished in 1969. When, a year or so later, the *Queen Elizabeth II* first crossed the bar, under the expert pilotage of Captain Freddy Brown, and was brought to rest alongside a newly built pier, it was a signal to all passenger ships of the world that the Port of Nassau was ready to receive them.

Along the beautiful beaches to the west of the city and on Paradise Island (Hog Island), now bridged to Nassau, many fine hotels have been built in recent years to accommodate the ever increasing flow of visitors. The growth of the tourist industry has been phenomenal indeed, surpassing even the most optimistic hopes of twenty years ago. Sir Stafford Sands had predicted that the magic figure of one million would be reached in 1970. Actually, this was achieved two years earlier, and in 1972 a total of one and a half million tourists came to the Bahamas.

The difficulty of getting New Providence going as a resort precluded any thought of the other islands until recent times. In fact, not until 1957 did the Out Islands begin to get much of an infusion of this life-blood of the country. Nassau still claims the lion's share of more than sixty per cent but, annually, more and more visitors are discovering the haunting beauty and restful quietude of the rest of the archipelago, now called the Family Islands.

Banking and Business

The massive advertising programme carried out by the Development Board (later, the Ministry of Tourism), and by private firms, drew world attention to New Providence. Of special interest to foreign businessmen was the favourable taxation climate. In the Bahamas there are no income taxes, death or succession duties or taxes on corporate profits. Furthermore, the legislation with respect to companies provides anonymity and surrounds corporate business with an impenetrable shield of secrecy because the public returns required by law are minimal.

Nassau, with its excellent climate, modern facilities and good communications, quickly became a favoured place among the world's tax havens. Foreign concerns established branches or head offices there by the score, and banking and business became the second most important industry of the Bahamas, albeit a distant second to tourism.

The concern of these firms is mainly with the Euro-dollar, that is to say the American dollar at work outside of the United States. Their activities are mainly international in nature, about which little is known locally. These companies benefit the Bahamas in a number of ways. Some direct benefit accrues to the Treasury by way of company formation and annual operating fees. The Bahamian people derive a great benefit through employment opportunities; a large sector of, what might be called, middle-class employment is provided by these companies. New Providence and the country as a whole benefits from the fact that Nassau is a financial centre; money which would not ordinarily be here is available for loans to individuals and businesses. Finally, these offshore companies contribute greatly to the favourable balance of payments position which the Commonwealth of The Bahamas enjoys. This allows an almost free flow of goods from abroad and results in an enviable standard of living.

The wave of prosperity generated by tourism and, to a lesser extent, by banking and business, was such as New Providence had never known before. Every sector of the economy was stimulated to new heights of activity. Thousands of people from England, Canada, the United States and other countries were brought in to help with the top jobs to which Bahamians had not yet attained, and even more thousands of labourers, chiefly Haitians, found their way here, legally and illegally, to help with the bottom jobs which Bahamians no longer needed or wanted.

In 1970, the population of the Bahamas was 169,000, and of these 102,000 lived in New Providence. At the same time, there were more than 10,000 non-Bahamians of working age residing in the capital island. An even better indication of the recent prosperity is the burgeoning revenue. Treasury receipts, which amounted to only $4,513,561 in 1950 climbed to $91,625,831 twenty years later. The largest part of this, by far, was contributed by New Providence. After a search which has gone on for three hundred years the people of this island seem to have found a smooth and peaceful road of prosperity—at last!

23
The Central Bahamas

We will now consider the rest of the Central Bahamas, beginning
with historic San Salvador.

San Salvador

Columbus spent but two days there and unfortunately he left no
enduring monument to mark the site of his triumph. Weather
and rot soon destroyed the wooden cross he had caused to be
erected with such great feeling and ceremony. Around 1680,
there was a pirate ship with the surprising name of the *Most Holy
Trinity*. The name was not used for blasphemy or in mockery,
for the crew, despite their calling, were strongly attached to the
Christian religion. Unfortunately, their captain cared little for
things divine so they deposed him and elected pious John Watling
to take his place. Captain Watling chose as a retreat one of the
Bahama Islands which stood outside the chain, uninhabited,
unfrequented and unnamed. This island took his name and went
on the maps as Watling's Island.

Inquisitive minds with a sense of history could not be content that the island crowned with the immortal glory of being the first landfall of Columbus in the New World, should remain unidentified. Perhaps through the sheer necessity of fixing the honour on some place, Cat Island was chosen. In 1791, however, a document was found which was thought to be irretrievably lost and which threw students of Columbus' first voyage into a flurry of excitement. In an old Spanish library was discovered a précis of the Admiral's *Journal* which had been abstracted from the original by a noted historian.

When this *Journal* was published in 1825, nothing in it was so widely and thoroughly analysed as Columbus' description of the island on which he stepped ashore on the morning of 12 October 1492. As time went by the majority of intelligent opinion was expressed in favour of Watling's Island. The Very Reverend Chrysostom Schreiner O.S.B. came to the Bahamas in 1891 to start a Catholic mission. After studying the *Journal* assiduously, reading the thoughts of many others, and exploring the area in sailing vessels a number of times, he became convinced that Watling's Island was indeed the real San Salvador. It was chiefly his persuasion which moved the Legislature in 1926 to restore the name which Columbus had bestowed on the island 434 years before.

If Columbus could return to San Salvador today he would find the island much as he last saw it. The Admiral, undoubtedly, would be much pleased to see three monuments commemorating his arrival there in 1492, each marking a different place where he first stepped ashore. He would probably point out the real exact spot of his landing which, of course, would call for a fourth monument.

After the abolition of slavery and the departure of the Loyalists, the ex-slaves and their descendants settled down to a life-style similar to that of the Lucayans. Some of the present inhabitants were almost as agape at the modern contrivances connected with a United States Guided Missile Base built there in 1951 as the Indians had been at the sight of the Spanish ships in 1492. That base, in fact, heralded a beginning of new hope for San Salvador. An airstrip, built in connexion with it, immediately placed the island within a few hours of Nassau. The base is closed now, but

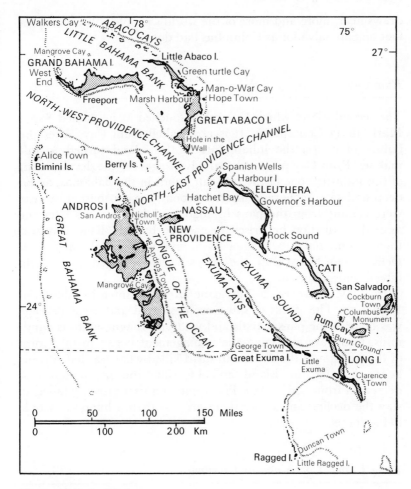

North and Central Bahamas

the airstrip remains and so do a number of buildings which were
turned over to the Bahamas Government for use as a Teachers'
Training College.

A few establishments have been opened in recent years, offering
modern accommodation to a score or so of visitors. But one can
be certain that this is just a beginning. As the quincentennial of
'The Discovery', one of the greatest events in the history of man,

draws near, more and more of the world's people will want to set foot on San Salvador as Columbus had done.

Rum Cay

The second island which Columbus touched at he named Santa Maria de la Concepcion. It is now called Rum Cay. After the failure of cotton the inhabitants of this island turned to salt making. Rum Cay possessed two advantages for the development of this industry: one of the best salt ponds in the Bahamas, and a deep and safe anchorage nearby. About 100,000 bushels a year were coming from the pans in 1840, and twelve years later the annual production had risen to 250,000 bushels. Rum Cay was then second only to Inagua as a producer of Bahamian salt. Delivered on board ship, the prices received ranged from ten to fifteen cents a bushel.

In 1853, however, a hurricane of great intensity shattered Rum Cay. The stocks of salt were destroyed and great damage was done to the pans, canals and wharves. Inagua with its windmills, tramways and energetic management began to take most of the trade, and the American tariff killed what was left. People began leaving the island and by 1886 the population had decreased from 800 to 350. Pineapple and sisal growing failed to stay the decline and today there are less than a hundred people living there.

Long Island, Cat Island and Exuma

Long Island, Cat Island and the Exumas were probably first settled by people from New Providence who fled when the pirates gained control. But here we are talking of only a few families on each island until the Loyalists came. The number of manor ruins still to be seen prove that these were favourite islands of the American refugees.

Each island has its store of loyalist lore. At Cat Island, Colonel Deveaux, of 1783 fame, staked his claim. It is reported that the interior of his mansion was lavishly decorated by a Frenchman

Exuma Cotton House (The only remaining Loyalist manor still occupied)

who had been brought to the island specifically for that purpose. The people of Long Island proudly point out the Dunmore Estate, once owned by the titled Governor, who was much detested by his fellow Loyalists. The Rolles of Exuma, all black, look upon the owner of their forebears as a great benefactor for, when his plantations failed, Lord John Rolle bequeathed his lands to his slaves and their descendants forever.

On Little Exuma Island, on an estate called the Hermitage, there is a plantation manor house still standing and still occupied. During its approximate 190 years of existence there have been many repairs and undoubtedly some structural changes. But it remains the solitary survivor of scores like it which once rose proudly above the white fields of cotton throughout the Bahamas. To a greater or lesser extent Long Island, Cat Island and Exuma participated in the succession of agricultural and marine industries which followed cotton. And when they all failed the people were reduced to little more than subsistence living from the soil and sea.

Exuma was awakened to the throb of modern life by the construction of an American sea-plane base near George Town during the Second World War. The purpose of this installation, built under terms of the Anglo-American 'Bases for Destroyers' Agreement, was to provide aerial surveillance of maritime activity in the Crooked Island Passage and its approaches.

The poet, Bliss Carman, during a visit to the Bahamas near the end of the last century, penned some very agreeable impressions of Nassau. But when he wrote

> Look from your door, and tell me now
> The colour of the sea.
> Where can I buy that wondrous dye
> And take it home with me?

surely he must have been thinking of the Exumas. For nowhere in the Bahamas, or perhaps in the world, is there water of such delightful shades and indescribable beauty. Americans began finding their way to this demi-paradise soon after the war. Today there are a number of modern resorts. The old cotton estates are being divided into home sites on a large scale, and many wealthy foreigners have built winter homes there.

Long before the Loyalists arrived, vessels from New York and Bermuda were making regular trips to Long Island to purchase salt. Recently, near a settlement with the unattractive name of Hard Bargain, there has been an impressive revival of this industry. The Diamond Crystal Salt Company has constructed a large and modern solar evaporation system, which provides employment for a number of people and produces annually about 250,000 tons of salt for export. Additional employment is provided by two resorts near the north end of the island. Otherwise the people live by farming and stockraising. More sheep have been reared there than in any other island of the Bahamas. A visitor to Long Island never fails to be impressed by the orderliness of the villages, the lush fruit orchards and the generous people of all colours who live and work together in remarkable harmony.

Cat Island is considered to be fertile by Bahamian standards. The first settlers met with disaster in 1720 when the Spaniards raided the island, murdered the men and carried off the children and slaves. A few years later, Woodes Rogers himself was anxious to start a plantation there, but he died before his plan could be effected. There is little economic opportunity for the inhabitants now. The people go about their farming chores and watch with interest a budding tourist industry which seems certain to grow well on this attractive and unspoiled island.

Ragged Island

On the western side of the Crooked Island Passage are a string of Cays called the Jumentos, a region of great beauty and a source of unending delight to yachtsmen who venture that far. Leading farther to the south is the Ragged Island Range which includes the inhabited Great Ragged Island.

Two prominent Loyalists, Major Archibald Taylor, who assisted Deveaux in the recapture of New Providence in 1783, and his brother Duncan Taylor, went to Ragged Island to develop salt pans there and the town which grew up was named Duncan Town after the latter. In 1886 this town of between three and four hundred inhabitants was said to be flourishing. Salt has remained the staple industry of the island until recent years. The people there were able to make a living from salt long after Inagua and Rum Cay had given it up, and even when it was selling for only five cents a bushel.

Next to salt making, Ragged Islanders were most renowned for their sea-going activities. In years past their salt droghers were familiar sights throughout the Bahamas, and they made trading voyages to Cuba and Haiti whenever there was a chance of profit. But all that is gone now and we are left to admire the resourcefulness of the 200 people remaining there who are able to eke out a living from their windswept and arid environment.

Eleuthera

We turn now to Eleuthera and the adjacent small islands where our modern history began. Over the centuries, Eleuthera has remained the fruit orchard and vegetable garden of the Bahamas and it is always a mark of quality to speak of Eleuthera tomatoes, Eleuthera oranges, Eleuthera pineapples.

When the American refugees went there, Eleuthera did not experience that explosive development which marked the strictly loyalist islands. For example, around 1812 when a smooth carriage-way, built years before, extended the length of Long Island, the Eleutherans were just beginning a horse-way to connect their settlements.

But Eleuthera had the Old Inhabitants with a century and a half of experience and dogged staying power. When this was blended with the energy, capital and business ability of the Loyalists Eleuthera was able to rise to great prominence during the latter half of the nineteenth century. Annually, dozens of ships would take cargoes of citrus fruit and pineapples to New York, Baltimore and other ports and return with foodstuffs, dry goods, building material and much else for domestic use. It is said that young ladies of Nassau would go to Governor's Harbour in those days to acquire the latest fashions in wearing apparel.

The inhabitants of Spanish Wells and Harbour Island have benefited from the Eleuthera soil, as have the Eleutherans. Each island has an allotted commonage on what their people call the

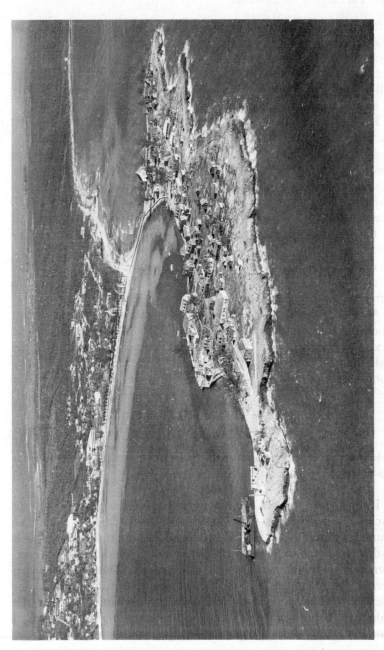

Governor's Harbour Eleuthera (Cupid's Cay in foreground)

'mainland'. That of Harbour Island is interesting in that it was granted primarily as a reward for the valuable assistance given to Deveaux in his recapture of New Providence. During the 1870's the population of Harbour Island stood at 2500. By 1943 it had fallen to 743. These figures, though exceptional, demonstrate in a striking manner the general decline of the area.

First attempts at revival were by means of agricultural pursuits. In 1936, a wealthy American, Mr Austin Levy, established a dairy and poultry farm at Hatchet Bay. His plan was to grow most of the required feed on the spot, and he conceived a new way to deal with the Bahamian soil. Machinery, much of which had to be improvised, was brought in and pitted against the stony ground. Some of the rock was torn up and cast aside and some pulverized to form a part of the soil. In this manner, acre after acre was transformed into tillable farmland. It was quite a day when the owner could look on his herd of dairy cattle, happily munching away on selected grasses which had been sown, fertilized and harvested entirely by modern machinery.

After Hatchet Bay, a number of other large scale farming and stock raising enterprises were launched at Eleuthera during the next fifteen years. But none of them could contend with the Bahamian soil. Mr Austin Levy, on first surveying his rocky domain, paused to pay a compliment to those who had worked it before him.

It should be to their everlasting credit [he remarked] that for centuries with almost unbelievable courage and skill, the farmers of the Bahamas have maintained themselves in the face of such great obstacles.

In 1947, Sir Roland Symonette constructed a small cluster of vacation cottages at a place near Governor's Harbour which he named French Leave. In that same year Bahamas Airways, which had been started earlier as a charter service by Sir Harold Christie, commenced regular flights to the island. These two events heralded the beginning of the modern tourist industry for Eleuthera. Today it is the third largest tourist centre in the Bahamas, being exceeded only by New Providence and Grand Bahama. Many of the people still rely on farming but increasingly they depend on tourism, winter residents and land development for employment.

Current Island

The small amount of history connected with Current Island indicates that its people must have enjoyed a very tranquil existence. It seems to have been granted during proprietary ownership, and over the years we hear nothing of pirates, foreign incursions or violence of any kind. The inhabitants carry on today as they have done for generations; all the men go fishing while the women take care of families and farms.

Spanish Wells

If asked to name a place in the Bahamas where pioneer blood is most concentrated, one would have to say Spanish Wells. Few Loyalists were attracted there, and the physical features of the all-white population reflect those of the Eleutherian Adventurers who waded ashore, a few miles away, three and a quarter centuries ago.

It seems likely that Spanish Wells was included in the Spanish depredations of 1680, and during the War of 1812 the settlement was plundered and partially burnt by Americans. Epidemics decimated the population and hurricanes rolled over the island time after time. It was probably because of these and other incidents that the inhabitants developed a clannish attitude. They never left home in large numbers as the Harbour Islanders did; nor have they been anxious to welcome outsiders to live on their island.

There is absolutely nothing like Spanish Wells in all the Bahamas today. A town of exquisite cleanness and beauty nestles beside a harbour which is a beehive of maritime activity. The fishing fleet, headquartered there, is the finest in the nation. Tourism has come to the island but it plays a minor role. The 1000 people who live there have raised themselves to a prosperous level by applying hard work to the oldest and most basic of Bahamian industries, fishing and farming.

Spanish Wells (St George's Cay)

Harbour Island

Oldmixon's assertion that Harbour Island was so named because of 'the goodness of the harbour' has the ring of truth. And we are justified in guessing that it was this harbour which Sayle was attempting to enter when his ship struck a reef. It received a good share of prominent Loyalists and they and their descendants have exercised great influence on the course of Bahamian events. The town itself was named after Governor Lord Dunmore who had a summer residence there and who took a great deal of interest in the island. During the nineteenth century, Dunmore Town was second only to Nassau in population and prosperity.

Perhaps no other patch of Bahamian soil has been so intensively cultivated as the 6000 acres of Harbour Island commonage on Eleuthera. Nevertheless, it was in maritime activities that the islanders made their greatest mark. A good harbour and a local shipbuilding industry were responsible for this.

A privateer named the *Primrose* was built there in 1792 and she provides a good example of what the island shipwrights could produce then. A single-masted vessel of seventy-four tons burthen, she measured nearly fifty-eight feet from stem to stern and more than eighteen feet at the beam. Ten cannon comprised the armament, some of them four pounders and some three pounders. Her complement was surprisingly large, fifty-six officers and men, including a 'linguister'. It was quite an advantage in plundering a ship to be able to communicate with her crew.

During the decade 1855–64, the twenty-six sloops and schooners launched at Harbour Island averaged forty-seven tons, while those built elsewhere in the Bahamas were less than half that size. But these were small compared to those built later for foreign trade in connexion with the citrus and pineapple industries; and smaller still compared to the lumber carriers of the present century. The 360 tons, three-masted, *Beatrice* was launched in 1908, and she was followed some years later by the smaller

Dunmore Town, Harbour Island—a century ago

Marie. J. Thompson *launched at Harbour Island in* 1922. *The largest ship ever built in the Bahamas.*

Corinthia, also three-masted. In 1922 came the queen of them all, the *Marie J. Thompson.* Carrying four masts and 696 tons in size, she remains the largest ship ever built in the Bahamas.

By the end of the Second World War shipbuilding was dead and Dunmore Town was dying. Dozens of deserted houses, some of them crumbling, were reminders of past prosperity. But no hope could be seen for the future. Then, in the late 1940's tourism came to the island as it did to Eleuthera, and hope was born again. Today, nine establishments offer a total of about 150 rooms. Many of the charming old houses have been bought by wealthy foreigners and beautifully restored. There is prosperity and optimism on the island now and the population of over a thousand is on the rise.

Andros

Andros is the giant of the archipelago. Until aeroplanes came along much of the interior had not been seen. Until recent times there was a legend that a primitive tribe, armed with bows and arrows, lived deep in the forest. Another legend concerning the chickcharney, a three-toed, three-fingered, human-faced elf which lives in pine trees, still lingers. Pirates are reputed to have had a headquarters there. 'They had an elaborate fortification' on South Andros, wrote Mr Elgin Forsyth, 'and preyed on Spanish commerce between Cuba and Florida. They even had a harem a half mile inland from the fort, and pastures for stolen Cuban cattle.'

The first permanent settlers are presumed to have come from St Andro on the Mosquito Coast, after it was ceded to Spain in 1783. Five years later, the colony which they founded consisted of 'twenty-two white heads of families and seven planters, with 132 slaves'. After the abolition of slavery, a number of blacks from Exuma and Long Island went to South Andros in search of farm land. And, during the 1840's, some people of mixed Indian and Negro blood, escaped from Florida and slavery, crossed the Gulf Stream, and settled in North Andros. Nothing much came their way after sisal growing and sponging until a few decades ago when the Bahamas Lumber Company established a mill there for the production of timber. A few years ago an American company, Owens-Illinois, of which we will hear more later, harvested the pine trees for pulpwood.

Andros, in recent years, has also had its modern pioneers in agriculture. Some very large farms, by Bahamian standards, were developed, and okras, tomatoes, cucumbers, strawberries, cantaloupes and papayas were grown with remarkable success. None of these enterprises, however, were financial successes. But it is interesting to note that failure was due more to labour, transportation and marketing problems than to the old bug-bear of Bahamian agriculture, a thin and difficult soil.

Just to the east of this island is a great submarine canyon called The Tongue of Ocean which was selected by the United States Navy as an ideal site for testing its underwater weapons and protective devices. After agreement with the British and Bahamian Governments work commenced on the project in 1964. The installation, close to Fresh Creek, is known as the Atlantic Underwater Test and Evaluation Centre. AUTEC, as it is abbreviated, has helped the economy by providing employment and by otherwise putting money into circulation.

A number of small tourist facilities and land development schemes have been started in recent years along the east coast with its refreshing breezes and fine beaches. Much can be expected from this large island in the years ahead.

Berry Islands

The Berry Islands had no permanent settlement before 1836 when Governor Colebrooke, who was anxious to resettle Africans taken from captured slave ships, laid out a town on Great Stirrup's Cay. It was named Williamstown in honour of William IV, and the Government must have expected it to amount to something for it was made a port of entry and a Customs House was erected there. Today, the ruins of this well-meant experiment can still be seen.

Sisal-growing and sponging had their day but the new trend for the Berry Islanders started in the 1930's when Miss Betty Carstairs, an English sportswoman, bought Big Whale Cay and transformed it into her own private Shangri-La. A few other wealthy people, including Mr Wallace Groves of whom we will hear more in the next chapter, did the same thing with other islands of the group. More recently two large developments of marvellous design and of the greatest potential have been started. These multi-million dollar projects are well planned centres of recreational activity for both tourists and home owners, and they provide good employment opportunities for the less than 500 people who live there.

North and South Bimini

There are two Biminis, North and South. Traditionally, North Bimini has been the place to live and South Bimini the place to farm. The area had long been a rendezvous for wreckers who kept an eye on Gulf Stream traffic. When wrecking increased tremendously toward the middle of the nineteenth century, some of the wreckers decided it would be better to live close to the scene of their business activities. Thus, in 1848, Bimini was settled by five wrecking families, totalling forty men, women and children. These people prospered because of their advantageous location, and by 1881 the population had grown to 663.

When wrecking faded out, the inhabitants took to fishing, sponging, and to growing sisal, coconuts and corn on South Bimini. And they carried on this way of life until the boom which came with American Prohibition. After rum running ended, the people commenced catering to wealthy sports fishermen who came that way to enjoy some of the best fishing grounds in the world.

Bimini today is one large tourist camp. A number of hotels and boarding houses offer a total of about 240 rooms; the water-front is packed with yachts, piers and marinas, and the town hums with buyers and revellers who crowd the souvenir shops, straw markets and night clubs. A special attraction of the island is the Lerner Marine Laboratory, a research centre operated by the American Museum of Natural History. There, one can see the colourful fishes of Bahamian waters at which Columbus marvelled so long ago.

24
The North-Western Bahamas

The Providence Channel separates the Little from the Great
Bahama Bank, and the north-western Bahamas from the rest of
the archipelago. Above the surface of the sea, the commanding
features of this area are the island group called Abaco and the
island of Grand Bahama with its adjacent Cays.

Abaco

We believe that a few Old Inhabitants were living at Abaco before
the Loyalists came. We are told that, in 1783, 1458 Loyalists
planned to go there from New York and 1500 from East Florida.
How many ever set foot on Abaco we do not know. They were a
fractious and footloose lot, made up mainly of disbanded troops,
always 'seeking some more promising region on the immense
continent in their vicinity, which, whilst it affords a various
choice, encourages a perpetual spirit of emigration'. By 1788 when
conditions had become somewhat settled, the population consisted
only of approximately 196 white inhabitants and 198 slaves.

Soon after that, Old Inhabitants began to move in. As far as the men were concerned, some say it was the pretty girls of Abaco who first attracted them, but they were also attracted by a larger and more resourceful area. The majority of them came from Harbour Island and today there is scarcely a white Abaconian who cannot claim an ancestor from that island.

The Loyalists from New York settled first at Carleton and later moved to 'Marsh's harbour'. 'Refugees and disbanded troops' from East Florida established themselves at 'Spencers-bite and Eight Mile Bay'. These mainland settlements did not flourish, and when the Old Inhabitants moved in and intermarried with the Loyalists, the 'conch' way of life was adopted by all and the cays became the preferred places to live.

By 1815, New Plymouth on Green Turtle Cay had become the principal settlement with 193 inhabitants. Forty years later a fleet of forty fishing boats and twenty wrecking schooners were owned by the islanders and the population had increased to a thousand. The people of this cay took to fruit-growing on the mainland and to foreign trade as did the Harbour Islanders. Green Turtle Cay became the industrial and commercial hub of Abaco and in 1890 there were 1700 people living there.

As the fruit growing industry declined, so did New Plymouth. By the turn of the century the centre of activity shifted to Hope Town, Elbow Cay, which with a population of a thousand, had developed into a town of shipbuilders and sea-farers.

Shipbuilding

Abaco shipwrights began building vessels soon after settlement and by the middle of the last century they were the chief ship-builders of the colony. During the ten year period 1855–64 they accounted for nearly one half of all Bahamian built vessels, 108 out of 230. Schooners of 50 to 100 tons were built for foreign trade during the fruit growing era, and larger three-masted schooners for the later business of lumber carrying. The *Perceler* of 150 tons was constructed in 1914, and the *Abaco* and *Abaco Bahamas*, 266 and 484 tons respectively, were launched in 1917 and 1922.

Ships were built at many places in Abaco but Hope Town

Hope Town, Abaco

became the centre of maritime activity. Apart from locally built vessels, a number of others, built elsewhere, were manned by the seamen of Hope Town. The series of hurricanes which commenced in 1926 wrecked, or severely damaged, many of these vessels. But by that time freight rates had fallen considerably and it was clear that sailing ships could no longer compete in the lumber carrying business. The decline and death of sponging completed the crippling of Elbow Cay's economy.

New Plymouth and Hope Town each have but a few hundred inhabitants today. When the Abaco wheel of fortune turned again, it pointed not to one of the cays but to the mainland where the Loyalists began their activities.

Timber

In building their vessels and houses the people of Abaco had always used the hardwood, which grows in good quantities on the mainland, for frames. But they had found little use for the more abundant long-leaf yellow pine or Caribbean pine. An American group, which did see some value in the yellow pine, obtained a 100 year Timber Licence with respect to the Crown pine-forests of Abaco, Andros and Grand Bahama and in 1906 they established a saw mill near the south end of Great Abaco. The town which grew up as headquarters of the operation was named Wilson City after Governor Sir William Grey-Wilson.

The Bahamas Timber Company, as the firm was called, turned out between fifteen and eighteen million board feet of lumber annually for local use and export. And it was the freighting of this lumber which gave employment to the large schooners of Hope Town and Harbour Island. Over the years the business changed hands several times, and the mill was moved to a number of different locations. Except for one short cessation of activity the lumbering went on until 1943 when the supply of large and accessible trees was exhausted.

In 1959, another American company, Owens-Illinois, came to Abaco to harvest the pine trees for pulpwood. Many hundreds of miles of access roads were constructed, and over these the pine-logs were hauled to a dredged terminal at Snake Cay. There, they were loaded on barges and freighted to Jacksonville, Florida. This cutting, hauling and shipping was to go on for nine years, a period of unparalleled prosperity and growth for Abaco, and especially Marsh Harbour which burgeoned into a little city. Nothing shows the effects of this company's activities on the island better than a few statistics.

A population of 3610 for all of Abaco in 1881 had fallen to 3407 in 1953, a decrease of 203 in 72 years. The census figure for 1963 was 6490, a remarkable increase of eighty per cent in ten years.

Owens-Illinois and Sugar Cane

While the Owens-Illinois people were still progressing with their logging, but with the end in sight, they conceived the idea of an agricultural enterprise on some of the deforested land, and they decided in favour of sugar cane.

Just prior to the commencement of this venture two other agricultural projects had been tried at Abaco. Citrus, avocado pears, cucumbers, pineapples and tomatoes, excelling in taste, beauty and size had been grown successfully. Problems of preparing the land, and maintaining its fertility, however, when added to those of labour, transportation and marketing proved too formidable and the plantations failed. Notwithstanding these failures Owens-Illinois, guided by the best advice and after the most thorough research, was confident that sugar cane would succeed.

Massive bulldozers were put to work to rip up tree-stumps, pulverize the rock and convert the terrain into tillable earth, as had first been done at Hatchet Bay. After generous quantities of fertilizer had been added, the crop was planted, and soon 18,000 acres of green canefields covered the land which had been home to the towering yellow pine. A modern mill and refinery were set up and the juice of the first year's harvest was converted into 15,000 tons of raw sugar, which was disappointingly low. The second harvest yielded 19,000 tons, which was not considered to be enough of an improvement. And that is as far as the company went. Slim prospects of future profits and the fear of adding more millions to an already large investment resulted in a decision to close down the operation, and the 1971 crop remained un-harvested.

Both the sugar cane property and refinery were put up for sale and it seems that Owens-Illinois might be finished with Abaco at least for the thirty-year period it will take the pine-trees to grow to the size of pulpwood requirements again. But during its time there the company poured many millions of dollars into the economy and it has left to the people many enduring benefits.

This was the largest single agricultural enterprise ever under-taken in the Bahamas, and its failure when added to so many of the past might lead one to despair of any great success with the Bahamian soil. But both Mr Claude Smith, the present Director of Agriculture, and Mr Oris Russell who preceded him, are convinced that modern, intensive farming will form an important segment of the economy one day. And that causes us all to be hopeful.

Tourism

During the 1950's Americans began to rediscover Abaco, and they saw it in a much more beautiful light than the Loyalists had done more than a century and a half before. On the mainland and on the cays many citizens of the United States, and some others, have built winter homes. Many more come to stay at a number of inns and small hotels which are sprouting up every-where. Abaco holds fourth place in the Bahamas for visitor accommodation, with 336 rooms now available to those who tour the area. And for those who want to own a private bit of Abaco a number of residential land developments offer a variety of interesting and beautiful sites.

Grand Bahama

The story of Grand Bahama is one of 'rags to riches', but the rags were in evidence a mighty long time before the riches came along. In 1803, McKinnen wrote that 'the Great Bahama is absolutely uninhabited'. In fact, it seems that no permanent settlement was attempted there before 1806. Fifty years later, an official report provides an insight into the life style which had developed there.

They raise cattle and horses to some extent, and cultivate corn, potatoes, etc. There are abundance of fish, lobsters and turtle . . . There are seven wrecking vessels and two schooners belonging to the Grand Bahama. For the fortnight before I visited it, there had been some fifty sail of wrecking vessels cruising about the great wrecking ground near Sandy Cay . . . On the north side of the Grand Bahama is some sponging ground . . .

The first economic boom of significance came in 1919, with United States Prohibition. The town of West End, being so close to the Florida coast, became one vast store-house of liquor. Major Bell who visited there in the early 1930's found the town and anchorage bustling with activity. There were

moored a fleet of grey, low-hulled motor-engined cruisers and some half dozen aeroplanes . . . outside the harbour was a pitching and heaving thirty footer with a gun forward and a big number on her hull plates . . . the inevitable Coast Guard vessel.

Americans, Englishmen and adventurers of other nations who flowed into West End during those hectic days discovered one product which they liked almost as much as the fine liquors stored there, the Bahamian spiny lobster.

Crawfishing

On the Little Bahama Bank, these lobsters or crawfish were so plentiful as to seem inexhaustible, and Florida, where a market developed, was just across the Gulf Stream. Crawfishing is now carried on throughout the Bahamas, and is the most remunerative of maritime industries. Over 1,000,000 pounds weight of tails, representing a catch of about $2\frac{1}{4}$ million lobsters, are shipped annually to the United States, and the local fishermen receive up to $3·50 per pound.

Soon after the Second World War had started, Mr Axel Wenner-Gren set up a crawfish canning business at West End, Grand Bahama which went under the name of Grand Bahama Packing Company Limited. A few years later his enterprise was taken over by General Seafoods of Boston, a subsidiary of General Foods Incorporated and renamed General Seafoods (Bahamas) Limited. This company went in for quick-freezing of lobster tails and grouper fillets, and the canning of bluefin tuna which were caught in the Gulf Stream. After a few years, it became evident that income from sales would never overtake the high cost of operations and, toward the end of 1946, the business began to close down.

The saw mill which had been working away at Abaco since 1906, with but one short interruption, was moved to Grand Bahama in 1944. Both the mill and the forestry rights were then owned by the Abaco Lumber Company. Logging headquarters were established at a place called Pine Ridge, about five miles to the east of Hawksbill Creek.

Billy Butlin

Soon after the saw mill began converting pine logs into building timber, an Englishman arrived on the island with a new and bold plan. This man, Billy Butlin, had made a great success of holiday camps in Britain. As he saw it, the western end of Grand Bahama Island, so close to the populous United States, was an ideal site for a resort of this type.

The £2,000,000 complex was to be called 'Butlin's Vacation Village' and it was planned to provide accommodation for one thousand guests by January of 1950, and for an additional thousand a year later. With the first phase still unfinished, it opened a month or so behind schedule.

By that time, however, the project had fallen into deep financial trouble. Actual costs had so far exceeded estimates that those who had invested their money refused to put up more. Consequently, much had to be done on a thin line of credit. Returns on the partially completed first phase were insufficient to meet the minimum demands of the creditors, who closed in and forced the company into receivership after less than a year of operation.

Billy Butlin's venture failed but his dream did not die. And as so often happens in the Bahamas, new adventurers came along to build on the foundation of past failure. Today, on property once owned by Butlin and his group, is the modern and thriving 500 room Grand Bahama Hotel, with its own airport, marina and golf course.

Wallace Groves

Mr Wallace Groves, an American, had been in this country for some years when in 1946 he bought the Abaco Lumber Company's mill and timber rights at Grand Bahama. Immediately he set in motion a number of improvements which greatly modernized and expanded the operation. A contract to supply pit-props to the mines of Britain was secured in 1951, and for the next several years many shiploads of these logs were sent across the Atlantic.

While his lumbering business was going on he conceived a visionary plan of great magnitude for Grand Bahama. This was made known to Bahamians when in 1955 an agreement was signed between the Bahamas Government and the Grand Bahama Port Authority. It was called the Hawksbill Creek Agreement. By its terms the Port Authority contracted to develop a deep water harbour at Hawksbill Creek. This was to be but the first phase in the creation of a free port and an industrial city.

The Government for its part agreed to the grant of 50,000 acres of Crown land on favourable terms; exemption of the port area from customs duties on non-consumable items, and from export, stamp and excise taxes, for ninety-nine years; and it further guaranteed that no personal or corporate income taxes, real estate or property taxes would be imposed for thirty years. Furthermore, the Authority and its business licensees were given permission to bring in whatever 'key personnel' were needed without recourse to the normal channels of immigration.

Soon after this agreement was signed, Mr Groves sold his lumber business so that he might devote his full time to Freeport. National Container Corporation, the buyer, proceeded to cut pulpwood for the next three years. This company was subsequently acquired by Owens-Illinois which, as we have seen, did so much for Abaco, a little later.

The big problem before Mr Groves, and those associated with him, was to get some momentum into Freeport. The harbour work was progressing well, a bunkering installation had been started, and there was talk of a cement plant. But what would come of these projects, no one could say, and not much else seemed to be going right. The failure of a number of enterprises which got an early start became a deterrent to others. Five years after the agreement was signed, a pall of despondency had descended on the embryonic town; and there were grave fears that the industrial city would never materialize.

With something akin to desperation, the promoters turned to tourism and residential land development as a source of hope. The Government was anxious to co-operate and, in 1960, a Supplemental Agreement was signed whereby the Authority was granted an additional 50,000 acres of land for a small sum, on condition that a 200 room hotel be constructed. There was then some concern that Freeport might not have sufficient attractions for the development of a tourist industry. Apart from a dredged harbour and mounds of limestone there was little else to see except a few roads and millions of pine trees. Those who pondered the problem became convinced that gambling casinos would more than compensate for whatever other deficiencies there might be.

As a result, application was made to the Governor-in-Council requesting that Freeport be exempted from the law prohibiting organized gambling. This was favourably considered and on 1 April 1963, a Certificate of Exemption was granted to a company by the name of Bahamas Amusements Limited for a period of ten years. And on the last day of that year the luxurious Lucayan Beach Hotel, replete with a sparkling casino, opened its doors.

Freeport

Sure enough, this turned out to be the touchstone of success. From that day Freeport began to move. Its forward march was astonishing to all who saw it or heard of it; it excited the imagina-

Bahamas Cement Company Plant, Freeport

Bahamas Oil Refinery, Freeport

tion of the business world. Unfortunately, space does not permit even the barest account of this phenomenal growth. We will have to be content with a sketchy summary at the end.

When the Progressive Liberal Party came to power in 1967, its leaders soon made it clear that there were some things they did not like about the Hawksbill Creek Agreement and about Freeport. Particularly distasteful was that the Port Authority and the licensees could employ almost any non-Bahamians they wished and that these expatriates were allowed to enter the area and remain there without Immigration approval. As to Freeport itself, they looked on this as a foreign enclave. Bahamians in general and blacks in particular were discriminated against with respect to business and employment opportunities and social activities.

A few years later, all expatriates were required by the Government to have regular work permits. This led to a storm of protest from those licensed to do business in Freeport. They considered this action to be a breach of the Agreement. The slowness of Immigration in the processing of permits and the uncertainty as to whether or not they would be granted, served to worsen the situation. When the licensees moved to force arbitration of the dispute, as provided for in the Agreement, the Government acted swiftly. By legislative action in February 1970, it unilaterally amended the Agreement and Freeport was brought under the same Immigration control as the rest of the Bahamas.

The momentum of Freeport was slowed considerably by the uncertain state of affairs which preceded this legislation and by its effects. Many enterprises failed; many others were forced to cease operations because of a shortage of trained personnel; and 'For Sale' signs sprang up everywhere. To those who knew the city during its period of spectacular growth, it looked somewhat like a ghost town in comparison. It should be understood, however, that although the growth rate is not what it used to be, Freeport is still very much a going concern. No one who sees the veritable miracle which has been wrought there in the short span of eighteen years can be anything but astonished. In 1955, there was nothing but pine trees, palmetto palms and scrub. Today, there is a well planned and well built city with broad avenues, beautiful buildings and spacious greens.

Where a small shallow creek once intruded on the shoreline is now a modern harbour dredged to thirty feet of depth, with large terminals, warehouses and offshore bunkering facilities. With 270 daily landings and take-offs, an International Jet Airport serves seven American, English and Canadian Airlines, in addition to the local national carrier Bahamasair.

There were only sixty persons and firms licensed to do business there in 1962. Today there are more than 1400. Prominent among the industrial concerns are a cement factory which produces six million barrels annually; an oil refinery which soon will be processing 450,000 barrels daily; a pharmaceutical manufacturing complex and a liquor distilling and bottling plant. A number of fine hotels have been built which offer a total of 3636 rooms to business people and tourists, none of whom can complain of a lack of attractions now.

When Freeport was first considered, the Government looked on it, hopefully, as a future source of employment for the people of Grand Bahama. That worthy, but limited, objective has long been surpassed. The magic city itself now has a population of more than 15,000; and Grand Bahama, which had a total of only 4095 people in 1953, could boast of nearly 26,000 in 1970. People from all over the Bahamas have found business and employment opportunities there and, of course, the Treasury receives substantial revenues from Freeport.

25
Colonial Government

To introduce the political history of the Bahamas, we will return to the Lucayans, the first inhabitants of these islands, who also felt a need for government.

Lucayan Government

Their situation, however, was blessed with simplicity. There were no racial or religious conflicts to be resolved; crime was almost non-existent, and there was no competitive striving after material possessions. Their customs and beliefs were the same, and each of them looked on life much as did the others.

Nevertheless, they were not without problems, as we have seen, and they felt the need, as perhaps all people do, of being guided through this world by one stronger, braver and wiser than themselves. The man who filled this requirement they called a *cacique* and the position tended to be hereditary. We do not know how many *caciques* there were in the Bahamas; the domain of any one might have been a village, an island or an island group.

All disputes were referred to him and he settled them in a manner most conducive to the welfare and happiness of his subjects. His word was law but he was not a tyrant. In matters of grave concern, he was careful to seek the advice of his medicine men and leading citizens. The people deferred to him in every way and never failed to show him the greatest respect and love. They considered it a great privilege to be able to present to him the best fish of the catch, the largest animals of the hunt and the finest produce of the harvest. Nevertheless, he was not a pampered monarch, for unlike the *caciques* in more populous lands, he joined in all the activities of his people, including their common labours.

Eleutherian Government

The political history of the Bahamas begins with the Eleutherian Adventurers, and it may be divided into three main periods. The first from 1648 to 1717 was a period of instability when those who controlled these islands were groping for some workable form of government. A relatively stable era was ushered in by Woodes Rogers in 1718 and this endured, with some interruptions, for more than two and a quarter centuries, ending with the recent period of party politics, rapid constitutional change, and Independence.

The Adventurers who came to the Bahamas had left behind them countries seething with bitter and bloody controversy, and their paramount hope was that these conditions would not be transplanted to Eleuthera. Being Puritans or Independents, they naturally believed, as did Cromwell, that the autocratic King was mainly responsible for the miseries which had engulfed England. Thus, in their New World colony, they were determined that power should be vested in the people and they called it a republic.

There are many who say that the actual machinery of government at Eleuthera did not measure up to the standards of a republic. But the slightest knowledge of republics of the world from that day to this is sufficient to demonstrate that a republic is almost anything that the government of a country chooses to call a republic. The Eleutherian Adventurers maintained that their colony was a republic and history must record it as such. We have to say further that it was the first republic in the New World and, indeed, the first in any English speaking country.

It was laid down in the *Articles and Orders* that the government would be composed of a Governor, a Council of twelve and a Senate of 100. The first hundred subscribers to the Company were to constitute the Senate in the first instance, and as members died or moved away the Senate would elect citizens to take their places. The first Governor and Council were to be elected in England and serve for three years, after which they would be elected yearly, by the citizens of Eleuthera, from the membership of the Senate.

Few of the requirements of this constitution could be implemented if only because of a paucity of people. Captain William Sayle was the first Governor and undoubtedly he was assisted by some kind of a Council. When he moved away, in 1661, he left the colony in the hands of his son, Nathaniel. And when Nathaniel departed, it seems that what was left of government soon disintegrated. Nevertheless, we are bound to look back with pride on the *Articles and Orders* of the Eleutherian Adventurers as the 'First Constitution' of the Bahamas. It was a very remarkable and enlightened document for the time, embodying as it did some vital germs of democracy.

Proprietary Government

On 1 November 1670, the Bahama Islands were granted to six men who, with two others, were already Lords Proprietors of Carolina. The grant made it clear, however, that these islands were not to be a part of Carolina or subject to their government, but 'absolutely separate and divided from the same'. Nevertheless, there remained this tie of nearly identical ownership. The Proprietors of Carolina and the Bahamas, anxious to have a stable form of government, had drafted what was called the 'Fundamental Constitutions'. They had been assisted in the preparation of this most curious document by the great philosopher John Locke, and the aim was that it should serve as a model constitution for those lands in America under their control.

An interesting provision is that which deals with the establishment of an aristocracy. Since it was forbidden to duplicate titles then existing in England, the 'Constitutions' suggested 'Palatine' for the senior of the Proprietors, and 'Landgraves' and 'Cassiques' for the rest of the Proprietors and their deputies. In contemporary documents, Lord Craven is referred to as the 'Palatine of the island of Providence etc.'. So there seems to have been some move toward the establishment of a Bahamian nobility. Otherwise, the 'Fundamental Constitutions' a semi-feudal instrument, was not applied to these islands and had no effect on them.

What really guided the framing of the 'Second Constitution' was the Royal Instructions to the Proprietors that they were to govern 'with the advice and assent and approbacon of the Freemen of the said islands'. This, in short, meant that there had to be an Assembly. Accordingly, the Proprietors, in a directive to Hugh Wentworth, the designated Governor, dated 24 April 1671, outlined the form of government. There would be a Governor, a Council of ten and an elected Assembly of twenty freeholders; and, ordinarily, the Assembly was to be called every second year in the month of November.

Here, we come against a curious twist of events which demonstrates very clearly the early attachment of Bahamians to representative government. Not waiting for the Proprietors to send out their instructions, the inhabitants had moved to call their own Assembly, and this Assembly had elected John Wentworth, brother of Hugh, as Governor. The matter was resolved when Hugh died and John was confirmed in the post by the Proprietors.

Nevertheless, John seems to have been proud of the fact that he was the people's man, and he must have informed the Proprietors that the people would have no other man. A clue as to how John actually had been elected is contained in Lord Shaftesbury's reply to a letter from him.

I desire to know [he wrote], whether you hold your place of Governor as chosen by ye people or us; for if you hold it from ye people we will quickly try how safe ye islands will be under another. I mention this because your letter expresses that ye Speaker told you in ye name of the country that they had chosen you for their governor and did not feel safe with another.

That there was a Speaker assures us, beyond all doubt, that there was an Assembly. We are unable to fix the exact date of this first Assembly but it seems most likely that it met during the year 1670. The seriousness with which early Bahamians regarded their Assembly is shown by the trouble which many of them took to cast their votes.

The inhabitants of these islands (Harbour Island and Eleuthera) [wrote Oldmixon], on Elections of Assembly-men and other Public Occasions, go to Nassau in Providence to give their votes. The Assembly consisted of 20 Members, chosen by the Inhabitants of all the Islands met together for that Purpose; for the Province not being divided into Precincts, they had no other way of choosing their Representatives.

When conditions allowed, Assemblies were summoned at intervals from 1670 to 1703, and the inhabitants became irate if the Governor failed to do his duty in this respect. One of the serious charges brought by the people against Cadwallader Jones, who was appointed Governor in 1690, was that 'he wilfully neglected to call a General Assembly till six months after the Time appointed by the Lords Proprietors' Instructions'. As would be expected, the privateers and pirates, who controlled the Bahamas between 1704 and 1717, had little use for 'ballotines' and assemblies, or government of any kind.

Almost from the very beginning English authorities had expressed dissatisfaction with proprietary government. Substantial bond was required to ensure the good behaviour of later Governors, especially in the proper enforcement of Imperial Acts relating to piracy and trade. The fact that the last two Governors to be selected by the Proprietors never assumed their posts was due as much to the difficulty of obtaining Royal approval as it was to the uninviting conditions existing in New Providence.

In 1708 official recommendations were made that the Crown should assume responsibility for government. In 1715 the Proprietors chose their last man for Governor, Roger Mosteyn. It was decided by the Crown that he should also be given a Royal Commission. Had he taken up the post, he would have been something of a hybrid, a combination Royal and proprietary Governor.

Royal Government

Woodes Rogers was the first Royal Governor and the Royal Instructions which he received called for a government on the same pattern as that of the proprietary period. The actual summoning of an Assembly was left in abeyance owing to the disturbed conditions then existing. But such a body was recognized as an essential ingredient of the law-making machinery, for he was told that 'you are not to take upon you to enact any Laws, till We shall have appointed an Assembly, and given you directions for your further Proceedings therein'. These directions came ten years later when Rogers was commissioned to be Governor a second time. Thus, we must look upon the Royal Instructions of 1718, combined with the Order in Council of 1728, implementing an Assembly, as the 'Third Constitution' of the Bahamas.

This form of government in which an elected Assembly shared authority with a Governor and an appointed Council was the common English colonial constitution granted during the seventeenth and eighteenth centuries. With Bermuda and Barbados, the Bahamas was ultimately to enjoy the distinction of the oldest assemblies in the British Empire. Those of the rest of the British West Indies were abolished during the nineteenth century.

The new Assembly of twenty-four members, sixteen for New Providence and four each for Harbour Island and Eleuthera, all elected in their own districts for the first time, met on 29 September 1729. This Assembly is of great importance in our history because it marks the beginning of a continuous representative body. There have been gaps, of course, but for no great length of time has the Bahamas been without an Assembly from 1729 to the present day.

The constitution was supplemented and amended from time to time by Letters Patent. Within the framework of the written instrument, procedural guidance was found in local precedents and traditions and in those of the Westminster model. Throughout, the Governor and his Council were the Executive Branch; but the Council, when it was a single body, also performed legislative functions. In 1841, an additional Council was created to deal solely with legislative matters. Government maintained a presence in the two legislative chambers, that is the Assembly and the Legislative Council, by appointing some of their members to the Executive Council as the Governor's Council was now called.

But this was a weak presence as far as the Assembly was concerned and its members in general performed the role of a stubborn Opposition. They looked with suspicion on all proposals which came from 'The Hill', and with anger at every move by the Legislative Council to thwart the will of the people's representatives. From the earliest days the Assembly had felt a strength which was frequently greater than its power. It saw itself as a champion of the people it had been elected to represent, and it performed this role with daring and boldness.

During Trott's time it took some brashness to vote for the abolition of certain imposts concerning which the House had no legal say. But it was prepared to offend both King and Proprietors for the simple reason that the taxes were burdensome to the people. The Proprietors congratulated the Governor for disallowing this in these words: 'You were much in ye right in not consenting to their bill for taking away ye King's Custome and Our Tenths of salt. . . .'

We can be sure that language of debate during proprietary years was of the saltiest. Assemblymen, however, did not restrict themselves to language when more forceful means were indicated. When Governor Cadwallader Jones tried to coerce the Assembly by having his son train the guns of an armed vessel on its meeting house, far from being browbeaten, members sprang to arms and clapped the Governor in irons.

Captain Elias Haskett was deposed in consequence of a popular uprising a few months after he arrived as Governor.

Throughout the rebellion, John Warren, the Speaker of the Assembly, played a leading part on the side of the people. He accompanied Read Elding and some other prominent inhabitants to Government House and when they forced themselves into the Governor's presence, Warren presented his pistol at the Governor. It was, however, brushed aside and the bullet wounded one of the conspirators. The Speaker then broke His Excellency's head with the butt end of the pistol.

Royal government was a much more settled and orderly

business. But the Assembly continued to exhibit an independent, and often an intractable, spirit. Even the iron-willed Woodes Rogers could not dominate the Chamber and felt it necessary to dissolve the House of 1729 little more than a year after he had called it. To show its disenchantment with Governor Tinker, the Assembly voted to discontinue his salary, and when the Speaker sided with the Governor he himself was voted out of the chair.

During the hectic period when the Loyalists were making strenuous efforts to gain political control, a protest signed by two of them was voted to be 'a most wicked, false and scandalous reflection upon the authority and dignity of this House'. It was 'ordered that the protests of Peter Dean and John Petty be burnt this day by the hand of the Common Hangman before the Courthouse door, which was done accordingly'.

At an early date the Assembly assumed the authority of dealing with those who insulted its dignity and especially those who misrepresented its proceedings. Such transgressors, including newspaper editors, public officials, its own members and even a preacher were summoned before the bar of the House. Those adjudged guilty were reprimanded or fined, and sometimes imprisoned.

The right of the House to act as its own court of law was not seriously questioned until 1817 and the celebrated 'Wylly Affair'. Attorney General William Wylly was arrested and imprisoned for misrepresenting the Assembly's proceedings in England in connexion with the Abolition issue. He was released on bail by the General Court pending a decision on the legality of the Assembly's action. The heated issue dragged on for three years during which time legislative activity was crippled. Finally, by the Speaker's casting vote, a so-called 'Healing Act' was passed wherein it was simply stated that the action of neither House nor Court should be looked upon as a precedent.

Traditionally, the House of Assembly has been referred to as the Lower House. But it has never been low in the esteem of those who aspired to political office. Both Peter Henry Bruce and Captain Frankland of the man-of-war *Rose*, refused the Governor's offer of seats in the Council, preferring to offer for the Assembly. As time went by, the serenity of the Councils came to be regarded as a reward for long and active service in the more vigorous Assembly.

The long and tumultuous history of the colonial House of Assembly contains much which could not be condoned at the time and much more which cannot be condoned by afterthought. The inhabitants of these islands often have had cause to be thankful for the guiding and restraining hands of good Governors and good Councils. But there is something about the Assembly's traditional attitude which claims our admiration. It always took special pride in the fact that it was the popular house, and its members always fought for the principle that real government should be vested in the representatives of the people.

When the 'Third Constitution' was applied to these islands it was similar to the political system then existing in England. But the Westminster model underwent continuous evolvement, becoming increasingly responsive to the needs and wishes of the people, while the Bahamas remained in a sort of constitutional limbo.

In his history of the Bahamas House of Assembly, printed in 1921, the Honourable Harcourt Malcolm, then Speaker, said

A form of Government in which there is no provision for the creation and maintenance of sympathy between the executive and the representatives of the people offers countless opportunities for deadlocks. It is striking testimony to the ability and commonsense of the inhabitants of these islands that, although their political constitution is unworkable in theory, they nevertheless have succeeded in working it with much satisfaction for a period of nearly two centuries.

And so this constitution went on and on, apparently with 'much satisfaction', until the demands of party politics and party government made it patently obsolete.

26

Party Politics and Independence

When the winds of change began to blow over colonial territories after the Second World War, little immediate effect was felt
in the Bahamas. Not until 1953 was the first Bahamian political
party formed, and even that event seemed unlikely to disturb
the tenor of the *status quo*. Few, if any, at the time could foresee
the great gusts the Progressive Liberal Party would generate;
but all could see that it was directed against the strongly en-
trenched ruling group. Before going further we will consider this
ruling group to see who they were and how they came to power.

Bay Street Boys

In the early days of the Assembly representatives came from the
districts they represented. Even when the number of populated
islands was greatly increased by the Loyalist refugees, this presented
no particular problem. For the House met infrequently, the
sessions were not long, and every island had men equal to those of
New Providence in financial means and political capability.

As industries failed, however, these qualified men quitted the Out Islands. Many left the Bahamas altogether, but some came to New Providence to try to make something of their lives in the capital. Because the Out Islands were denuded of political talent, some of the planters and businessmen who had moved to Nassau offered themselves for the districts which they had represented while residing there. Not infrequently, their descendants continued the connexion and it became the accepted thing that representatives of the Out Islands should be drawn from the business and professional class of New Providence. Along the main street of Nassau most of the representatives had their shops and offices and they came to be called the 'Bay Street Boys'.

There had been black representatives in the Assembly since four were elected in 1834 when free blacks voted for the first time. But their number had not increased much by the end of the Second World War. In fact, the racial composition of the House was almost in inverse proportion to that of the population. Thus, when the P.L.P. was formed in 1953 its target was clear enough, the white 'Bay Street Boys'.

Harmony was not a traditional characteristic of the ruling group. Throughout, they were inclined to divide into hostile factions. The most notable example of this was the long and bitter wrangle which resulted in disestablishment of the Church of England in 1869.

But the first indications of a challenge to their authority in the early 1950's produced a remarkable cohesiveness. Rebels remained among them, but, thereafter, there was a clinging together, a proceeding by consensus. The challenge presented by the P.L.P., however, demanded even stricter disciplines and, in 1958, they banded together to form the United Bahamian Party. This event signalled the beginning of party politics in the Bahamas. The P.L.P., led mainly by political novices, offered no new philosophy except, vaguely, that of majority rule. In the early years of its existence, that party was not taken seriously by many, and even its staunchest supporters found it difficult to be confident of success.

From the beginning, the U.B.P. was headed by capable and influential men who were also seasoned politicians. The country at that time was experiencing an encouraging economic upswing, and many Bahamians who had known nothing but hard times were then finding rewarding employment. Therefore, the message which the U.B.P. had for the people was that they should not 'rock the boat'.

Progressive Liberal Party

Among the leaders of the P.L.P., however, were a few men of uncommon persistence and, with the aid of a party newspaper, they continued to 'rock the boat' as vigorously as they could. The main barb of their propaganda was that the ruling group were interested only in their own businesses and professions and the white minority, and had no sympathetic feelings for the struggling blacks. They hammered relentlessly at certain inequities in the social life of the country and in business and employment opportunities, all of which hampered the advancement and fulfilment of blacks. They hammered, too, at defects in the representative system which were advantageous to the U.B.P.

Two events during the latter half of the 1950's were of great assistance to the P.L.P. in its bid for power. In 1956, Sir Etienne Dupuch bulldozed an Anti-discrimination Resolution through the Assembly. Sir Etienne is not a revolutionary but a reformer, with a strong distaste for racial discrimination, who has profoundly influenced the Bahamian scene. With the object of promoting equality and concord between the races, he had organized the Bahamas Democratic League a year before. This multi-racial party never got very far because, at that time, the whites were still hoping to hold on to power and the blacks were sensing that they might gain it.

His anti-discrimination Resolution had the effect of opening up to blacks all public places, such as hotels, restaurants and theatres, which formerly had been closed to them. Men think as much of their dignity as they do of their bread and, because of this, blacks began to think of themselves, for the first time, as first class citizens.

A few years later, there was a general strike which we mentioned earlier in connexion with the opening of Windsor Airport. This strike was led by the President of the Bahamas Federation of

Labour, Mr Randol Fawkes, lawyer, politician, and the outstanding pioneer of Bahamian trade-unionism. The economy of New Providence was brought to a virtual standstill, and the striking workers who were nearly all black were made aware of the power that was in their hands. Mr Fawkes was not then a member of the P.L.P., but leaders of the P.L.P. soon made common cause with him and with the strikers, and that party thereby gained lustre as a champion of the working man.

As an aftermath of the strike, certain electoral changes were introduced on the compelling advice of the British Colonial Office. Among them was the creation of four additional seats in the 'black belts' of New Providence, all of which the P.L.P. won in the ensuing by-elections. These, added to the six gained in the General Election of 1956, constituted a sizeable Opposition.

The Development of Party Politics

As the General Election of 1962 drew near, unbounded optimism prevailed in the P.L.P. and the U.B.P. was fearful of the outcome. The results, however, were surprising to all; of twenty-nine seats the P.L.P. took only eight, which was only two ahead of its showing six years before, and two less than its strength after the by-elections of 1960.

During the campaign, both parties had stressed the need for a new constitution, one better adapted to the age of party politics. At a conference in London the next year, where all parties were represented, the 'Fourth Constitution' was hammered out. It became effective on 7 January 1964. By its terms, the Executive Council was abolished; the Legislative Council became the Senate, with Sir George Roberts as its first President; ministerial government was introduced, and real power was vested in a Cabinet formed out of the majority party of the Assembly.

Sir Roland Symonette was chosen by the U.B.P. as the country's first Premier. This man had had very few advantages in his youth but, through sheer grit and hard work, he had built up a number of successful business enterprises. His ability, vigour and restless energy, combined with a most likeable disposition to make

Sir Roland T. Symonette, Kt, J.P. M.P. First Premier of the Bahamas

him a popular choice. Sir Stafford Sands, the brilliant and
capable wizard of tourism, was given the second highest post,
that of Minister of Finance. Thus led, the Bahamas went forward
into the untried realm of responsible government.

Leaders of the P.L.P. maintained that it was unfair electoral
boundaries which had caused their defeat in 1962, and on this
issue they concentrated their attention and propaganda. A
favourite stratagem of some P.L.P. Assemblymen, to gain sym-

His Excellency Sir Milo B. Butler, G.C.M.G. takes the salute after being sworn in as the first Bahamian-born Governor General of the Bahamas (August 1973).

pathy, was to violate the rule of closure and so force the Speaker to have them bodily ejected from the House. Mr Lynden Pindling, Leader of the Opposition, executed a more dramatic form of protest by throwing the Speaker's Mace out of a window, to be broken up below. He was followed by Mr Milo Butler (now Sir Milo) who likewise disposed of the Hourglass used for timing speeches. And while the country was wondering what, if anything, the Speaker would do about these consistent violations of rules and the destruction of his symbol of authority, the Opposition decided to boycott the House.

The boundaries were redrawn, not entirely to the P.L.P.'s liking, and a General Election was called for 10 January 1967. The P.L.P. had some very valuable assistance in waging its campaign. The racial factor loomed larger than before, chiefly because of the much publicized struggle of American blacks for social justice; and some local black religious leaders entered the fray, having seen some connexion between the election date and the time of year when the Israelites had fled Egyptian bondage. Perhaps the most powerful propaganda weapon in the hands of the P.L.P., however, was the disclosure in the foreign press that a number of prominent leaders of the U.B.P. had been receiving 'Consultants Fees' from the Freeport Port Authority. This was particularly damaging to the U.B.P. because these payments had started soon after it had been agreed to permit casino gambling at Freeport.

The General Election of 1967 was fought under a very broad franchise. A property qualification for adult males had been discarded and, in 1961, after some years of agitation by a group of suffragettes, notable among whom was Dr Doris Johnson, now President of the Senate, women were given the vote. The election resulted in a dead heat between the two major parties. Of the thirty-eight seats, the U.B.P. and P.L.P. gained eighteen each, the Labour Party one, and one Independent member was returned. Holders of the latter two seats, Randol Fawkes and Alvin Braynen, threw in their lot with the P.L.P. enabling it to form a government.

Named Premier was Mr Lynden Pindling, who had become a member of the P.L.P. soon after its inception and who had been leader of that party in opposition. Although he had risen above the masses, he maintained an empathy with them which made him the most popular figure in his party. He soon proved himself to be one of the most capable and charismatic political figures the Bahamas has ever produced. Mr Arthur Hanna, who had joined the party in its early days and who was regarded as a fearless champion of the black and the poor, was appointed Deputy to the Premier.

The P.L.P. had only a small majority and, when one of its House members died early in 1968, another General Election was called for 10 April. This was won by a landslide, the P.L.P. gaining twenty-nine of the thirty-eight seats. To the discerning, it was then clear that black rule was here to stay, and the essential correctness of this could scarcely be disputed in a country where eighty-five per cent of the people are black.

Soon after these elections, the ruling P.L.P. sought further constitutional advance. Once again the politicians went to London, and the 'Fifth Constitution' in Bahamian history came into effect in 1969. This was substantially the same as that of 1964. Among other changes, the Government was given an overall majority in the Senate, the Premier became a 'Prime Minister', and the Bahamas was officially designated 'The Commonwealth of the Bahama Islands'. In addition, the Bahamas Government was given more responsibility for internal security and provision was made for the delegation to the Bahamas Government of limited responsibility in external affairs. This took the Bahamas as far as the British Government would allow, short of complete Independence. And this last step, Britain made clear, the Commonwealth could take any time its people so desired.

Independence

The Bahamian people had never exhibited any great enthusiasm for Independence. The shackles of colonialism as they were felt in these islands were more gossamer than steel. Thus, when in the early part of 1971 the Prime Minister announced that his Government would seek Independence not before the next General Election and not later than 1973, there was no dancing in the streets and no bonfires of joy. But there was something of inevitability about Independence, in the minds of those who favoured it and those who did not. The idea had come of age, and had found strong expression in subject countries and in the United Nations, that colonialism should be brought to a speedy end. Britain had demonstrated repeatedly that she would thwart none of her possessions which wanted to run their own affairs.

In fact, Britain seemed to go a bit further than this and, in the Bahamas, there was the distinct feeling that she was more anxious to co-operate with those who wanted Independence than with those who preferred to remain dependent. She turned a cold shoulder to those who suggested a plebiscite and insisted that the matter be decided by a General Election. If both major parties had favoured it, Independence would not have been an issue. But the Opposition, while not objecting to Independence *per se*, took the stand that 1973 was too soon and that the Bahamas should gain some further experience in responsible government before taking that final and irretraceable step.

The Opposition which faced the Government in this contest was not the same old U.B.P. we have come to know. After its crushing defeat in 1968, there was a general feeling among the leadership that the U.B.P. belonged to a time and age that had passed forever. That redoubtable warrior, Sir Roland Symonette, its Leader, was stricken with illness and the mantle of leadership fell on Mr Geoffrey Johnstone, a practical-minded and clear-sighted young man who does not enjoy the comfort of illusions. He knew, beyond doubt, that the U.B.P. could never again gain the strength to form an alternative government or even to mount an effective opposition. But the U.B.P. was the only party opposed to the Government with real grass roots strength, amounting to more than a quarter of the registered voters. He, therefore, bent his efforts toward an amalgamation of all opposition parties so that this strength might be preserved as a foundation upon which a new party with a future could be built.

In the opposition field at the time, apart from the U.B.P., were the Labour Party, led by Mr Randol Fawkes, which had never been able to get off the ground, the National Democratic Party led by Mr Paul Adderley, which had little support, and the Free P.L.P. led by Mr Wallace Whitfield, which was still untried. The latter two were splinter parties of the P.L.P.

Negotiations toward a union of some kind were fruitless until both the U.B.P. and Free P.L.P. were given a severe trouncing by the P.L.P. in a by-election held late in 1971. Thereupon, the need for unified action was clearly seen and serious talks began

Prince Charles, representing Queen Elizabeth II presents the Constitutional Instruments signifying the attainment of nationhood, to Prime Minister I. O. Pindling on Independence Day.

before Christmas. They resulted in the formation of the Free
National Movement, early in 1972. In its final form, this party
was made up of the former Free P.L.P. and U.B.P., and a majority
of the N.D.P. Chosen as Leader was Mr Cecil Wallace Whitfield,
a dynamic political figure, who had shown consummate skill in
welding the disparate units together.

A General Election was called for September 1972 and the
campaign proved to be the most heated the Bahamas has ever
known. Many issues were brought out, but surmounting them
all was that of Independence. Essentially, the people were asked
to vote for the 'P.L.P. and Independence', or the 'F.N.M. and
No Independence'. When the results were made known, the
F.N.M. was seen to have won only nine of the thirty-eight seats.
The Bahamian people had clearly opted for the 'P.L.P. and
Independence'.

All that remained to be done before Independence, the date
for which had been set already, was to go to London, for the
last time, to formulate a Constitution. Mr Whitfield had lost his
Assembly seat and Mr Kendal Isaacs, Q.C., a capable and
experienced man, but relatively new to party politics, was elected
as Leader of the F.N.M. Under his guidance, the party decided
that the Government had received a valid mandate from the
people to take the Bahamas into Independence and that the issue
was dead. Despite a great deal of opposition to this point of view,
the consensus of the party's council was that the most valuable
service the Opposition could render the country at that particular
time was to co-operate with the Government in working out the
best possible constitution for an Independent Bahamas.

In this respect, the framers were eminently successful. The
Honourable Eugene Dupuch, Q.C., himself one of them, and an
authority on constitutional law, had this to say

The Constitution of The Bahamas, and I say this with the greatest
respect, is a far more literary, legalistic, reasoned and democratic
document than the Constitution of the United States of America . . . .

We have gone out of our way to protect the rights of the under-privi-
leged while not losing sight of the human apprehensions of the privi-
leged. We have endeavoured to give equality under the law to the
majorities and the minorities, the rich and the poor alike.

We have preserved and affirmed the fundamental rights and freedoms of the individual, irrespective of race, place of origin, political affiliation, creed or sex, subject only to the rights and freedoms of others and the public interest.

Few nations indeed can make this noble boast.

Under the Independence Constitution, the sixth in the history of these islands, The Bahamas was pledged to be a part of that great Commonwealth of which Queen Elizabeth II is head. It was agreed that her representative in this country would be a Governor-General; and the first man to be given this post was Bahamian-born Sir Milo Butler, a longtime social and political fighter, much loved and respected by the masses of the country.

On the night of 9 July 1973, thousands of Bahamians gathered on the Fort Charlotte Grounds in New Providence to witness a sight which could be seen only once. During those last few seconds before midnight, the Union Jack, enveloped in darkness, was lowered from its pole to mark the end of an era which had begun 325 years before. Next, the floodlights blazed to reveal the black, gold and turquoise of the Bahamas flag slowly ascending the mast. On reaching the top, it fluttered gently in the morning breeze as a signal to the world that a new nation had been born.

Sources and Suggestions
for Further Reading

1 Primary Sources

Many important documents dealing with Bahamian history are in the
Public Records Office in London and other places in England. These
are listed in Bell, H. C., and Parker, D. W., *Guide to the British West
Indies Archive Materials in London and the Islands* (Washington, 1926).
It also lists many of the documents available in Nassau. The most
important of these are to be found in the Department of Land and
Surveys, the Registry and the Department of Archives and in the
records of the House of Assembly Library.

2 Newspapers and Magazines

Bahamas Gazette 1784–1857
Nassau Guardian 1844–
The Tribune 1904–

Bahamas–Nassau, Freeport and Resort Islands (originally published as
Nassau Magazine of the Bahamas by Mary Moseley (1933). Now published
bimonthly)
Bahamian Review 1952–

3 Secondary

Bacon, E. M.   *Notes on Nassau* (New York, 1926)
Bacot, (Surgeon Major) S.   *The Bahamas: A Sketch* (London, 1869)
Barratt, P. J. H.   *Grand Bahama* (Devon & Pennsylvania, 1972)
Bell, H. MacL.   *Bahamas: Isles of June* (New York, 1934)
Benjamin, S. G. W.   *The Atlantic Islands* (New York, 1878)
Bethel, A. T.   *The Early Settlers of the Bahama Islands* (Nassau, 1914)
Britton, N. L., and Millspaugh, C. F.   *Bahama Flora* (New York, 1920)
Bruce, P. H.   *Bahamian Interlude* (London, 1949) originally part of
    Memoirs of Peter Henry Bruce, Esquire (London, 1782)
Burns, (Sir) A.   *History of the British West Indies* (London, 1954)
Carse, R.   *The Age of Piracy* (London, 1959)

Cochran, H. *Blockade Runners of the Confederacy* (New York, 1958)

Cottman, E. W. *Out-Island Doctor* (London, 1963)

Craton, M. *A History of the Bahamas* (London, 1962)

Curry, R. A. *Bahamian Lore* (Paris, 1928)

Defries, A. *The Fortunate Islands* (London, 1929)

Dowling, A. *A Report on the Bahamas and Biminis* (published privately by Marion B. Carstairs, 1942)

Dupuch, (Sir) E. *Tribune Story* (London, 1967)

Dupuch, E. Jr. (Pub.) *Bahamas Handbook and Businessmen's Annual* (Nassau, 1960)

Dupuch, S. P. (ed.) *Sun 'n Sixpence* (Nassau, 1964)

Durrell, Z. C. *The Innocent Island: Abaco in the Bahamas* (Vermont, 1972)

Esquemeling, J. *Buccaneers of America* (Amsterdam, 1678, reprinted in English translation London, 1893)

Feiling, K. *The Life of Neville Chamberlain* (London, 1946)

Frick, G. F., and Stearns, R. P. *Mark Catesby: The Colonial Audubon* (Illinois, 1961)

Gosse, P. *The Pirates' Who's Who* (London, 1968, reprint of 1924 edition)

Harvey, T. C. *Official Reports of the Out Islands of the Bahamas* (Nassau, 1858)

Holmes, F. *The Bahamas during the Great War* (Nassau, 1924)

Horner, D. *The Blockade-Runners* (New York, 1968)

Ives, C. *The Isles of Summer or Nassau and the Bahamas* (Connecticut, 1880)

Jane, C. (ed.) *The Journal of Christopher Columbus* (London, 1960)

Kent, R. (ed.) *Letters from the Bahama Islands: Written 1823–4* (London, 1948)

Kline, H. (ed.) *Yachtsman's Guide to the Bahamas* (originally compiled by Harry Etheridge. Now published annually, Florida)

Klingel, G. C. *Inagua* (London, 1944)

Langton-Jones, R. *Silent Sentinels* (London, 1944)

Lefroy, J. H. *Memorials of the Bermudas* 2 volumes (reprinted London, 1932)

Little, B. *Crusoe's Captain* (London, 1960)

Loven, S. *Origins of the Tainan Culture, West Indies* (Goteburg, 1935)

Malcolm, (Sir) H. *A History of the Bahamas House of Assembly* (Nassau, 1921)

Manwaring, G. E. *Woodes Rogers, Privateer and Governor* (Nassau, 1957) originally published as introduction to Rogers, W., *A Cruising Voyage Round the World* (reprinted London, 1928)

Marx, R. F.   *Shipwrecks of the Western Hemisphere*, 1492–1825 (New York, 1971)

McKinnen, D.   *A Tour through The British West Indies* (London, 1804)

Miller, W. H.   'The Colonization of the Bahamas, 1647–1670', *William and Mary Quarterly*, 3rd Series II (January 1945)

Mitchell, C.   *Islands to Windward* (New York, 1948)

Morison, S. E.   *Admiral of the Ocean Sea* (Boston, 1942)

Moseley, M.   *Bahamas Handbook* (Nassau, 1926)

Oldmixon, J.   *The British Empire in America* (London, 1708); part reissued as *History of the Isle of Providence* (London, 1949)

Peggs, A. D.   *A Short History of the Bahamas* (Nassau, 1959)

Peggs, A. D. (ed.)   *A Relic of Slavery. Farquharson's Journal* (Nassau, 1957)

Peggs, A. D. (ed.)   *A Mission to the West Indian Islands, Dowson's Journal* (Nassau, 1960)

Peters, T. P.   *The American Loyalists and the Plantation Period in the Bahama Islands* (Florida, 1960)

Powles, L. D.   *Land of the Pink Pearl* (London, 1888)

Rathbun, F. H.   *Rathbun's Raid on Nassau* from *Proceedings U.S. Naval Institute* November 1970 (Annapolis, Maryland)

Rigg, J. L.   *Bahama Islands* (New York, 1949)

Rogers, W.   *A Cruising Voyage Round the World* (London, 1712) reprinted 1928 with introduction by G. E. Manwaring

Rutter, O.   *A Traveller in the West Indies* (London, 1936)

Sharer, C. J.   *The Population Growth of the Bahama Islands* (PhD Michigan, 1955)

Shattuck, G. B. (ed.)   *The Bahama Islands* (New York, 1905)

Shepard, B.   *Lore of the Wreckers* (Boston, 1961)

Siebert, W. H.   *The Legacy of the American Revolution to the British West Indies and the Bahamas* (Ohio, 1913)

Stark, J. H.   *History and Guide to the Bahama Islands* (Massachusetts, 1891)

Tannehill, I. R.   *Hurricanes* (Princeton, 1938, revised 1951)

Taylor, T. E.   *Running the Blockade* (4th ed. London, 1912)

Tebeau, C. W.   *A History of Florida* (Miami, 1972)

Thompson, T. A.   *A Short Geography of the Bahamas* (Nassau, 1944)

Tribune Publication   *The Murder of Sir Harry Oakes, Bt.* (Nassau, 1959)

Whipple, A. B. C.   *Pirate: Rascals of the Spanish Main* (London, 1957)

Wigley, H. de W.   *With the Whiskey Smugglers* (London)

Williams, N.   *Captains Outrageous* (London, 1961)

Wilkinson, H. C.   *Bermuda in the Old Empire* (London, 1950)

Wilson, J. *Survey of the Bahamas* 1783 (Ms in Public Library of the City of Boston)

Winston, A. *No Purchase, No Pay* (London, 1970)

Wright, B. S. *The Frogmen of Burma* (Toronto, 1968)

Wright, J. M. 'The Wrecking System of the Bahama Islands' *Political Science Quarterly* Vol. XXX, No. 4, December 1915

Wylly, W. *A Short Account of the Bahama Islands* (London, 1789)

Young, E. *Eleuthera, The Island Called Freedom* (London, 1966)

Index